communication for IT

communication for IT

ACCESS SERIES

Boston   Burr Ridge, IL   Dubuque, IA   Madison, WI   New York
San Francisco   St. Louis   Bangkok   Bogotá   Caracas   Kuala Lumpur
Lisbon   London   Madrid   Mexico City   Milan   Montreal   New Delhi
Santiago   Seoul   Singapore   Sydney   Taipei   Toronto

McGraw-Hill Australia 

A Division of The **McGraw·Hill** *Companies*

Reprinted 2002, 2003
Copyright © 2002 McGraw Hill Australia Pty Limited
Additional owners of copyright are named in on-page credits.

National Library of Australia Cataloguing-in-Publication Data

Access ESD.
   Communication for IT.

   Includes index.
   ISBN 0 07 471034 6

   1. Communication of technical information. 2. Information Technology. I. Ellyard, Sue. II. Koritschoner, Edna. III. Braham, Bronwyn. IV. New South Wales. Technical and Further Education Commission. Access Educational Services Division. V. Title. (Series: Access series (Roseville, N.S.W.)).

004.0711

Published in Australia by
McGraw-Hill Australia Pty Limited
Level 2, 82 Waterloo Road, North Ryde NSW 2113 Australia
Sponsoring Editor: Michael Tully
Production Editor: Leanne Peters
Editor: Leanne Peters
Cover Design: Lucy Bal
Internal Design: Claus Huttenrauch
Typesetter: Kim Webber
Illustrator: Greg Gaul
Printed by: Pantech Ltd, Hong Kong

CONTENTS

PART B
WORKING IN TEAMS

PARTICIPATING IN AND LEADING WORK TEAMS

MEETINGS

PART C
INTERACTING WITH CLIENTS

COMMUNICATING WITH CLIENTS

PRESENTATION SKILLS

PART D
WRITING FOR INFORMATION TECHNOLOGY

PRINCIPLES OF EFFECTIVE WRITING

WORKPLACE DOCUMENTS

WRITING REPORTS

GRAPHIC COMMUNICATION

PREFACE

Communication for IT is a new text specifically written to develop communication skills for the specialised needs of IT and computing students, in recognition of the unique experience and challenges of the IT environment. By using a variety of case studies, illustrations, graphics and authentic workplace activities in an Australian context, the text enables learners to:
- understand fundamental communication concepts
- relate communication concepts to an IT environment and current workplace practices
- develop communication-related competencies from the Information Technology Training Package.

The book's structure, layout and use of plain English support accessibility for students of various backgrounds and skills. It helps students understand the concepts of communication and offers clear and comprehensive guidelines for tasks and activities. The text is suitable for use in the classroom, guiding interactive group learning, and as a resource for students working alone. The different facets of communication in the IT workplace are addressed, including client interaction, working in teams, workplace writing, meetings, conflict resolution and negotiation skills.

This book has been developed by TAFE NSW—Access Division for the university and Vocational Education and Training (VET) sectors. Access Division develops curriculum products and resources, including professional development programs, and strategic advice for access and general education. Access Division is active in the national VET arena, and has worked in partnership with the Australian National Training Authority (ANTA) and VET providers in other States and Territories.

The authors have extensive experience in the development and delivery of communication teaching in vocational education and training, the university sector and in industry.

Sue Ellyard is Program Manager, Communication, at Access Division. She manages the development of communication courses and resources for all TAFE NSW Institutes. She previously worked as a head teacher of Communication in TAFE NSW and a lecturer in teacher education.

Edna Koritschoner teaches communication at TAFE NSW and the School of Community Medicine at the University of New South Wales. She previously worked as an audiologist.

Bronwyn Braham is a teacher of English and Communication at TAFE NSW. She has interest and experience in developing contextualised communication teaching and learning resources for a range of vocational applications.

Some of the features within the text include:

Competencies: cross-references content to the Information Technology Training Package.

Topics discussed: outlines the chapter in point form.

Chapter introduction: summarises the information in the chapter.

Activity: provides individual or group learning strategies.

Case study: describes IT workplace examples, scenarios and issues.

Checklist: enables you to mark off what you have learned, and what you still want to learn.

Action points: highlights what you can do to develop your skills.

Summary: provides a summary of the chapter.

Training log: tests your learning at the end of each chapter.

Action plan: suggests strategies to help you apply communication knowledge and skills.

ACKNOWLEDGMENTS

In writing this book we sought and obtained assistance from a number of individuals to whom we would like to express our gratitude.

Firstly, we would like to thank the colleagues who provided feedback and advice on the drafts, particularly Agnes Vukovic of TAFE NSW—Information Technology, Arts and Media Division. We would also like to thank Marsha Berry, Royal Melbourne Institute of Technology, Mary Gurgone, Central TAFE, Perth, Marilyn Enders, TAFE Division, University of Ballarat, Sue Robertson, Holmesglen Institute of TAFE, Nick Westley, TAFE NSW—Information Technology, Arts and Media Division, Lynn Beauregard, TAFE NSW—Illawarra Institute.

Finally, we would like to thank the team at McGraw-Hill who assisted us in the development of this text: Michael Tully, Sponsoring Editor, and Leanne Peters, Production Editor.

GUIDED TOUR

Clear agenda

Relevant training package codes are referenced within each specific chapter.

This chapter is linked to **elements** c⟨
in the Information Technology Traini⟨
- Receive and Process Oral and Wr⟨
- Create User and Technical Docun⟨
- Interact with Clients ICAITS009B⟨
- Relate to Clients on a Business L⟨
- Confirm Client Business Needs IC⟨
- Develop and Present a Feasibility⟨
- Establish and Maintain Client Use⟨
- Record Client Support Requireme⟨
- Determine Client Computing Prob⟨
- Record Client Support Requireme⟨
- Provide One on One Instruction ⟨
- Assist with Policy Development f⟨
- Apply Skills in Communications ⟨

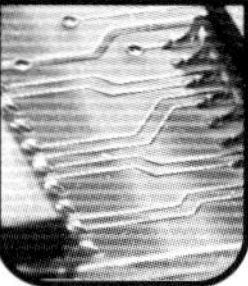

k team
n development

in a team environment
ecision making in teams
he plan
n progress and outcomes

Topics discussed and aims

Each chapter opener clearly states discussion topics and aims.

ask members of the group to fill out reaction forms at preu⟨
videotape interaction with clients (with their permission, of ⟨
ask individuals to act as observers of meetings, team activiti⟨
conduct formal surveys
ask team members to keep a journal, focusing on specific a⟨
share information

Checklist 3.1

How to be a more effective leader

There are several group processes which help the team d⟨
and cohesion. The team leader plays a critical role in all⟨
the following using your current work team or experience⟨

Group process

1. Does the team leader facilitate effective communication—to ensure⟨ people have the information they need to get the job done?
2. Is there a group identity through the use of inclusive language (a 'we⟨ rather than 'I' approach)?
3. Does your team leader plan and/or encourage events that build up th⟨ team's identity and traditions?
4. Is there a focus on teamwork rather than the achievement of 'stars'?
5. Do individual team members give informal recognition to each other ⟨ work well done?
6. Does the team leader set clear, attainable short-term team goals, to ⟨ which all team members can relate?
7. Are there formal team rewards such as letters of commendation to th⟨ team, dinners and social events that reinforce the role of the team in⟨ outcomes?
8. Does the team leader acknowledge the skills of all team members an⟨ provide opportunities to apply them;
9. Does the team leader delegate tasks and roles so that the full potent⟨ of each team member is utilised?
10. Does the team leader orient new team members well?

Case studies

Case studies are scattered throughout chapters, allowing the learned to practice and further develop skills.

Checklists

Use these checklists to track your learning as you go.

Living application

IT examples test your knowledge in each chapter, ensuring you develop the skills to successfully complete each learning objective.

- management or supervision style in the wor
- experience or training among the team mem
- opportunities for all team members to gathe

Activity 3-2

Finding solutions as a team

Select one of the following scenarios and wo a solution to the problem.

Scenario 1: Software selection

Your group has been asked to work make a client is a large insurance company that sell software does not link well to the website a when using the website. At this stage the tea will recommend to the Manager's meeting ne

Using the checklist plan the approach yo solution. Your task is not to find the solut strategy or plan that would enable the group

1. identify the problem
2. agree on a goal
3. establish the criteria for success
4. identify the issues/factors/information
5. identify resources
6. decide on the preferred strategy
7. plan the action
8. decide on a feedback process

Scenario 2: Furnish the office

SUMMARY

eople committed to
accepted rules and
d roles aimed at achieving the goal'. An
non goal or purpose, clear strategies,
e leadership, rewards, and feedback
people need a wide range of skills, such
ct management skills.

stablished by management to deal with
k. The purpose of the work team needs
the mission statement of the company.
goals and the role of the team in the
basic meeting procedures are followed.
uses a step-by-step, analytical format to
ning the problem; defining the end goal;
lternatives for action; and selecting the
he gathering of information from various
elated to presenting their report in the
eam processes in today's organisations
nd service, and pressure to offer quality

ning process. Effective planning involves

Summary

Make sure you get what you need out of each chapter by using the detailed summary at the end of each chapter.

TRAINING LOG

to participate
tion to teams
kills of others
ll need to ask another member of a team
n skills. This person my be a member of:

beginning of this chapter
complete the activities
ntribution to the team by completing the

	OFTEN	SOMETIMES	RARELY
	☐	☐	☐
	☐	☐	☐
	☐	☐	☐
	☐	☐	☐
?	☐	☐	☐
	☐	☐	☐
	☐	☐	☐

Training log

A final chance for you to test your understanding. Use these activities as a work environment simulation.

Case study 3-1

Sysdan specification problem

The new product development team at SYSDAN has bee
customer information software for a national retail chain.
team has been dealing with a conflict arising from mistake

Peter, one of the design engineers, is respon
specifications from data supplied by the client. He has
data, which means that at least two weeks of work has b

The deadline for the product is looming and pen
mean the company could lose money on the job. To add
is due to start work on another contract on the date sche
one. Most team members are very angry about the situa
some of them are very high.

Jill, the project team leader, has kept in close
throughout the project and has been able to argue that th
do something special. Her view is that if money is to be lo
spent getting it done on time than being hit with the p
would damage relations with the client.

Jill has arranged for the team to work for four
Monday set aside for relaxation. She has also convinced th
marketing managers along for the sessions to help with t

The time has been planned so that team membe
result in the three days. In addition to planning the work
with individual team members, enlisting their help
relationships between team members.

Imagine that you areHow can Jill and have the pro
to manage the team from now on as well as planning the

Case study activities

INTERPERSONAL SKILLS

CHAPTER 1

COMMUNICATION CONCEPTS

COMPETENCIES

This chapter is linked to elements contained in the following competencies which are in the Information Technology Training Package.

- Receive and Process Oral and Written Communication ICAITD003B
- Communicate in the Workplace ICAITTW002B
- Interact with Clients ICAITS009B
- Determine Client Business, Expectations and Needs ICAITAD041A
- Apply Problem Solving Techniques to Achieve Organisational Goals ICAITS010B
- Participate in a Team and Individually to Achieve Organisational Goals ICAITTW011B
- Coordinate and Maintain Teams ICAITTW026B
- Apply Skills in Human Resources Management BSX154L406
- Guide Application of Human Resources Management BSX154L506
- Manage Human Resources BSX154L606

The aim of this chapter is to provide an understanding of communication concepts necessary to work effectively in an Information Technology (IT) environment. The issues discussed in this chapter are about relationships between people. Positive relations in the workplace not only improve morale but also improve efficiency and job satisfaction.

In particular it will help you answer questions such as these:

- Why is it sometimes so hard to make people understand us?
- Is it possible to be a better 'communicator'?
- Can we make people 'hear' what we are saying?
- What are the main obstructions to effective communication?
- How can we use communication to build better business relationships?

TOPICS DISCUSSED

- Communication at work
- Skills of a good communicator
- The communication process
- Sending and receiving
- Non-verbal communication
- Questioning skills
- Active listening
- Empathy
- Cultural awareness

INTRODUCTION

What is communication?

When you explain an idea to someone, you are trying to share that idea. If your communication is successful, then both you and the other person have a common understanding about that idea. If the communication is unsuccessful, then you may have a misunderstanding that can affect your working relationship and your business. In essence the real communication that occurs is not merely the words spoken or written by you, but also what another person understands about the words or actions you have used.

In the IT industry you may have to:

- explain technical information
- understand and implement policies
- answer the telephone
- respond to enquiries from clients and colleagues
- negotiate solutions to hardware and software problems, service agreements, supply issues, etc.
- implement ethical work practices and procedures
- represent yourself, your team and your organisation to clients
- educate others about new technology.

These are only some of the many communication tasks you will need to undertake.

Different ways of communicating

Each type of communication needs different skills and techniques. Subsequent chapters describe many techniques you can use in the following situations:

- person-to-person, e.g. face-to-face, reading a letter, making a phone call
- in a small group, e.g. planning, solving problems, making decisions
- in a meeting, e.g. negotiating agreements, presenting, bargaining
- in an organisation, e.g. emailing, writing reports and memos, using noticeboards, supervising, managing people and projects
- in the mass media, e.g. speaking in public, on radio and/or television; writing for the media, in papers, journals, books; advertising and public relations
- to larger groups, e.g. when training, teaching, entertaining (art, cinema etc.)

'Communication' and 'communications'

'Communication' and 'communications' are two separate terms, and it is particularly important in the IT environment to be able to distinguish between them. You will deal daily with communication systems, communication equipment and technology; however, the communication skills developed in this book will help you interact effectively with the people you come into contact with at work.

The distinction followed throughout this book, and the one now accepted by most Australian authorities (including the *Macquarie Dictionary*), is as follows:

The singular word, 'communication', refers to the process of communicating and involves an exchange that must involve two or more individuals. The plural word, 'communications', refers to the technology, the organisations that deal with message transmission, and the electrical and mechanical systems used to carry messages (e.g. communications satellites are used for image, data and voice transmission).

COMMUNICATION AT WORK

We spend a lot of our time communicating in the workplace. We do this in many ways.

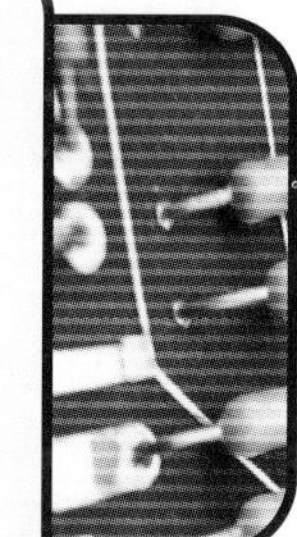

Activity 1.1

Communication at work

Complete the following table by considering your communication at work over the last two days.

Who did I communicate with? (e.g. client, colleague, manager)	Why did I need/want to communicate? (e.g. collect information, promote a product, socialise)	How did I communicate? (e.g. telephone, email, fax)

From your list in Activity 1.1 you can see that in any day you will communicate with many different people, for different reasons and in different ways. This is why employers in all industry groups value communication skills so highly. Not only does successful workplace communication increase productivity through maximising efficiency and increasing employer satisfaction, it also reduces time lost in safety or procedural breakdowns and in settling disputes.

SKILLS OF A GOOD COMMUNICATOR

Effective communicators may display the following qualities:
- speaks and writes clearly
- listens actively to other people
- shows that they understand the other person's ideas by giving feedback
- looks at the other person when speaking or listening
- gives the other person time to say what they want to say
- shows respect for the views of others
- asks questions to show interest and makes sure they understand the other person
- uses appropriate non-verbal behaviour such as gestures and facial expressions
- does not interrupt or speak over the top of the other person.

We will now look at these skills in more detail.

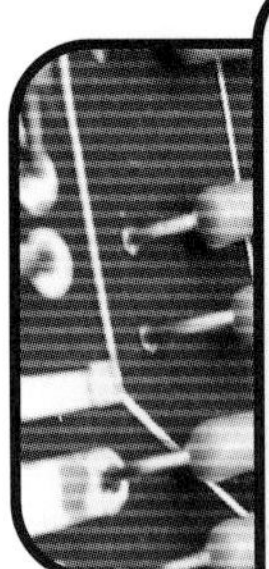

Activity 1.2

Communication skills

Think of someone you know personally who you believe is a good communicator.
1. What skills do they have that make them a good communicator?
2. Share your ideas in a small group and produce a list of communication skills.
3. Compare your responses with the list in the text. Can you add anything more?

THE COMMUNICATION PROCESS

Figure 1.1
The communication process. Communication is a dynamic, two-way process that involves creating shared meanings using workplace or community cultures available through networks and technologies.

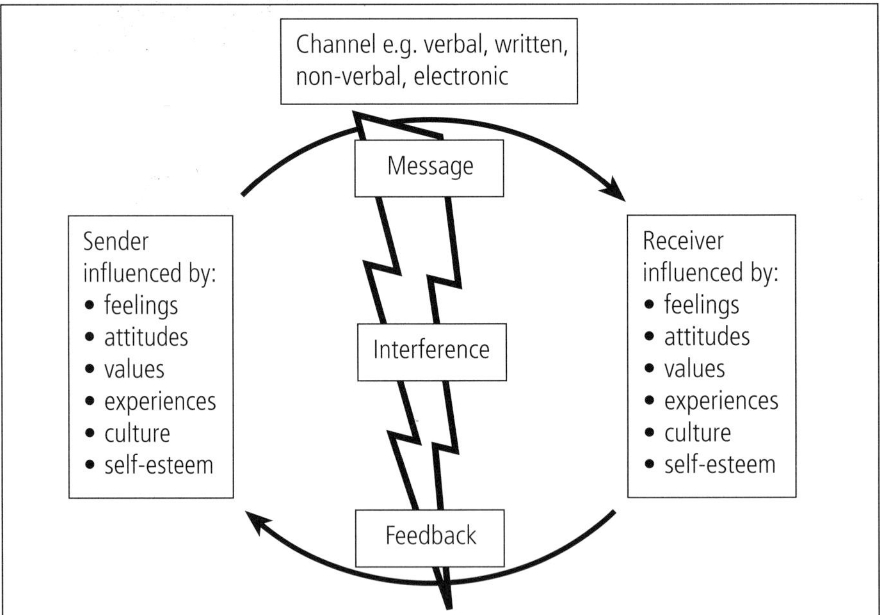

As Figure 1.1 shows, there are six different elements in the communication process.
1. **Sender.** The person/s giving the message.
2. **Receiver.** The person/s needing to understand the message.
3. **Message.** What you say, write, etc.
4. **Channel.** How the message is given—spoken, written, signs, etc.
5. **Feedback.** How both the sender and receiver know if the message has been understood.
6. **Interference.** The barriers, noise or other things that block communication or cause misunderstanding.
    The entire process takes place within the information technology environment.

SENDING AND RECEIVING

Both the sender and receiver need effective skills so that the message means the same thing to both sides. Think about the following questions:

- **What makes a good sender and a good receiver?**
- **What do you need to do to make sure others understand what you mean when you speak?**
- **How do you make sure that you have received the message accurately?**

It may be helpful to watch people talk and see what they do well and not so well.

Think of a person who you consider to be an effective communicator. What do they do when they are sending or receiving messages to make sure the meaning of the message is a shared meaning? Activity 1.3 highlights some of these methods.

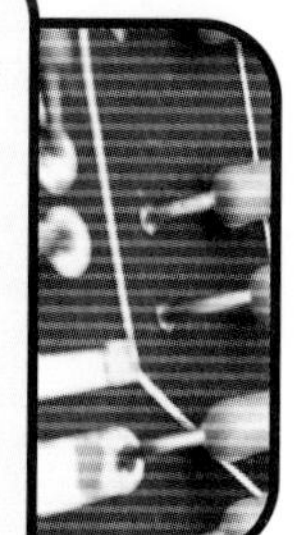

Activity 1.3

Creating a shared meaning

Complete the following table by adding those skills you think necessary to convey your meaning accurately when communicating.

Sender	Receiver
Speak clearly	Pay attention
Ask for feedback to check understanding	Give feedback such as a nod or 'yes' to show understanding and ask for clarification when you do not understand

What affects the sender and receiver?

There are many factors that affect how you give and interpret a message. Figure 1.1 suggests that some of the following influence your communication:

- Feelings. For example, assume you have just spent two hours trying to fix an urgent software problem, are feeling frustrated, and someone approaches you for a social chat. Your response may not be very friendly.
- Attitudes. For example, a person who believes they know more than you about a hardware problem (although they have no experience in fixing the problem) may be more difficult to convince about the solution required.
- Values. For example, convincing an Apple Mac user to change to an IBM PC may be difficult.
- Experiences. For example, someone who has experienced several problems with a new piece of software will not be convinced of its suitability.
- Culture. For example, in one-to-one instruction a person may say they understand rather than ask a question or request that the instruction be repeated.
- Self-esteem. For example, it may be difficult to train an older person in a new piece of software if they lack confidence in their ability to use computers in general.

Understanding and misunderstanding—interference or communication barriers

Understanding is achieved if the sender's original idea is conveyed without alteration and the meaning is shared by the sender and receiver. However, this is the ideal situation; in many instances the meaning sent and the meaning understood do not match.

Two of the most common forms of communication breakdown occur when:

- the sender's message does not reach the receiver
- the receiver misunderstands the sender's message.

For example, you ask Alberto to construct a computer package for you. Two weeks later, when the client takes delivery of a package in which the hardware and software configuration does not conform to their request, it is obvious Alberto misunderstood your instructions.

Who is affected by this situation? You might feel a bit foolish in the eyes of others for not being able to get people to do their job properly. Alberto might feel put out because he has wasted his time. The customer may be angry because they have not received what they ordered. What may have contributed to this breakdown?

Figure 1.2
Barriers to communication

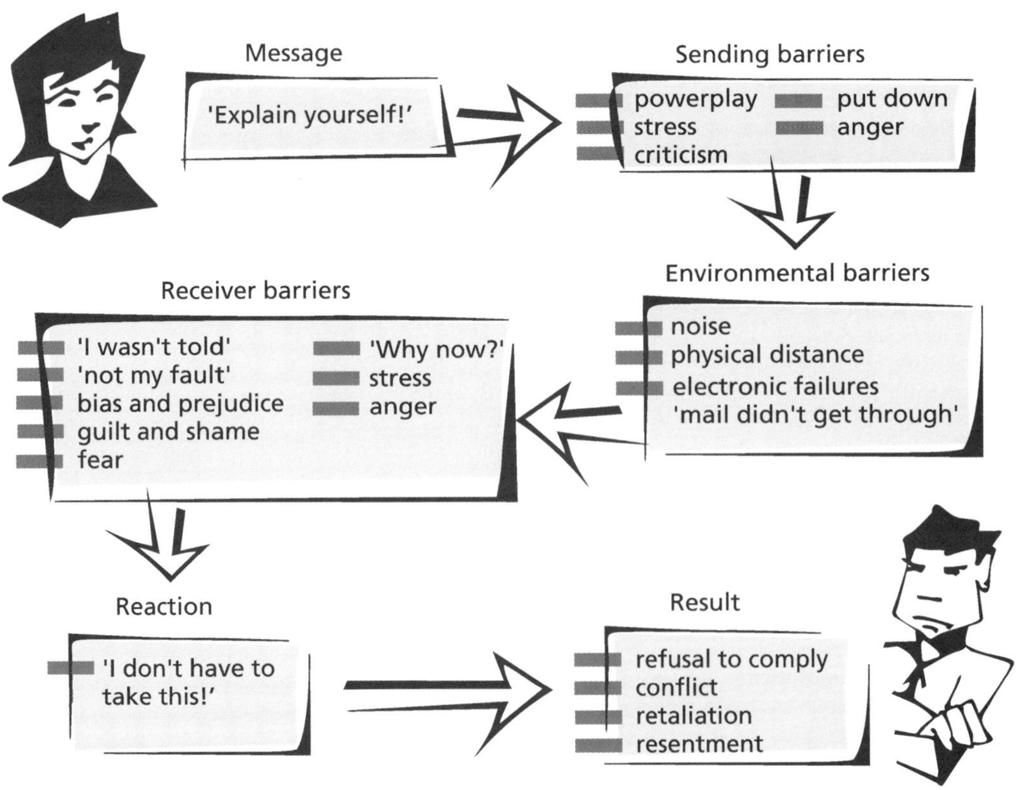

Here are some examples of **interference** or barriers to communication that can affect how a message is received (or whether it even gets through).

- **Rank, status, power.** People may feel too intimidated to give their opinion openly to senior management.
- **Equipment failure.** An email or fax does not go through.
- **Wrong channel.** An office memo may not be the best way to announce a major change in work practices.
- **Ambiguity.** The message is unclear and open to interpretation.
- **Bias or prejudice.** The receiver draws conclusions according to who sent the message rather than the content of the message.
- **Emotional state.** Anger, stress, pressure, etc. can all influence how effectively we send or receive messages.
- **Fear of change.** People worried about change may interpret any alteration or adjustment to work practice as a threat.
- **Denial.** Blocking out or ignoring messages we would rather not receive.

Activity 1.4

Interference and barriers

1. Think of specific examples of interference you may experience in an IT work environment when sending or receiving messages. Organise your examples under the following headings:
   (a) **people**, e.g. office hierarchy, staff training
   (b) **technical**, e.g. equipment failure
   (c) **physical**, e.g. closed doors, distant locations
   (d) **spatial**, e.g. arrangement of work stations.
2. List some other barriers you have experienced either in your workplace or socially.

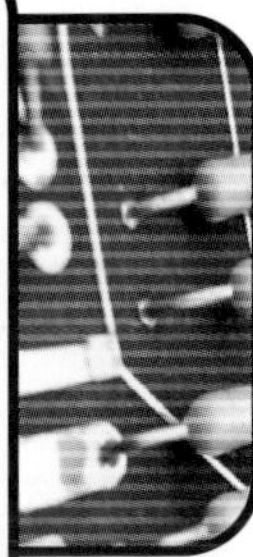

Case study 1.1

Overcoming communication barriers

You have been asked to help set up computers and provide basic instruction to three new staff members who work in different sections. They need instructions on the network procedures although they are all familiar with the word processing and database applications.

Case study activities

1. List the barriers to communication that could occur in this situation.
2. What communication skills would you use to overcome these barriers?

It is sometimes surprising that we are able to communicate as well as we do. Physical barriers, like closed doors, affect transmission, while language barriers reduce understanding.

Even if a message is received, personal barriers can reduce cooperation and agreement. You will be able to find a way around most barriers, but it usually means spending extra time, effort or money.

Understanding is achieved if the sender's original idea is conveyed without a change in meaning, but no matter how carefully you choose your words, all too often the message produces unintentional meanings. In reality, the meaning sent and the meaning understood are seldom identical. Figure 1.3 shows some of the forms of interference that may occur in an IT workplace.

Figure 1.3
Forms of interference

Feedback messages

When you reply to a message, your response will probably include some reaction to or comment about the sender's original idea. Similarly, the sender looks for some reaction from the receiver to ensure that the message has been understood.

Ask 'how?' instead of 'what?'

Ask how the listener intends to carry out your request. The response will give you a better idea of what they have really understood.

Ask the receiver to repeat your message

Some are happy to do this; some are not, since your request could imply distrust. However, with friends—or someone you are helping—this is an excellent way to avoid misunderstandings.

Explain why you need feedback

Since you are studying communication breakdowns, it will help to obtain open and direct feedback about misunderstandings as often as possible. Explain this to receivers, and ask for their cooperation in providing it.

Do not ask 'did you understand?'

This type of question adds to the problem. Few people will openly admit their failure to understand, especially if they are trying to impress you. An alternative is to ask new employees, for instance, to repeat the skill you have been demonstrating. In more formal contexts you might say 'OK, that should cover all the possibilities, let's just go over it one more time to make sure we haven't left anything out. Why don't you read out the steps and I'll check them off on my list.'

If you are the receiver, do not wait to be asked for feedback

Volunteer feedback. Say 'Let's see if I can remember it all. First I have to ...'. This also encourages others to volunteer feedback.

Activity 1.5

Feedback

1. How do you know if someone has understood your message? What kinds of behaviour do you notice in the other person?
2. Think of a work situation when you know a message has not been interpreted correctly. What indicators told you that the message was misunderstood?
3. List the ways in which you get feedback to check if a message has been understood correctly.

NON-VERBAL COMMUNICATION

In the IT industry, it may be tempting to forget the power of non-verbal communication and only rely on electronic or technical means. Successful managers and leaders in the industry know that skilful non-verbal communication is a powerful tool.

Non-verbal communication does not use words. It includes body language such as:

- eye contact
- facial expressions
- the way we stand or sit
- gestures
- how far we stand from people.

Non-verbal communication also includes voice characteristics such as:

- tone, pitch and expression
- volume and speed
- emphasis and intonation.
  Information may also be communicated through:
- spatial arrangements, e.g. the way furniture or equipment is arranged
- design/decor of the room
- your dress and grooming
- signs or symbols in the room.

Non-verbal signals

We depend on non-verbal signals in many situations, especially when we are not familiar with what is going on or when we do not know the people.

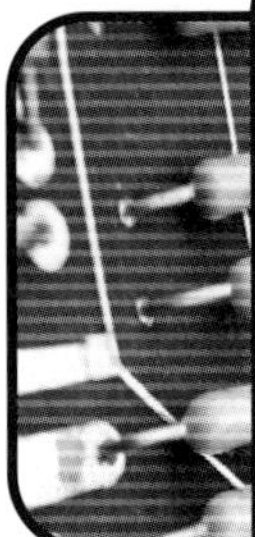

Activity 1.6

Non-verbal signals

Recall or imagine your first day at work.

1. List three non-verbal signals that:
   (a) encouraged you to communicate with people you met in your workplace
   (b) discouraged you from communicating with people you met in your workplace.
2. Discuss your results with others and do the following.
   (a) List some other non-verbal signals that made it easier to talk to new people.
   (b) List some other non-verbal signals that put you off talking to someone.

The importance of non-verbal communication

Over 70 per cent of meaning is expressed non-verbally. We cannot always tell what people intend to communicate just by what they say or how they look. We need to interpret their verbal and non-verbal signals.

The meaning of non-verbal communication can vary widely according to people's cultural background. It is important to be sensitive to the non-verbal behaviour of other people in our work place. If we misinterpret non-verbal signals, communication breakdown may occur.

Non-verbal communication at work

Non-verbal signals are important indicators of what a workmate is really feeling, or of what they think or want. In times of emotional tension or in difficult situations, understanding non-verbal behaviour can help reduce conflict at work.

The behaviour you normally use with fellow employees may be different from your behaviour in other situations. Think about the non-verbal communication (body language, tone of voice, etc.) that you use in different situations and the behaviours that you observe in others.

Figure 1.4
The way your workspace is set up will have an impact on how you communicate with other people.

QUESTIONING SKILLS

You can enhance your communication skills if you ask questions in the manner most appropriate for the workplace situation.

Types of questions

You need to use different types of questions to help you get the information you need, as shown in Table 1.1.

Table 1.1
Types of questions and their uses

Type of question	Examples	Purpose
Closed: usually elicits a yes, no or one-word answer	Are you the only one using the computer? Has this problem occurred before? Are you connected to a network?	to get single facts to confirm or check you have correct information to re-focus a talkative client
Open: usually prompts a longer answer	What is this meeting about? How do you feel about the new voice mail system? What do you use your computer for? What features are important for you?	to explore and gather information to encourage a more detailed answer to promote conversation
Probing: helps you to obtain specific information you require for a thorough service delivery	What kind of environment (temperature, exposure to sunlight etc.) are the computers located in? What did you notice when this problem started? When does it get worse? When does it improve?	to direct or guide the client to find out when, where, how, what and why

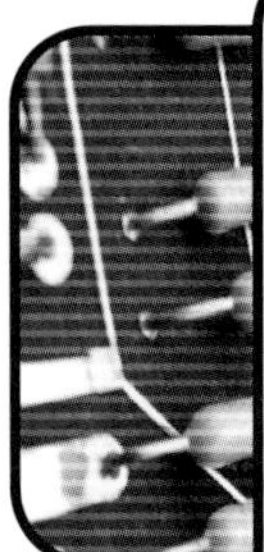

Activity 1.7

Questioning skills

Asking too many closed questions can waste time or turn an interview into an interrogation.

1. Design a series of three questions to find out the nature, source and extent of some workplace problems. Use the following problems or others from your workplace:
   (a) computer will not boot up
   (b) password will not let client into network
   (c) email cannot be sent.
2. Evaluate the effectiveness of your questions by trying them out with a partner.

ACTIVE LISTENING

One essential characteristic of good communicators is that they are great listeners. Listening accurately and carefully is essential if you want to:

- understand a complex situation
- recognise the emotions underlying an issue
- understand the other person's perspective on an issue
- determine the needs and problems of clients
- solve both technical problems and those involving people
- broaden your perspective on any issue
- work effectively with others.
    You are engaged in active listening when you are:
- 'hearing' what the other person is saying rather than working on your reply
- asking questions for clarification
- using non-verbal communication to send a message that says 'I am listening to what you are saying'.

    Active listening is a skill you learn by practice. It takes more effort than plain 'hearing', but the benefits make it well worthwhile.

Benefits of active listening

There are many benefits of active listening.

- You enjoy two-way benefits. When people notice how well you listen to them, they usually reciprocate and try to understand you better.
- Relationships within a group improve. Members develop a more positive attitude towards each other, so personal support and teamwork is strengthened. Friendships develop and deepen.
- You receive more accurate information. People explaining a problem are more inclined to give you the whole story. The more confident they are that you are listening, the happier they will be to share facts they would not reveal to a poor listener.
- People encouraged by your active listening often discover solutions to their own problems. The opportunity to talk things over in depth—or just the chance to put a problem into words—is all they need to see the issue in its proper perspective.
- You get on better with people. Disagreements are more easily settled when people listen to each other. Active listening combined with empathy makes it easier to solve problems or at least reach a compromise.
- You can find out not only what people are saying, but why they are saying it. You acquire vital information and discover more about what is really going on.

Barriers to effective listening

Interrupting

You may disagree with what is being said; however, it pays to hear the other person out. Interrupting to inject a counter-argument is a non-verbal signal. It suggests that for you, scoring a point of disagreement holds a higher priority than finding what issues you agree on. **If you listen without interrupting and then in turn make your point, the other person will be more inclined to listen to you.**

Letting your emotions control your listening

If you get too emotional you will be more inclined to jump to conclusions or interpret words and actions wrongly. This distorts the discussion and hinders clear understanding.

Inadequate background knowledge

Often when people begin to speak they assume you know exactly what they are referring to. If this appears to happen, stop the speaker and ask for clarification.

Understanding what you hear

As you listen, you will need to extract the main ideas from among the other points. People cannot always serve their spoken messages to you in neat, organised packages; that is one reason they write important messages—to sort out ideas before presenting them.

Listen for key 'topic' ideas. They need not always be facts. Facts, data and examples may have been added only to support the main topic, which might be non-factual but vitally important—for instance, how others feel about a controversial issue. The average person speaks at about 100–250 words a minute. You can hear and understand over 400 words a minute and can think at an even faster rate. Use this spare thinking time to concentrate on summarising main points, clarifying meanings and checking non-verbal signals.

Consider the context in which you are listening, the power ratio and other background signs before deciding what the main topic really is. **Then use feedback to find out whether what you think you understand is in fact the key issue.**

Activity 1.8

Listening at work

Think about a recent incident or issue at work that affected you or the work you do. It should be an issue you feel strongly about. Perhaps you disagreed with a decision that affected the work of the team, or perhaps you had a problem with a workmate.

1. Describe the incident or issue and your point of view.
2. Did your workmates/other people listen to your point of view?
3. What happened to you after they listened to you? How did you feel? What did you do? How did it affect the work of the team?

Skills needed for active listening

Active listening means effective listening. It is more than just hearing the message; it is about understanding the content and feelings behind the words. Active listening is made up of attending, following and reflecting skills as shown in Table 1.2.

Table 1.2
Active listening skills

Attending skills	Following skills	Reflecting skills
These are the skills that show another person you are prepared and willing to listen. They include: • using body language that shows you are paying attention (e.g. facing the person, looking interested) • appropriate eye contact • minimising outside distractions and noise (e.g. turning off a radio or television)	These skills show that you are interested in what is being said and encourage the person to expand on the message. The skills include: • friendly interested questions to open the conversation (e.g. 'Do you want to tell me about … ?') • minimal feedback to encourage the speaker i.e. the short words or sounds that people often use in a conversation almost automatically (e.g. 'mm', 'Yes', 'right') • attentive silences • infrequent questions	These are the skills that show that you not only have heard what has been said but also understand the feelings and intentions of the message. You can show this by: • restating the essential parts of what has been said (useful if it is a long and complicated issue because it ensures that you have understood correctly) • reflecting feelings and content back at the speaker (e.g. 'You seem upset about what happened.') • summarising the major concerns

Activity 1.9

Listening skills

This activity involves the different active listening skills—attending, following and reflecting—and can be completed with a partner or in a small group.

1. Make a list of some topics to talk about. They should be topics you are interested in and have some strong opinions about. Examples could include:
   (a) your interest in the IT industry
   (b) the effect of the GST on the IT industry
   (c) benefits and pitfalls of e-commerce
   (d) what kind of job you would like to have
   (e) things that annoy you about your job
   (f) the future of computers in the home
   (g) software improvements in your area of expertise
   (h) any other work-related issue.
2. Have one person choose a topic and talk about it for 1–2 minutes while the other person listens actively by:
   (a) **attending**: showing you are paying attention
   (b) **following**: offering encouragement
   (c) **reflecting**: summarising to show you understand.
3. Swap roles and rate each other's listening skills.

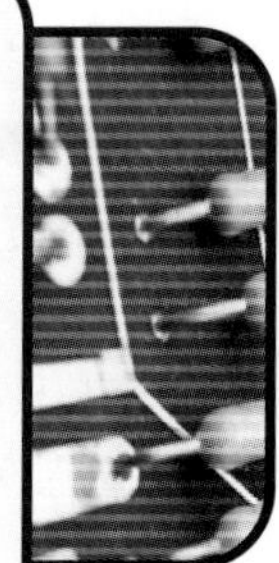

EMPATHY

Empathy is an important concept that underpins effective understanding. Empathy is often confused with sympathy.

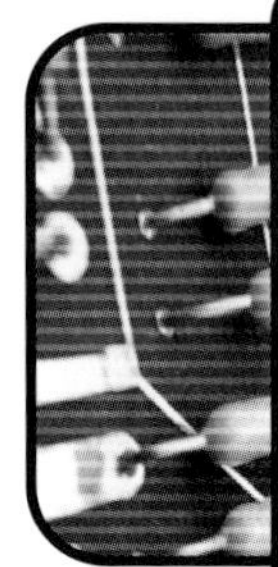

Activity 1.10

Empathy and sympathy

What is your understanding of each of these terms? Ask two other people for their definitions of each term and look at the similarities and differences in their answers. Use this information and a dictionary to accurately define the terms for yourself.

Sympathy is when ____ ?

Empathy is when ____ ?

It is easy to feel empathy for someone with a similar worldview. The challenge is to feel empathy when someone thinks in a very different way!

Creating empathy

Empathy is sensing another's feelings and attitudes as if we had experienced them ourselves. It is our willingness to enter another's world, and our ability to communicate to that person our feelings of sensitivity towards them. It is not blind sentimentality; it always retains some objectivity and distance. We do not lose our own identity, though we discover our common humanity. Figure 1.5 shows the value of creating empathy.

Create empathy by:

- taking other people's needs and concerns seriously
- valuing feelings and attitudes
- respecting others' privacy, experience and values
- listening actively
- encouraging further elaboration and clarification
- using open body language and a warm vocal tone
- reserving judgment and blame
- displaying interest in what others communicate
- withholding unsought advice
- supporting others' attempts to find a solution
- making affirming statements and gestures.

CULTURAL AWARENESS

Australia is often described as a multicultural society. This means that our society is made up of many diverse cultural groups. People from over 160 different countries of origin are represented in Australia today. Cultural identity may be based on political or religious beliefs, gender, education or interest groups, as well as on racial or national origin.

Figure 1.5
The value of empathy

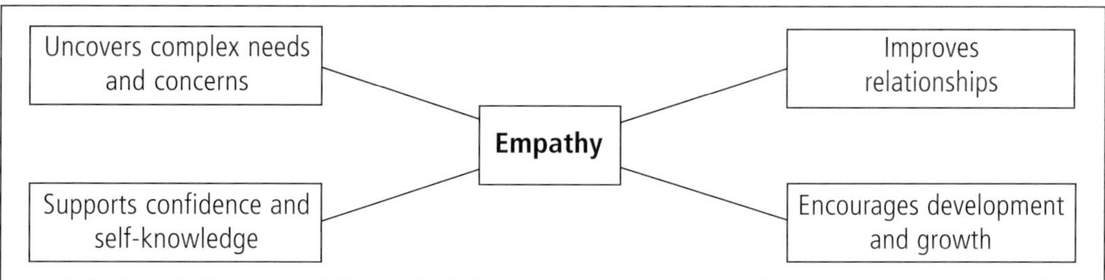

Your workplace may include people from a variety of cultural backgrounds. Many Aboriginal families have been here for over 2000 generations, while non-indigenous Australians have been here for only a maximum of eight generations. Many of the latter are the first or second generation of their family to live in Australia.

In the workplace you need to be tolerant of differences in values, beliefs and attitudes and the behaviours that reflect them. If you are aware of cultural differences you will be able to help your team to work effectively. Working effectively together requires an understanding of how culture can influence behaviour and communication styles.

Generalisations

When we have little experience of people from other cultures we tend to make generalisations based on this limited knowledge or understanding.

Activity 1.11

Making generalisations

Choose a person in your workplace who you do not know very well, and who you believe comes from a different cultural background to yourself. Answer the following questions:

1. What type of music would this person be more likely to enjoy?
2. What kind of car would this person be more likely to drive?
3. Does this tell you something important or does it stop you from understanding people properly and create a negative image?

Stereotypes

Generalisations can lead to stereotypes. Stereotyping occurs when you assume that you know something about a person because you know their cultural background. We all use stereotypes to a certain degree to help organise our ideas about people. However, in the workplace it is important that stereotypes do not interfere with communication.

Stereotypes can lead to pre-judging or prejudice. Instead of relating to team members as individuals, we judge their appearance or behaviour on the basis of the stereotype we have of their cultural group. In a work team this results in communication breakdown and can lead to inefficient or even dangerous work practices.

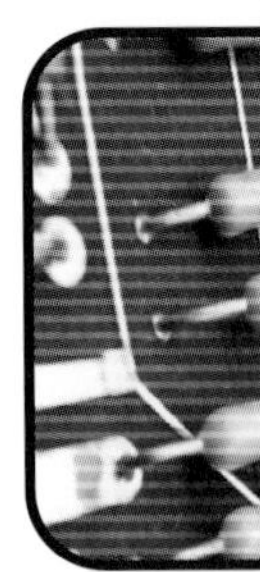

Activity 1.12

Stereotyping

1. What judgments could people make about your work performance based on your appearance or dress?
2. List what you would think about somebody in your work team who:
   (a) drives a prestige European car
   (b) refuses to wear the standard uniform
   (c) seems to miss a lot of team meetings
   (d) has tattoos
   (e) spends meal breaks alone
   (f) seems to take a lot of days off.
3. List the diverse cultures that are represented in your workplace. (Remember, cultural identity may be based on political or religious beliefs, gender, education or interest groups, as well as on racial or national origin.)
4. List the benefits to you and the workplace of having a culturally diverse workforce.

ACTION POINTS

> Plan your communication—be aware of the needs and wants of all involved in the communication.

> Sit in the receiver's chair.

> Avoid background signals that confuse your communication.

> Be aware of any barriers to effective communication.

> Divide messages into logical topics or points.

> Send messages clearly, at a level and pace the receiver can cope with.

> Use a range of channels in important communication situations.

> Use feedback to ensure messages are received.

> Build understanding and agreement through positive communication.

> Use active listening as a tool to build understanding.

> Give and ask for feedback to confirm agreements and outcomes.

> Be clear on the follow-up steps to your communication.

> Be aware of different rules and customs in other cultures.

> Use language that respects the beliefs and values of others.

SUMMARY

Communication makes it possible to share ideas and feelings with other people. Most communication involves more than just sharing meanings. Usually it has a direct effect on the relationships between the people involved.

Communication channels are the media or devices by which messages move. All at some stage involve basic senses—sight, hearing or touch. The effective sender thinks about who is receiving the message, why it should be shared and how best to share it. This means that messages need to be planned.

The meaning understood by the receiver is seldom exactly the same as the one in the sender's mind. Feedback helps to indicate how accurate the level of understanding really is. Consequently, two-way communication is far more effective than one-way communication because it allows feedback between both parties.

Anything that delays a message or makes it harder to convey meaning to another person is a communication barrier. People who are not clear about their purpose in communication usually send unclear messages that lead to breakdowns. Denial—a result of bias, prejudice or an unwillingness to receive the message—also leads to blockages and barriers.

Any response to a message is 'feedback' and can be verbal, non-verbal, positive, negative, or involve action. One kind of negative feedback—error feedback—is especially important. It tells you whether your messages are 'on target' and, if not, how to set them right. Encourage error messages in order to find out exactly when and where problems are occurring. Use feedback to diagnose breakdowns, and do not wait to be asked; when communicating, give feedback as a matter of course. This encourages others to do the same. Business relationships can be kept active through follow-up feedback. However, do not assume that all feedback is accurate—some people use it to mislead you.

Use empathy: 'sit in the receiver's chair' to discover the causes of misunderstandings and breakdowns. Tuning in to people adds to your ability to understand others and helps others to understand you. Your empathy also encourages others to agree with you by showing them how your message will help them to meet their current needs. Empathy on the part of both sender and receiver marks the difference between ordinary understanding and excellence in communication.

It is hard to change beliefs and attitudes, but opinions can be altered. Empathy helps you to decide whether people are expressing only an opinion, or strongly held views based on beliefs and values. Use empathy in communicating with difficult customers or prejudiced opponents. You do not have to like people or agree with them in order to empathise with them.

Messages have a better chance of successful reception if transmitted via a combination of several channels. Typical non-verbal channels include body movement, facial expressions, posture, clothing, symbols, colours, vocal tone and pictures. Mass-media channels are ideal for one-way, impersonal communication, particularly in carrying messages for the general public. Personal channels are preferable for communication with a small number of people. They use more time and energy but create better relationships, and are helpful in achieving cooperation and agreement.

TRAINING LOG

Cultural awareness

1. Collect five pieces of information that directly relate to how people communicate with each other at work. This information may come from internal or external websites or from printed sources. You might consider policies or guidelines related to equal opportunity, anti-discrimination, WorkCover, or occupational health and safety. The information could also be a customer service policy or mission statement from your workplace or one you know. Ask your teacher, trainer or workplace supervisor for further advice.
2. Describe four main features of your workplace that affect how people communicate. Describe one feature for each of the following: personal, environmental, technical and cultural.

Action plan

1. Find five job advertisements for positions you would be interested in applying for now or when you have completed your training. Use a job website and the IT employment section of a newspaper.
   (a) Give the title of each position.
   (b) Make a list of the specific communication skills each position requires. Be sure to differentiate between **communication** skills and **technical** skills.
2. Interview a person in a managerial or recruitment position in an IT work environment. What communication skills do they look for in prospective employees?

CHAPTER 2

CONFLICT RESOLUTION AND NEGOTIATION SKILLS

COMPETENCIES

This chapter is linked to elements contained in the following competencies which are in the Information Technology Training Package.
- Interact with Clients ICAITS009B
- Relate to Clients on a Business Level ICAITTW027B
- Determine Client Business Expectations and Needs ICAITAD041A
- Confirm Client Business Needs ICAITAD042A
- Apply Problem Solving Techniques to Achieve Organisational Goals ICAITS010B
- Participate in a Team and Individually to Achieve Organisational Goals ICAITTW011B
- Coordinate and Maintain Teams ICAITTW026B
- Apply Skills in Human Resources Management BSX154L406
- Guide Application of Human Resources Management BSX154L506
- Manage Human Resources BSX154L606

The aim of this chapter is to provide an understanding of conflict resolution and negotiation skills. The issues discussed in this chapter will help you solve problems or differences between yourself and others. We need to be able to solve conflict and negotiate suitable solutions in a wide range of contexts. These skills are about maintaining positive relationships with all people.

In particular it will help you answer questions such as these:

- Why do many people feel uncomfortable in conflict situations?
- Is it possible to 'plan' the way you manage conflicts?
- How can conflict be used to achieve positive outcomes?
- Can you achieve your goals in conflict situations?
- How can you develop strategies to make it easier to handle other people's anger, threats or distress?
- Do you have the skills needed to constructively manage conflict?
- How can you plan your negotiations?
- What makes a successful negotiator?
- What can be done if the negotiation does not go according to plan?
- How can you improve the chances of implementing the agreement?

TOPICS DISCUSSED

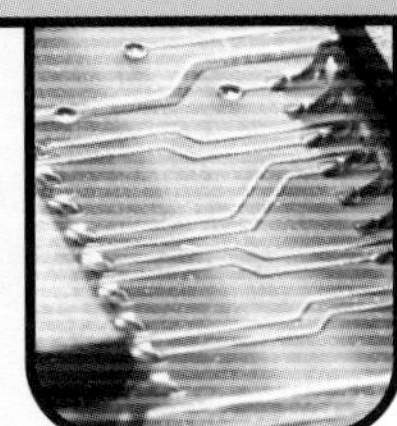

- What is conflict?
- Causes and signs of conflict
- Stages of conflict
- Factors that affect the development of conflict
- Responding to conflict
- What is negotiation?
- Preparing for the negotiation
- Conducting the negotiation
- Evaluating the effectiveness of the negotiation

INTRODUCTION

This chapter examines the factors that contribute to conflict in the workplace, signs of conflict, stages the conflict moves through, and factors that influence conflict. It describes strategies for managing conflict situations to generate positive outcomes. Managing conflict does not always mean that conflict will be resolved, because this often requires more sophisticated negotiation skills. Therefore this chapter also examines the processes involved in successfully negotiating with others in a wide range of situations. In particular it highlights the processes applicable to any negotiation situation.

You may be required to resolve conflict and negotiate suitable outcomes for any of the following examples:

- client service agreements
- work standards
- work methods
- software development projects
- funding arrangements
- complaints from clients about technology problems
- deadlines for the completion of work
- budgets for the implementation of new technology
- hardware and software requirements for a specific situation
- between staff about discriminatory behaviour in the workplace.

An effective outcome based on constructive responses leaves the people involved in the conflict feeling as though their needs have been respected and avenues for further communication are left open. Negotiation skills are essential for resolving conflicts successfully and helping you and other parties to agree on the best outcomes. The best outcome is one that is accepted by the parties as meeting their needs and achieving the criteria for an effective solution.

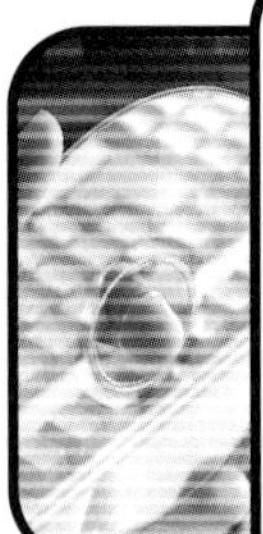

Case study 2.1

Identifying issues

Dale and Sandy work for a CD duplication company specialising in quick response CDR replicating. One day you are walking past the office when Sandy storms out and collides with you. You ask her what the problem is and have the following conversation.

Sandy: Dale is a real pain in the neck—he's always taking credit for things I've done and then puts me down in front of Lee. I can't stand him! I try to avoid him but Lee has put us both on that Collins job and now he's acting as if he's in charge of it.

You: Hmm, I don't seem to have any problems with Dale. Have you tried talking to Lee about this?

Case study activities

1. What are some of the issues in this situation?
2. What might happen if the situation is not dealt with effectively?

WHAT IS CONFLICT?

Most people use the term conflict as a description of a negative or difficult state. It does not usually conjure up a positive image.

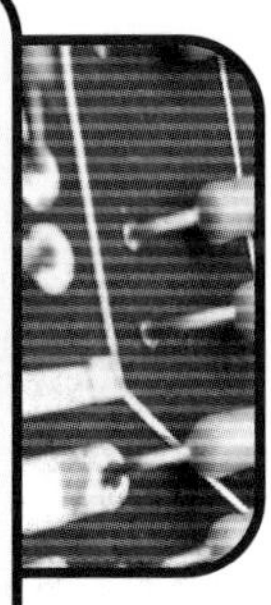

Activity 2.1

Understanding conflict

Think about your experiences of conflict both at work and in other relationships, then write or draw your answers to the following questions.

1. What does the word conflict mean to you?
2. What feelings, colours and images do you experience and associate with conflict? Form small groups of four and discuss your answers to the first two questions. In the group, answer the next four questions.
3. What are some of the common images, feelings and meanings associated with conflict?
4. Why do a lot of people see conflict as negative?
5. What reactions/behaviours are triggered by conflict?
6. What are the positive outcomes of conflict?

Conflict can be defined as:

the state in a relationship or interaction when two or more people are attempting to have differing needs met in a way that creates discomfort and results in negative reactions or responses.

Conflict occurs at some point in most, if not all, relationships. If it is perceived as a negative state it usually means that for at least one of the parties a negative experience may have occurred recently or in the past that may still affect the relationship.

People do not cope easily with conflict situations. Conflicting needs, discomfort and negative reactions from other people often cause responses that make the situation worse. In many cases, people follow predictable patterns which range from hostile aggression to passive resistance or capitulation.

Activity 2.2

Attitudes to conflict

Consider the following statements. Do you think they are true? Explain why you do/do not believe the statement.

Statement	T/F	Reason
Conflict at work means that the team and/or the organisation is not functioning properly.		
Conflict is caused by poor communication between people.		
If avoided conflict will eventually go away.		
All conflicts can be resolved.		
Conflict always results in a winner and a loser.		

Goals versus relationships

Conflict can occur when there is a sufficiently large gap between one person's goals and those of another to affect the relationship between them. One person may want something that appears to be incompatible with another's needs. The need may be a simple one such as wanting to be left alone or a complex one involving deeply emotional issues.

People's needs are an important factor in conflict situations. If the problem is simple it may be possible to ignore the situation and the discomfort it causes, to be aware of what is happening but leave things as they are without incurring serious consequences. There are, however, instances where serious problems have been ignored because someone has wanted to avoid conflict at any cost. A classic example involved an airliner attempting a landing under difficult conditions. The plane crashed because the copilot was not prepared to tell the captain that the latter's instruction to abort a landing was inappropriate as the plane was out of fuel. The copilot would have had to insist that they were in an emergency situation and demand an immediate landing. In this highly dangerous situation obsessive protocol and deference overrode good judgment.

Avoiding conflict can also create problems. The cockpit of a plane is an excellent example of a situation where high levels of communication and cooperation are essential, but where personality and workplace culture can create havoc. Our own work situations may not be as dramatic, but the same principles apply. Airlines have begun to recognise this and are now spending more time teaching communication skills to air and ground crews.

Look for active and passive signs of conflict. Conflict has a number of recognisable signs. These include things like shouting, harsh tones of voice, and people storming off. Passive behaviours such as silence and refusal to engage or compromise can also be signs of conflict but may be harder to recognise. On the surface, these behaviours seem aimed at pleasing, but are in fact ways people cope with extreme discomfort.

The two faces of conflict

If conflict is going to be resolved in a successful way then it is important for each person involved to view the situation as an opportunity to change something or to learn something. People's needs are an important factor in conflict situations. If the problem is simple it may be possible to ignore the situation and the discomfort it causes. There are, however, instances where serious problems have been ignored because someone has wanted to avoid conflict at any cost.

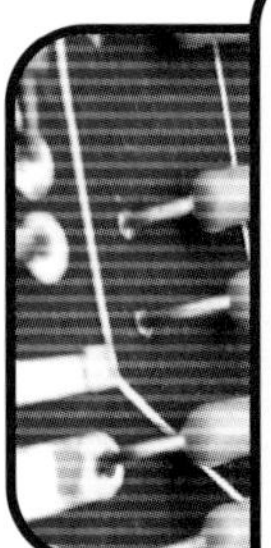

Activity 2.3

Avoiding conflict

Think about the IT workplace. Make a list of potential problems that could result by people avoiding conflict. List some examples of what can occur if people avoid conflict. The first one has been done for you.

1. A talented employee may decide to leave the workplace, resulting in a loss of skill and expertise for the company.

2. ____

____

3. _______________________________________

____

4. _______________________________________

____

Conflict is not in itself a bad thing. People can manage conflicts without interfering with their relationships and ability to get on and do their job. Conflict is a very important feature of all relationships. It can be a safety valve that helps to release emotions built up by the demands of work, parents, children or financial problems. In families, for example, it helps children (and adults) identify the boundaries of behaviour. As children grow up they need to practise more demanding and complex roles, and it is only by coming up hard against parents' and other people's values that they develop a sense of where the limits are.

Resolving conflict requires effort on both sides. You need to use active listening, good questioning skills and empathy. You also need some additional skills that will be discussed later in this chapter.

Figure 2.1
Conflict in the workplace

CAUSES AND SIGNS OF CONFLICT

You know that you have a conflict on your hands when someone is behaving angrily or aggressively towards you. You may not be responding directly, but the conflict situation exists nevertheless. Types of behaviour may include:

- anger
- physically aggressive acts
- verbal threats or aggression
- signs of distress
- intimidation, sarcasm or ridicule
- resentment.

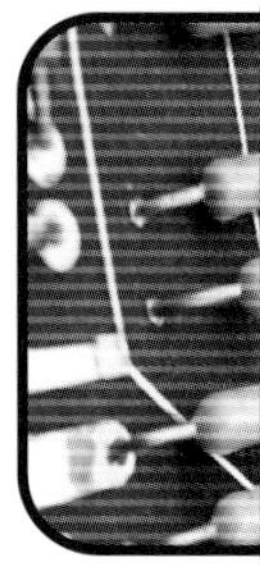

Activity 2.4

Signs of conflict

Think about situations where you have experienced conflict at work or have observed it in others. Here are some examples:

- you hear that a co-worker has complained about you to your line manager
- your suggestions about improved customer service are ignored.

    Choose an example from your own experience.

1. How did you feel?
2. What happened?
3. What types of behaviour have you witnessed during other conflicts?

If you want to resolve conflicts you need to acknowledge that there is a problem. It is easy to recognise your own feelings but it is even more important to recognise them in others. You may not believe that there is a problem but it does not follow that no problem actually exists. Open and positive communication in the workplace can alert you to issues that need resolution.

At work, conflict signals that all is not well and things need to be looked at. It is also an important ingredient of the change process in organisations. As new technologies or processes are introduced (e.g. when a company is restructured), people's traditional views or ways of doing things are threatened and this can be a cause of conflict. People's reactions and the type and level of conflict emerging can be a vital source of information for managers, who can use it to manage the change and help people adapt themselves or the processes.

Conflict on the job is usually contained because power relationships make continuing the conflict in a destructive way a potentially job-threatening experience. In other cases the underlying professional respect that two people might have for each other acts to contain the damage. There are different styles of communicating that keep conflict at a constructive level. People who have a positive attitude to relationships and a commitment to a longer-term view will do things like:

- listen to what others are saying
- use inclusive language that does not put others down
- observe what is going on around them
- clarify their goals and the strategies for achieving them.

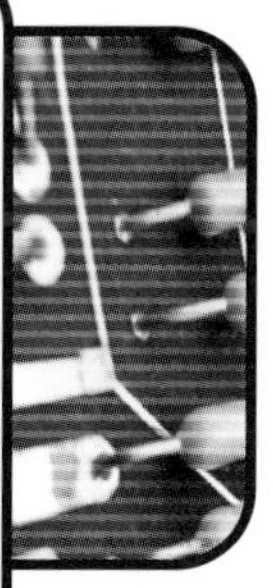

Activity 2.5

Personal experiences of workplace conflicts

Think of a situation in your workplace where you felt there was a conflict. It may be one you were involved in or one that you observed.

1. What was the conflict about?
2. Why did the conflict occur?
3. List the negative outcomes of the conflict (e.g. delay in meeting deadlines due to the time taken to resolve disputes).
4. List the positive outcomes of the conflict (e.g. improvements in procedures).
5. Discuss your answers in small groups. List some of the common areas where conflict may arise in your organisation.

There is always an element of anger in conflict; people usually fight for or about the things that make them angry. In some cases the problem arises because someone gets something that another person feels they are entitled to, or something is taken or used without permission. Other causes might be a person being attacked unfairly or accused of doing something they did not do, or not performing to some sort of standard. In all these cases conflict arises because one person believes that the other did not live up to some sort of expectation.

Different expectations and uncertainty can cause conflict. People feel comfortable when events fit their expectations. When accepted patterns are changed people experience uncertainty, frustration and sometimes fear. These feelings cause strong reactions against the people seen as the cause of that uncertainty. An example of strong reactions in the face of ambiguity occurs when there is uncertainty about finance for a job or project that might affect the jobs of contract staff.

Many of the circumstances that give rise to ambiguity occur in the external environment, which intensifies the participants' feelings of powerlessness. This can come out as aggression towards people who are innocent bystanders. When the economy is in recession, sales fall off, creating uncertainties regarding employment. Not only do levels of conflict in the workplace increase, but people often take their anger and frustration home and inflict it on their families and friends, who struggle to deal with it because a large part of the problem is outside their control.

Activity 2.6

Conflict situations

List some of the situations specific to an IT workplace that may cause conflict.

1. Keeping up with advances in technology.
2. Lack of technical service or maintenance.
3. _______________________________________
4. _______________________________________

STAGES OF CONFLICT

The nature of the IT industry means that you will need to work closely with lots of people on numerous projects, managing client needs as well as organisational needs. Conflict often moves through stages. It is sometimes possible to identify what triggers the move from one to another, but mostly the transition occurs without people being specifically conscious of the shift. Dealing with a potential problem early can avoid a bigger problem in the future.

There are four main stages of conflict: discomfort, trigger, general tension and misunderstanding, and crisis.

Discomfort

Discomfort is an early sign that conditions for conflict to emerge exist. Events that do not seem important by themselves can build up and cause resentment. For example, meeting times are changed at short notice without consulting those involved, or a technical officer fails to follow up on a customer enquiry and the customer complains to the manager about the poor quality of service. Good communication skills will often help you identify the source of the concern and deal with it constructively before things worsen. If you are feeling uncomfortable ask yourself: 'Is there something I could do now about this feeling?'.

Trigger

A trigger or series of events makes you feel uncomfortable with the person. The reaction to some incident, often trivial in nature, is exaggerated in its intensity. The effect of discomfort has led to interpreting behaviour in a negative way. For example, someone postpones making changes to an online program because they know it will be more efficient to do it later when a number of other changes have to be made. The supervisor sees that the change has not been made and confronts the employee then and there.

General tension and misunderstanding

A lack of trust develops due to non-resolution of the problem. All behaviours are interpreted as negative and reinforce the poor relationship. If this continues, things can only get worse for the relationship from here. Two workers may be arguing about a software problem when a line manager intervenes to resolve the dispute by organising things for them. If the tension between the two has been growing because the company is being restructured and one of them may have to leave, then solving the software problem will do little to resolve things.

Crisis

The relationship is so poor that communication is misinterpreted. If the relationship is in crisis it is obvious that conflict exists. You know that you have a crisis on your hands when someone is behaving angrily or aggressively towards you. You may not be responding directly, but the conflict situation exists nevertheless. Types of behaviour related to this stage include:

* anger
* physically aggressive acts
* verbal threats or aggression
* signs of distress.

At this stage the conflict may affect others not directly involved such as fellow workers, management, family and friends.

Figure 2.2
Stages of conflict

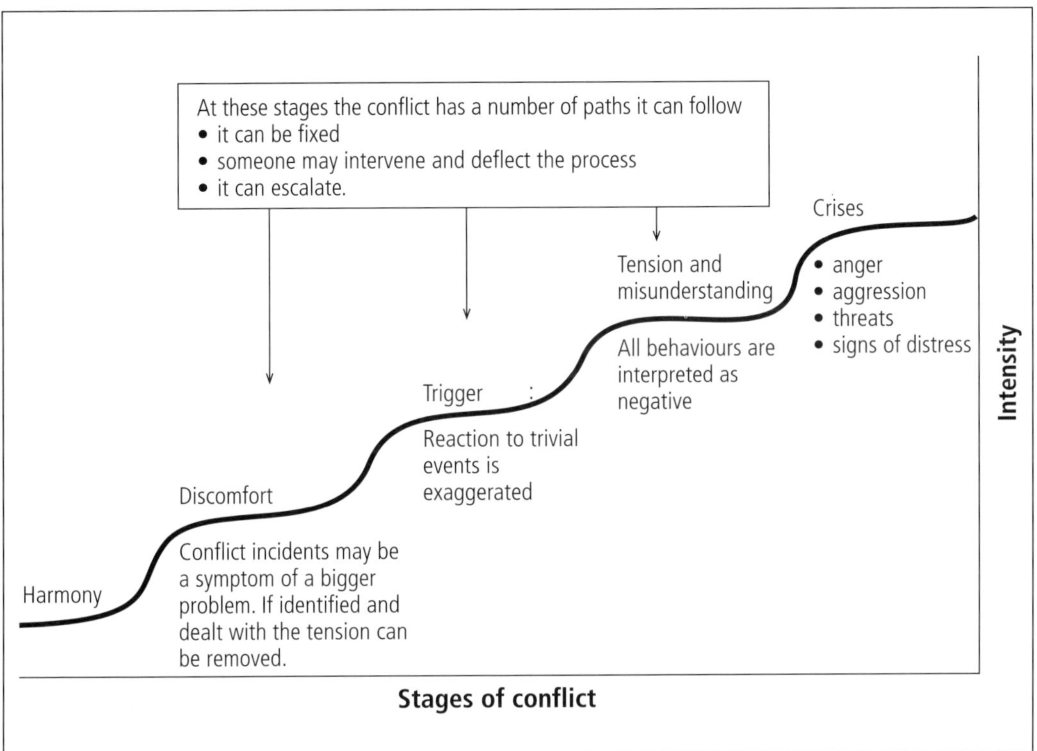

The real insight is to deal with a potential conflict at a low level before it turns into a crisis. In the early stages, the conflict will still have a number of paths it can follow and early intervention may help to avoid the crisis. Dealing with the conflict may not necessarily remove it; the conflict may simply move back to a stage where it is not as obvious, or people are less concerned about its effects. Understanding what stage the conflict has reached helps with deciding whether it is likely to be managed easily, or if it has moved beyond simple remedies and needs more sophisticated management.

Full-blown conflicts can become 'institutionalised' and there are many examples available. Institutionalised conflict is where people have come to accept conflict with another person as a normal part of the way they operate and everything they do has accommodated to that fact. Productivity may be down, but people seem to be getting on with things. The temptation (or should we say tendency?) is to leave things as they are and hope that the problem or those causing the problem will just 'go away'. Experience has shown that they rarely do.

FACTORS THAT AFFECT THE DEVELOPMENT OF CONFLICT

Sometimes it is easy to focus only on the actual events of the conflict situation and miss seeing other factors that might be the real cause of the problem. This is a bit like the situation where you can smell smoke so you hunt around for a fan to blow it out of the room, instead of first looking for a fire to put out. If there is a fire, dealing with the smoke is not going to solve the problem.

Asking whether there is more to the situation than meets the eye helps identify other options for dealing with the conflict and ensures you are addressing the real problem rather than its symptoms. It is sometimes useful to look at the problem from a *people* and *environment* perspective.

Personal and environmental factors both affect the development of a conflict. Our work style—the way we operate at work—is determined by a complex combination of personality, worldview and work environment factors. It may also be a source of conflict.

People factors

Factors such as needs and wants, self-concept, past experience, and health all fit under this heading.

Needs and wants

If the outcome of a conflict situation affects basic needs and wants, such as income or job security, people will fight a lot harder than if the outcome is less important, such as whether or not their idea for the design of a customer service questionnaire is accepted rather than someone else's.

Self-concept

Constructive outcomes to conflict are difficult to achieve and long-term solutions are almost impossible where a poor self-concept plays a part. A positive self-concept allows people to accept a wider range of outcomes and handle conflict more effectively; they are less threatened by uncertainty, and more inclined to consider a wide range of options in any situation. They will canvass other people's ideas. People with a low self-concept cannot put themselves in the other person's shoes, which results in a rigid approach to problem solving, making it hard to consider options.

Past experience

Prior experience in conflict situations plays an important role in determining how people will respond when confronted by conflict. A history of positive outcomes will ensure a higher chance of future outcomes being positive. Of course the reverse also holds true. People who have had significant problems when dealing with conflict will assume the worst in many situations and be more inclined to use negative tactics.

Health

People's health as well as the existence of specific illnesses will have a marked impact on the course of a conflict. The most obvious example is tiredness, which can severely hamper a person's capacity to respond effectively, resulting in actions that are out of character. This can undermine all the planning and good work done to manage a particular conflict.

Other impediments to managing conflict effectively include excessive consumption of alcohol and drugs, and emotional crises in relationships. These diminish a person's ability to respond rationally, let alone resolve conflict situations.

Commonsense says that people in good health are more likely to cope with stress, of which conflict is just one cause and/or outcome. The implications of this are wide ranging for organisations interested in improving productivity through increases in efficiency or improved levels of customer service. It is a recognised fact that good health lowers stress levels and improves job performance. As a result of this knowledge some employers have provided services designed to lower stress levels for their employees. Examples of some of the services include fitness, recreation and child-care facilities. Good health and fitness improve people's ability to manage conflict.

Environmental factors

Environmental factors are those over which the participants may have no direct control. The management culture of the organisation, the state of the company's business, pressures from clients, and even the weather are environmental factors that affect the way people manage conflict situations.

Management culture

Some organisations place a strong emphasis on consultation and effective communication. Experience in implementing changes in areas of workplace safety and quality management has shown that when communication channels are ineffective, stress levels during periods of change increase, resulting in higher levels of conflict. Where organisations foster a strongly competitive culture, people will tend to reflect that approach in their dealings with each other through behaviour designed to 'beat' the other person. **A culture of cooperation and collaboration reduces conflict.**

All organisations have formal and informal structures and processes that have been consciously put in place, or have emerged in response to specific needs and then become permanent. Examples include:
- conciliation processes
- approaches to staff induction and training
- accountability mechanisms
- reward systems (formal and informal)
- leadership styles.

Uncertainty

Uncertainty about systems and processes increases the incidence of conflict. Informal processes for things like conciliation and reward systems can generate conflict if these systems operate erratically and if people are never sure how the systems will react to their problems. Informal processes create uncertainty as to the amount and kind of support that can be expected.

An overemphasis on structures, which happens in organisations with strong bureaucracies, can also foster conflict because the system is too inflexible. So when people get frustrated with the constraints, they bypass the 'system', which often brings a strong negative reaction from those with a vested interest in maintaining the existing structures.

State of business

When business trends are uncertain, the stresses of trying to cope or the uncertainty of whether people will keep their jobs pervades the organisation.

Pressure from clients

Clients' behaviour can influence employees' threshold for managing conflict, especially if clients are very demanding and the time frame for a response is unrealistic. In the IT industry, the client's business may rely on the operating system. It is generally accepted that the larger and more expensive the equipment the less available in-house support will be; this means the supplier is relied on for support. For the client any technical failure would be considered an emergency and they may expect immediate technical support.

Weather

Research has shown that particular weather patterns affect people's moods and this shows up in increased levels of tension and irritability. Thunderstorm activity and long, hot spells are obvious examples.

Individual/personal styles

People will bring their natural style to a given situation, but it will be influenced by the context in which it is used. Examples of styles that people use include:

- denial that a conflict exists
- hiding from conflict situations
- smoothing things over at all costs
- aggression
- cooperative, or people-centred
- problem solving.

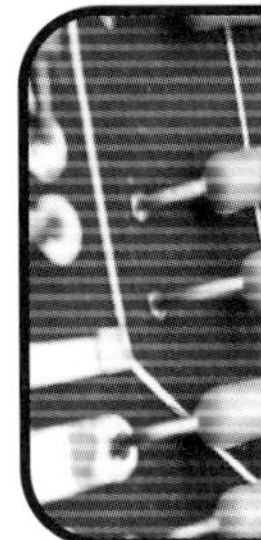

Activity 2.7

Work style questionnaire

Tick each statement that describes how you usually operate at work (not how you would *like* to operate).

There are no correct or incorrect answers, so tick as many or as few as describe your work style. No work style is more valid than any other. All sets of characteristics are needed for an organisation to function effectively. Ideally, we should all develop the best characteristics of each work style.

1. Add up your score for each quadrant. The quadrant with the highest score should tell you something about your work style. Consider the advantages and disadvantages of each quadrant as a work style.
2. List three features of your work style which you think are helpful in dealing with conflict.

____

____

____

Orderly and systematic	☐	Results oriented	☐
Deliberate and unassertive	☐	Accepts challenges	☐
Enjoys study and analysis	☐	Strong willed	☐
Critical thinker	☐	Takes the initiative	☐
Detailed and thorough	☐	Willing to confront	☐
Well organised	☐	Makes decisions easily	☐
Likes accuracy	☐	Ambitious	☐
Weighs alternatives	☐	Sense of urgency	☐
Needs standard operating guidelines	☐	Assertive	☐
Steady quiet manner	☐	Likes solving problems	☐
Dislikes sudden or abrupt changes	☐	Questions the status quo	☐
Eager to please	☐	Persuasive	☐
Helpful	☐	Socially outgoing	☐
Lacks interest in goal setting	☐	Sees possibilities	☐
Not highly competitive	☐	Informal	☐
Has difficulty saying no	☐	Fun loving	☐
Loyal	☐	Energetic	☐
Calms excited people	☐	Creative	☐
Good listener	☐	Lack of concern for details	☐
Needs security	☐	Likes participating in groups	☐
Lets others take the initiative in social situations	☐	Creates a motivational environment	☐
		Does not like to be hemmed in	☐
Patient	☐	Open with feelings	☐
Enjoys assisting others	☐		

Source: Conflict Resolution Network. P. O. Box 1016, Chatswood, NSW, 2057. Phone: 02 9419 8500, fax: 02 9413 1148, email: crn@crnhq.org, website: www.crnhq.org.

Case study 2.2

Conflict in the workplace

PC Manager

You are the PC Support Manager responsible for the maintenance of all PCs for your organisation. Several months ago, you issued all staff with guidelines for the use of PCs in your company. You have since found viruses on several systems, and think you have worked out who may have introduced them into the system. You have ensured that the virus scan is up-to-date but on occasions this has not helped. You are annoyed at the extra workload as a result of these staff members' actions.

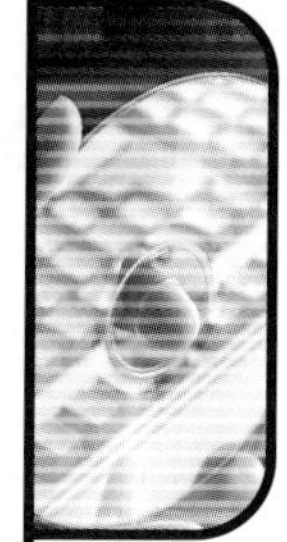

You are also accountable for the licensing of software used within your company. You feel that the staff members who are downloading software from the internet and/or using email for private purposes at work probably are not as productive as other staff.

You have arranged a meeting with the accounts clerk, who you suspect is one of those staff who has introduced viruses into the system.

Accounts Clerk

You work hard at your job updating data into your company's client base. At times you are bored when work is slow, so you work quickly and allow yourself time to take a break, during which you love to play games, email friends, or search the internet for software suitable for your home computer. You feel you are entitled to this because you nearly always complete your work on time. You also maintain that it is a constructive way to use your breaks, because it keeps your brain stimulated.

You usually bring disks in from home, where you have downloaded items from a bulletin board. The trouble is, you have accidentally introduced several viruses over the past couple of months. You know this is a problem, but are not too worried, because **you** know that the PC Manager regularly updates the virus scan software.

The PC Manager wants to see you about the viruses being introduced into the organisation's system. You think the PC Manager is making a big deal out of the issue.

Case study activities
1. What is this conflict about?
2. What are the conflicting needs and wants of each of the stakeholders?
3. What are the behaviours or signs that indicate that a conflict exists? Look at these from the point of view of the key people involved.
4. What level is the conflict at now? What other levels has it progressed through?
5. In your opinion, at what level could this conflict have been resolved? How?

RESPONDING TO CONFLICT

It is easy to fall into the trap of believing that all conflict involves aggression or some other form of outward signs of negative behaviour. There are as many ways of responding to conflict situations as there are styles of behaviour. Some styles used by people in conflict situations include:
- acting in a self-righteous manner
- avoidance
- compromise
- smoothing over
- aggression.

Activity 2.8

Methods of dealing with conflict

1. Write down the advantages and disadvantages of the following methods of dealing with conflict. Consider the short- and long-term effects.
    (a) Withdrawal. You decide to simply get out of the picture. 'It's not my problem!'
    (b) Suppression. You decide the conflict is not worth dealing with. 'Business as usual.'
    (c) Win/lose. One side is convinced of their correctness and will do anything to prove their point.
    (d) Compromise. Both parties give up on aspects of their proposed solution.
    (e) Win/win. Everyone gains something from the outcome. Both sides are comfortable with the result.
2. Use the workplace conflicts that you identified in activities 2.4 and 2.5 to answer the following questions.
    (a) What was the conflict about?
    (b) What method was used (withdrawal, suppression, win/lose, compromise, win/win)?
    (c) What was the effect?
3. Discuss your answers in small groups and record what you found useful.

Assertive behaviour

Effective communication is essential in solving problems. In the previous chapter we looked at questioning skills, active listening skills and using empathy, all of which are important in solving conflict. They help in understanding the situation from the other side of the fence. Let us now look at what skills are relevant in order for you to get others to understand your perspective on the problem.

When conflict arises people often behave in ways that are not helpful. People may shout at you (be aggressive) or may find it difficult to speak up (be passive). Using assertive behaviour is a good method to help solve problems.

Assertion is a way of communicating where an individual expresses their own thoughts, feelings and needs honestly and directly and with respect for the thoughts, feelings and needs of the person to whom they are talking.

Characteristics of assertive behaviour

The basic message of **aggressive** behaviour is:
- 'This is what I think—you're stupid if you don't agree with me.'
- 'This is what I want—what you want doesn't matter.'
- 'This is what I feel—your feelings aren't important to me.'

The basic message of **passive** behaviour is:
- 'I don't count—you can decide for me.'
- 'My feelings aren't important—what you feel is more important.'
- 'I'm wrong—you're right.'
- 'You're more important than me.'

The basic message of **assertive** behaviour is:

- 'This is what I think.'
- 'This is how I see the situation.'
- 'I'm interested to know what you think.'

When there are problems or issues to be solved, it is worthwhile knowing how to respond using assertive behaviour. It is important to listen and understand what both people see as the problem and be clear and polite when giving opinions.

There are many advantages in using assertive behaviour, but there can be problems when it is used inappropriately. As we saw, the basic message of assertive behaviour is stating how you feel and how you see a situation. Other advantages in being assertive include:

- increasing your self-esteem
- being able to give effective feedback
- clarifying information or instructions.

Assertive behaviour is not always appropriate and disadvantages, such as the following, do exist.

- Inconsistent assertive behaviour. If you are not consistent in your assertive behaviour, it can appear to be aggressive.
- The use of assertive behaviour with sensitive people can also seem aggressive.
- Assertive behaviour should only be used at appropriate times. This depends on who you are talking to and the subject of your discussion/conversation.

Activity 2.9

Advantages and disadvantages of assertive behaviour

List advantages and disadvantages of assertive behaviour that you have observed in your workplace or community.

____

____

____

When we respond with assertive behaviour, we need to do the following:

- be clear, honest and to the point, with words and behaviour that match the message
- speak about our own feelings/wants/beliefs, without making judgements about those of others
- feel OK about ourself, our needs and our actions
- respect the rights and needs of others
- use an 'I' message.

'I' statements

'I' statements are a useful assertiveness tool. They allow you to express how you feel about a situation, without blaming or attacking the other person. For example, when saying 'I feel really frustrated when I come in and find you have borrowed my laptop', it is also a good idea to state clearly what you would like to happen: '... and I would like you to ask first'.

There are, therefore, three components to 'I' statements:

1. How you feel.
2. The situation.
3. What you would like to happen.

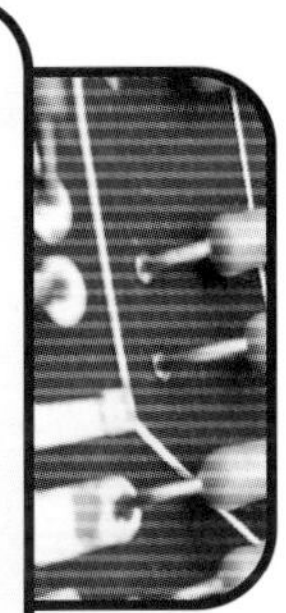

Activity 2.10

Assertive responses

1. Translate the following aggressive, attacking 'you' statements into assertive 'I' statements.
   (a) 'You never do anything properly. Why can't you get your act together and finish the manual for the client?'
   (b) 'You just decided on the software requirements without even asking me. I'm part of this team too, you know!'
2. What would be a passive, aggressive, and assertive response to each of the following situations?
   (a) A workmate has been using your computer when you are not there and has changed some of your settings.
   (b) You are having lunch with a potentially important client who tells you a joke you find really offensive.
   (c) A workmate always dismisses your suggestions about solving hardware problems in front of other staff.
   (d) A client calls you on your mobile at weekends asking questions about issues that you consider non-urgent.

Case study 2.3

Use of personal power

Sam is employed in an IT section and is currently working on a large application program for a client. The section has been beset by the latest outbreak of flu, leading to a backlog of work. This has resulted in the team leader asking people to do extra hours on the weekend to catch up. Sam has worked the last four weekends because of the project for the client and does not want to work another weekend. A memo arrives from the team leader. She has made a roster and Sam is to work this weekend for six hours. Sam feels upset and decides to talk to the team leader.

Case study activities

1. Where is the source of the conflict for Sam?
2. Where is the source of the conflict for the team leader?

   Sam speaks to the team leader who shouts at Sam that it is not her fault that people are sick, she is just trying to do her job and Sam should do the same.
3. At what level is the conflict at now?
4. What skills does Sam need in this situation?
5. List the ways in which people try to exert power over others or try to influence them to do something, e.g. standing over the top of someone when talking, or shouting.

Methods of exercising power

Some common ways people exert power inappropriately in a conflict include the following (add any others you have observed):

- aggressive behaviour such as shouting, yelling or threatening
- manipulative behaviour such as lying or bluffing
- making false promises
- behaving in a patronising manner
- playing on your sympathy
- ignoring you
- praising you excessively, e.g. 'You're so good at doing this. You really should be the one to do it.'
- implying terrible consequences, e.g. 'If you don't do this then ...'
  You can also be 'powerful' if you are open, assertive and willing to listen.

How to use assertiveness appropriately

Assertiveness in conflict situations works best when those with whom you are communicating have the skills to respond in a positive way. There are times, however, when you may have to be more circumspect. People who are shy, sensitive or insecure may experience difficulty in coping with assertive communication unless introduced to it gradually. Use assertion only in those places and at those times appropriate to the people and the situation involved.

Conflict between cultures

Some cultures use open communication only in close family situations. Be careful using it unless you are sure it will be accepted and appreciated. A great deal has been written about the importance of understanding how different cultures communicate, especially in conflict situations. **The important thing to remember is that good observation and listening skills will help you deal with most situations.** Regardless of the culture that people come from, they respect those who show empathy and do not try to force their views or style on others. No amount of understanding, knowledge or empathy will help you in situations where the other person automatically labels you as hostile to their culture.

Develop your assertiveness skills by persisting, practising, exchanging information, changing old habits, believing in what you are standing up for, working for equality, knowing the right time and place, and respecting cultural differences.

Confronting powerful people

- Do not take personal criticism on board. Turn the attack on you into an attack on the problem.
- Use your active listening skills to show you have heard and understood their point of view.
- Ask yourself what you would think if you were in their shoes.
- Use assertive messages. Be clear about your purpose and ideas.
- Use **and**, not **but**.

Figure 2.3
Use assertive messages

Steps for managing conflict

You find yourself in the middle of a conflict situation. Perhaps you have a sense of it happening or there may be more obvious signs. Whatever stage the conflict is at, you decide it has to be dealt with and you are in a position to do something about it. What next? The answer lies in how you systematically tackle any problem in your day-to-day work or personal life.

Firstly, **break the problem up into a few logical, easily managed steps, and then implement the steps**. Key ingredients for success lie in understanding the problem, keeping your goals firmly in mind and knowing that things may not go according to plan.

Six steps you will find useful in dealing with conflict are shown in Figure 2.4.

1. **Acknowledge your emotions.**
2. **Identify the problem.**
3. **Plan.**
4. **Communicate effectively.**
5. **Use an effective close.**
6. **Follow up the outcomes.**

Figure 2.4
Steps for managing conflict

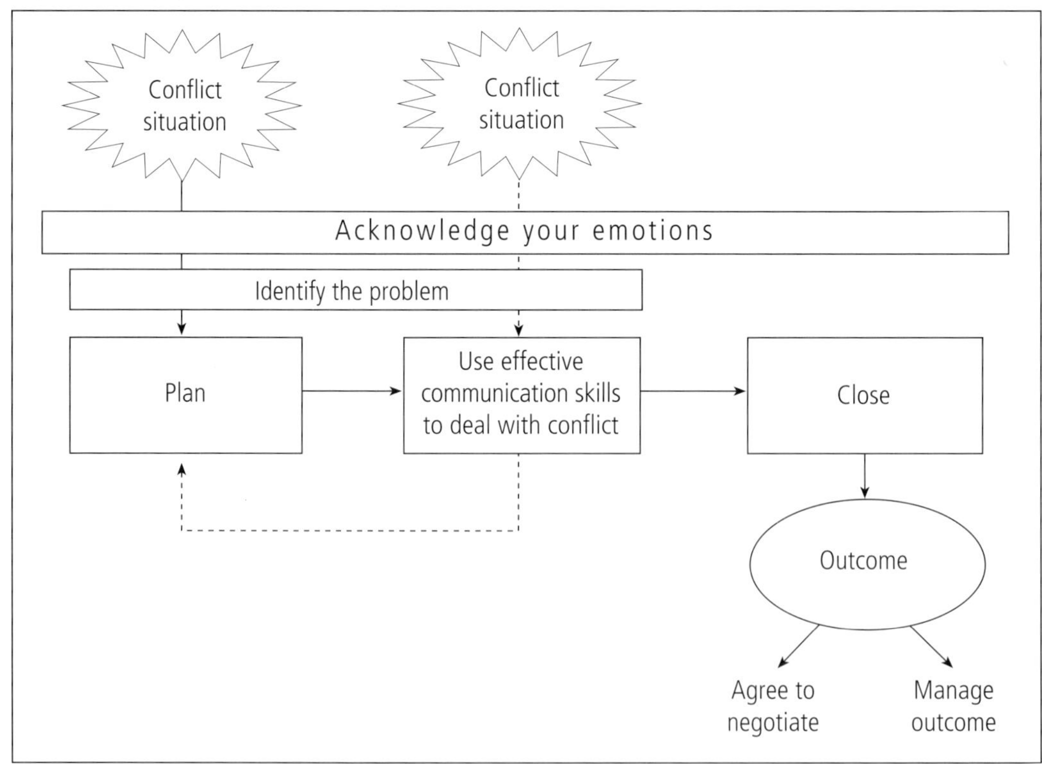

Conflict can be handled more effectively if you can see the process as a series of steps to be tackled.

Acknowledge your emotions

Your emotions affect your ability to deal with conflict. It is important to stop and reflect on these feelings before you decide what you are going to do or say. Stop to think before you react.

Identify the problem

Having a clear picture of the problem is central to dealing with any conflict. It is pointless to harass the warehouse staff over delays to orders if they are not getting the correct information in the first place. You have to ask yourself whether you have really identified the problem. Could there be another, more basic problem? Are there other ways of finding out?

Imagine two people arguing over whose work should have priority with the technician. The problem could be that:

- management has not adequately defined areas of responsibility
- one of the people could be under pressure from a client to complete some paperwork
- each is trying to prove they are more important than the other
- they do not like each other.

Each interpretation can result in a different answer as to how the conflict should be handled, either by the participants or others.

Plan

The following tasks will help you when planning to manage conflict:

- identify your goal/s for the situation
- list the relevant issues
- identify participants' needs and wants
- identify the main options for approaching the situation
- select the most appropriate solution.

Identify your goal/s for the situation

Know precisely what it is you want to achieve. You are not likely to set out on a journey without knowing where it is you are heading—otherwise, how would you know when you had arrived? In conflict situations, **clear goals help you know when particular issues or behaviours are not relevant to the process**. One way to focus on the goal would be to say to yourself: 'I will know I have successfully dealt with this situation when ...'

List the relevant issues

Factors influencing the conflict and relevant information about the people involved should be identified. As you list issues, you may see a solution to the problem, someone who can advise you, or pointers to the real cause of the problem. This stage gives you a guide to some of the forces operating and paths that might be worth exploring to help manage the conflict.

Identify participants' needs and wants

Participants are the people involved in the conflict, those directly influenced by the outcome, and the main people likely to have an influence on the process. **Identifying their needs and wants** helps you put yourself in their shoes (remember the skills of empathy). You may not agree with what they want, and you may not even be completely correct with your interpretation of their views, but at least you are better placed to **anticipate responses and think of ways in which their needs, as well as yours, can be met.**

Identify the main options for approaching the situation

There is no magic 'how to' method for dealing with the actual conflict. The approach you use will be determined by how effectively you have planned and by the behaviour of other people involved. With careful planning, you will find that there is a wide range of options for any conflict situation.

Select the most appropriate solution

Once you have looked at the implications of using a range of options, you can select the one most likely to help you achieve your goals and those of the others involved. Experience will tell you that things often do not go according to plan, so **it is important to have at least one contingency plan.** This may be as simple as knowing when to say that you are uncomfortable about the way things are going and asking to call a halt, or it may be more complex and involve someone on stand-by who can help if things get out of hand.

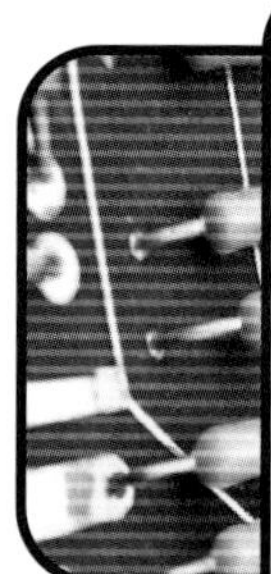

Activity 2.11

Mapping conflict

Reread Case study 2.3 about Sam who was directed to work on the weekend. Map the progress of that conflict under the headings listed in the text.

	Sam	Team leader
Goals		
Issues		
Needs and Wants		
Options		
Appropriate solution		

Communicate effectively

Having a plan is not by itself enough to increase the chances of a successful outcome. An important part of the process is knowing that you do not simply walk up to someone and say 'Look here you, we've got a problem!'. This is not effective communication. **Knowing the best time and place to address the problem is almost as important as the way in which you go about it.**

Effective communication in conflict situations is essential and depends on following a number of simple rules:
- get agreement on the problem
- clarify each other's goals
- use effective communication skills to discuss the problem.

Get agreement on the problem

How often have you heard people arguing and thought to yourself that they seem to be arguing about different things? Halfway through the argument someone says 'Hey, that's not what I said, what I really mean is ...' and they realise that they are in fact in agreement about the issue. This happens when people have not properly clarified the problem.

Focusing on the problem at the beginning does not mean saying 'Now look here, you seem to have a problem!'. Nothing is more likely to get a bad reaction than that sort of attack. You need to ensure that you are both on the same wavelength and dealing with substantive, rather than trivial issues.

Clarify each other's goals

Having reached agreement on what the conflict is about, the next step is to ensure that those involved are heading in a compatible direction. For example, if there is a clash between staff concerning whose work gets priority, one approach is to say 'Look, I understand the concerns you have about your work being given a lower priority; what I would like to do is get agreement on an acceptable process for managing priority jobs'. This tells the other person that you understand their position and gives them a chance to either accept or reject your position. However, claiming to understand when the other person does not believe you may inflame the situation. If it is obvious that you are both heading in different directions, move quickly to the next step. You are going to need time to consider the options and establish the basis for a negotiated outcome.

Use effective communication skills to discuss the problem

During a conflict it is very easy to react to the tone of what is being said and the way it is presented, and miss hearing exactly what the other person is trying to say. One way to deal with this problem is to ask the other person, 'Now what do you see as the problem?' and then wait for them to answer. It is very useful to paraphrase what they are saying. This means repeating what they have said in your own words: 'Now as I understand it, you are concerned that I am pushing my work on to the office staff at the expense of yours.'

Paraphrasing, or the technique of restating the comments that you have just heard from the other person, is a very powerful tool that can put a brake on some of the anger that often starts a conflict. It also helps you clarify concerns. Another interesting benefit comes when you or the other person hear the problem stated out loud. This can lead to an opportunity to clarify the problem, which deflects attention from the specific incident. It also clearly signals to the other person that you are listening to them. **Listening** plays a very important role in conflict management, particularly in the early stages when issues and views are being aired. See Chapter 1 for more on effective communication.

Use an effective close

Whatever the outcome of the conflict situation, the close is important because it determines the note on which you finish and what direction the conflict (if not resolved) will take. **An effective close is essential when dealing with conflict.**

The key elements of the close are:
- summarise the outcomes
- get agreement on the next stage
- record the outcomes (where appropriate).

If you feel the discussion has gone as far as it can at this stage, you can say 'We have reached a point where ... (summarise the main understandings) ... and I would like to think about the implications. When would it suit you to get back together on this?'.

Sensing that the conflict has reached a point where you believe it can only get worse, the most sensible option is to say 'I understand why you are angry at the situation, but I don't feel this is the best time (and/or place) to deal with this. Would tomorrow at one o'clock in my office suit you?'. They could reject your offer, so you have the choice of persisting or putting it back on them by saying 'Well, what do you think will help us sort this out in a fair way?'.

Writing down the outcomes helps when you are planning the next stage or needing help with remembering what you have to do. You may remember times when you have walked away from a difficult encounter and then forgotten the details of the outcome. A written record of the outcomes can be one you both agree to, or it can be something you do for yourself in order to manage repercussions if the end is acrimonious.

Follow up the outcomes

You may think this is self-evident but it is surprising how much goodwill has been undermined because one or both parties have not followed up on what they agreed to do. One of the main causes for incomplete follow-up is not getting agreement on the precise outcomes. If you do not have an understanding of who is to do what, how and when, the chances of later misunderstanding increase.

One of the features of good follow-up is effective feedback. Having reached agreement on what is to be done, it is useful to agree on how to monitor progress. This may be done next time you get together, or it may involve other forms of communication, such as emails or phone calls.

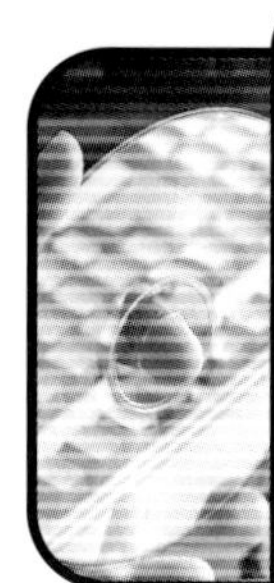

Case study 2.4

Outsourcing versus in-house

You are an Operating Systems Administrator for an IT support organisation which provides various IT services to clients, including PC support, which is your own area of IT specialisation.

You have been situated at the site of a client's manufacturing business, full-time, for the past two months, under a contract between your organisation and the client's business. Your contract is coming to an end, as it was originally negotiated for a total of three months. However, you realise that there are still many changes and upgrades to make to the operating systems. You believe the business is losing time and money without these upgrades, and that a further contract should be drawn up for another three months.

You have heard that the client is anxious to end the contract, as they no longer wish to continue paying the high price of full-time on-site support, and that they are thinking about employing their own in-house Operating Systems Administrator to attend to their IT needs. You have experienced some hostility from users, saying that they cannot understand why their company does not employ their own IT specialist and, although they have no complaints about your work, they also believe it is a waste to have an 'outsider' gain the necessary knowledge and skills of their company's business, and not have that IT specialist working directly for the company.

The Financial Accounting Manager, who is responsible for all IT applications at the manufacturing business, has asked you to attend a meeting with them to discuss whether the business should renew the contract when the three month period is up, or whether they should terminate the contract and employ an IT specialist directly. The Financial Accounting Manager has appeared to be hostile with you in the past, intimating that there is not enough being done, quickly enough.

You have had a very big job, trying to bring this business 'out of the dark ages', and into more up-to-date IT applications, which, you believe, will enhance their business and profit-making capabilities. You also realise that this will be a much longer job than originally thought, as so much needs to be done.

Case study activities

1. Identify the signs, stages and possible causes of the conflict.
2. List the major needs and concerns in the situation from the perspectives of yourself, the Financial Accounting Manager, and the other employees of the company.
3. What options could you present to the manager at the meeting?
4. Prepare a role play of the meeting with another workmate.

Organisational methods of resolution

Problems or disputes in the workplace can be resolved in a variety of ways.

1. **Management/executive decision.** Direct order from management which relies on the power of its formal authority.
2. **Direct negotiation.** Informal discussions between the parties involved in the dispute to reach agreement.
3. **Facilitation.** The facilitator acts to bring the parties together (often at a formal meeting) to seek resolutions. The facilitator often acts as the chair and may not necessarily be neutral.
4. **Mediation.** An informal and confidential process where the mediator, a neutral third person selected by the parties in dispute, assists them in negotiating a settlement agreement.
5. **Independent arbitration.** A private but formal process that involves a hearing of the evidence by a decision maker selected by the parties. The decision maker will make a resolution of the dispute based on the merits of each case. This is binding on the parties.
6. **Conciliation.** A formal process, where an independent person appointed by a tribunal or court makes a recommendation as to the best solution to the parties' dispute. The parties can decide whether or not to follow that advice.
7. **Litigation.** Legal proceedings involving court-determined, legally binding decisions.
8. **Expert evaluation.** A process in which a neutral expert enquires into the merits of a dispute during its early stages. The third party evaluator may offer non-binding conclusions regarding the probable outcome of the matter, which may assist the parties in their negotiations.

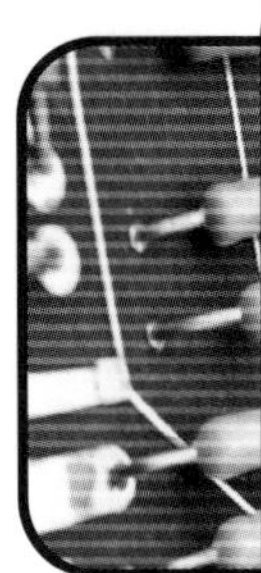

Activity 2.12

Methods of resolution

Complete this table with examples from your workplace or personal experience.

Method	Situation
Management/executive Decision	
Direct negotiation	
Facilitation	
Mediation	
Independent arbitration	
Conciliation	
Litigation	
Expert evaluation	

WHAT IS NEGOTIATION?

Negotiation skills help you and other parties agree on the best outcomes. The best outcome is one that is accepted by the parties as meeting their needs and achieving the criteria for an effective solution.

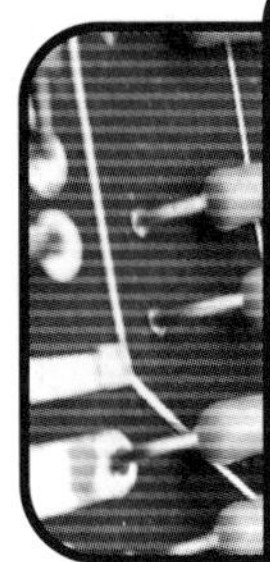

Activity 2.13

Concept of negotiation

1. List words that you associate with the concept of negotiation.
2. In small groups discuss the words you chose. Decide on a few key terms that summarise the concept of negotiation for your group.

Your definition should include the following principles:

- **negotiation involves two or more people who want to achieve a solution to a problem**
- **negotiation is a joint agreement on the settlement of differences about a particular issue**
- **negotiation is a process consisting primarily of communication.**

Negotiation is used to achieve agreement about the goals and the outcome of a situation. It is a communication process that we are involved with every day at home, at work and socially, as we attempt to reach agreement with others. Negotiation involves discussion about such things as allocation of goods and services, and opportunities and issues related to conditions and timing. These discussions can end in more conflict if the negotiation process is not successful, so you need skills for dealing with conflict as well as needing to be aware of the signs and causes of conflict too.

Working in the IT industry will require you to negotiate with clients when designing a new/additional system, taking into account the current system's functionality, geography, environment, client/user, and cost restraints.

Skills needed for effective negotiation

You need a range of specific skills to negotiate and achieve an agreed outcome. **Good interpersonal skills are an important part of successful negotiation.**

Other essential skills are:

- planning and preparing thoroughly before a negotiation
- having an understanding of the negotiation process
- being able to use appropriate techniques during negotiation
- knowing how to follow up processes
- evaluating the effectiveness of a negotiation.

This chapter looks at how to achieve an agreed outcome; this means that the needs of all parties are catered for in the outcome. For that reason, power plays and some of the more devious negotiating techniques are not covered here. Generally they are not helpful in achieving an agreed outcome. As you become a more experienced negotiator it is useful to be familiar with these techniques so that you can identify and counter them when they are used by others during negotiations.

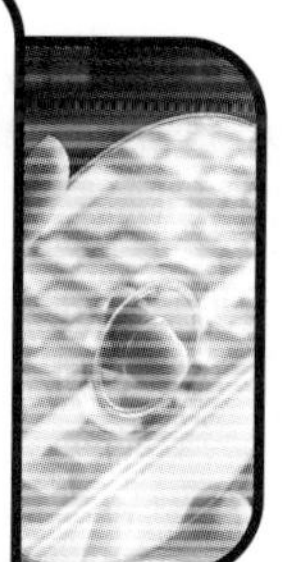

Case study 2.5

Mike and Jean

Mike and Jean are members of a new project team dealing with an important client. Jean is the project leader.

As part of her planning, Jean has come up with a number of problems.

- Mike's workspace is two floors down from where Jean works and she is anxious for all team members to be in the same area because they will need to share files.
- Previous experience with a project where team members were separated showed that communication was difficult, documents went astray, and it was always hard to get people together quickly if something had to be discussed.
- The project will be managed using a new software package, and it is common knowledge that Mike is not happy with the software selected.
- Mike will not be keen on moving because his workspace is in a prime location with good light, a view and a fair amount of privacy. He would have to give these up to move to Jean's area, which he regards as crowded and noisy.

Case study activities

1. What are some of the issues for Jean in this situation?
2. What are some of the issues for Mike?
3. What are some of the ways in which this situation could be negotiated and what might happen in each of them?

PREPARING FOR THE NEGOTIATION

Most people will agree that the success of any venture depends very much on the quality of the planning. This is especially true for negotiation because it involves getting other people to agree to an outcome that they do not necessarily see as being in their best interests initially. **A successful negotiator will gather information about the problem, find out about people involved in the negotiation, and be aware of the need to prepare for contingencies, all of which is then built into a plan.**

This section looks at how to plan for a negotiation by considering the issues and the goals of the negotiation. The preparation stage is essential to the successful outcome of any negotiation, and involves the following steps.

1. **Identify the problem.**
2. **Define the goal.**
3. **Gather and record all relevant facts about the negotiation situation.**
4. **Map the negotiation.**
5. **Anticipate possible outcomes.**

Identify the problem

When you identify the problem in a negotiation, you are trying to describe the overall issue and identify the challenge facing the negotiators. It is one of the most important steps because it ensures you are addressing the 'right' problem.

Define the goal

Defining your goal in a negotiation means making a statement about the best outcome that you can achieve in the situation. If you can clearly state your goal then you will be more likely to keep the discussion focused, and eventually achieve your goal. A clear goal will help you to present your position to others, and also to think about and anticipate their goals.

Relationships versus goals

Your goal for the negotiation should always state the best outcome for you. However, when planning for a negotiation and identifying the goal or outcome, it is important to consider your relationships with the others involved in the negotiation. Sometimes the status of the person in the workplace and your status in relation to that person will affect your goal. If you will be continuing to relate to and work with others involved in the negotiation, then it is important to take that factor into account when setting goals. If you will not have to maintain a long-term relationship, then you might be prepared to work harder for your goal.

Here are some of the criteria that a goal statement should satisfy. The goal should:
- focus on the outcome that you want from the negotiation
- deal with the major issues of the situation
- be achievable
- be clearly defined.

Gather and record all relevant facts about the negotiation situation

This requires thorough information gathering to help you identify the range of issues, needs, goals, options and facts relevant to the particular negotiation.

Figure 2.5
A must/should/could get chart

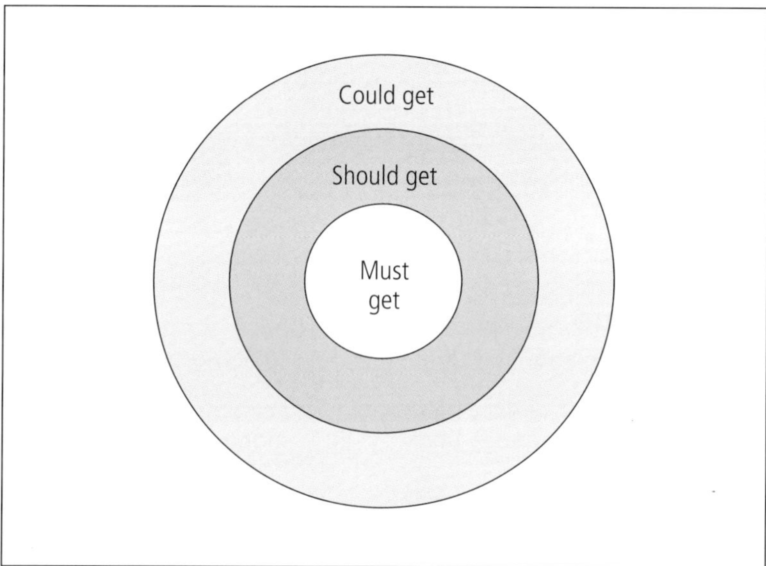

The chart in Figure 2.5 focuses on the outcomes that you want from the negotiation, and is drawn as three concentric circles. The centre circle lists the outcomes that you **must** obtain from the negotiation. The next circle contains the outcomes you think that you **should** gain from the negotiation, and the outer circle contains the outcomes that **would be a pleasant bonus** if you achieved them but they are not essential outcomes.

Map the negotiation

Use the information (both objective and subjective) you have gathered to create a 'picture' or map of the negotiation. In preparing a map of a negotiation situation there are four steps that you need to take.
1. Describe the problem of the negotiation.
2. Identify the people who are involved in the situation.
3. Use empathy to analyse the situation.
4. Think about each person in turn, including yourself, and record their needs and fears about the problem.

In the example of a negotiation map in Figure 2.6, a dot com company has hired a consultant to plan for implementing a restructure program. She is about to negotiate the introduction of her proposal with representatives from the technical and marketing teams. Using a map like this the consultant is able to ensure that all factors were addressed. The negotiator can also check that all bases are covered.

Anticipate possible outcomes

Consider and evaluate as wide a range as possible of likely outcomes before the negotiation starts. This is a key step to effective planning. Your ability to use empathy to think about the situation from the other's perspective is essential in a negotiation. This is the communication skill described as 'putting yourself in the other's shoes' so that you can view the situation from where they are standing. During the mapping stage of the negotiation, use empathy to think about their needs, concerns, goals and possible behaviour.

Principled negotiation starts from the needs and interests of the people or parties involved and it aims to achieve a mutually acceptable outcome.

Figure 2.6
Example of a mind map used to identify the needs and fears of those involved in addressing the quality assurance problem.

CONSULTANTS

NEEDS	FEARS
– acceptance of quality ideas	– being discredited in eyes of management
– support from workers and management	– losing contracts with other companies
– quick decisions	– that negative views will undermine quality systems
– accurate information	

CHANGE MANAGEMENT

WORKERS

NEEDS
– clear information
– incentive to change
– respect for ideas
– opportunities to communicate

FEARS
– increased workload
– identification of work group weaknesses
– reduction in the number of workers required
– change, pressure
– job losses

EMPLOYERS

NEEDS
– improved quality
– increased client numbers
– avoiding conflict
– clear documentation

FEARS
– high costs
– decreased output
– identification of poor management structure
– industrial action

Brainstorming method 1: working alone
This is sometimes called 'drawing a mind map'. Write the problem on a sheet of paper. Working out from the problem, list all the relevant issues (the order and placement is not relevant), making notes on them as you go. As you map the issues and facts, make a note

of resources that may be useful in addressing the negotiation. These may include people, information, documents and so on.

Brainstorming method 2: two or more people

Set a fixed time limit (3–5 minutes) for recording ideas, but do not allow any discussion of the ideas suggested. When the time starts, record the ideas that you and the group think of about the topic. Ideas can be expanded or rejected later but during the brainstorm all ideas are accepted and recorded.

Brainstorming method 3: de Bono's PMI (plus, minus, interesting)

This approach has been developed from a de Bono thinking tool and works best with five or more people. It uses the same methods as above, but three timed sessions are used (allow 2–4 minutes per session). In the first session, only positive ideas about the topic are stated, in the second session only negative ideas are stated, and in the third session points of interest about the topic are stated. The ideas are recorded on three separate lists.

At their simplest level, these approaches will yield useful ideas. For more sophisticated adaptations of these techniques refer to one of the books on problem solving listed in the bibliography.

CONDUCTING THE NEGOTIATION PROCESS

Setting up the negotiation

How you set up the negotiation situation (if you have control over this aspect) can have a major effect on the course of the negotiation. Getting any of this wrong sends a powerful signal to those with whom you are negotiating. If they feel you are trying to 'stage manage' the situation, or not planning carefully, then trust will be harder to establish. Key elements in setting up the negotiation include:

1. **Time.** Organise an agreed time for the negotiation which suits everyone involved. This avoids interrupting other important work and allows all people involved to attend the negotiation. It is important to select a date that is not too close to deadlines to allow people to explore all the issues, unless you want to force others into a quick decision. However, a quick decision may not result in a principled outcome!

2. **Location.** Select a location where people can give their attention to the negotiation and not be interrupted by other work demands such as telephones. You may need to consider asking people to switch off mobile phones or pagers. The location should suit the purpose of the negotiation; a quiet non-threatening location is best.

3. **Furniture and seating.** Furniture should be adequate for the group. Avoid physical barriers between participants (such as desks), and make sure the seating arrangements do not exaggerate the status of any of the parties. A round table is effective for seating people during a negotiation.

4. **Team members.** Ensure that:
   - all the people involved in the negotiation are available for the meetings
   - all parties are adequately represented in the discussions
   - the people with power to make the decisions are at the negotiations.

     This is the only way to ensure that everyone knows the relevant information and that the agreement is accepted by all. It also avoids delaying tactics.

Figure 2.7
A selection of problem-solving techniques

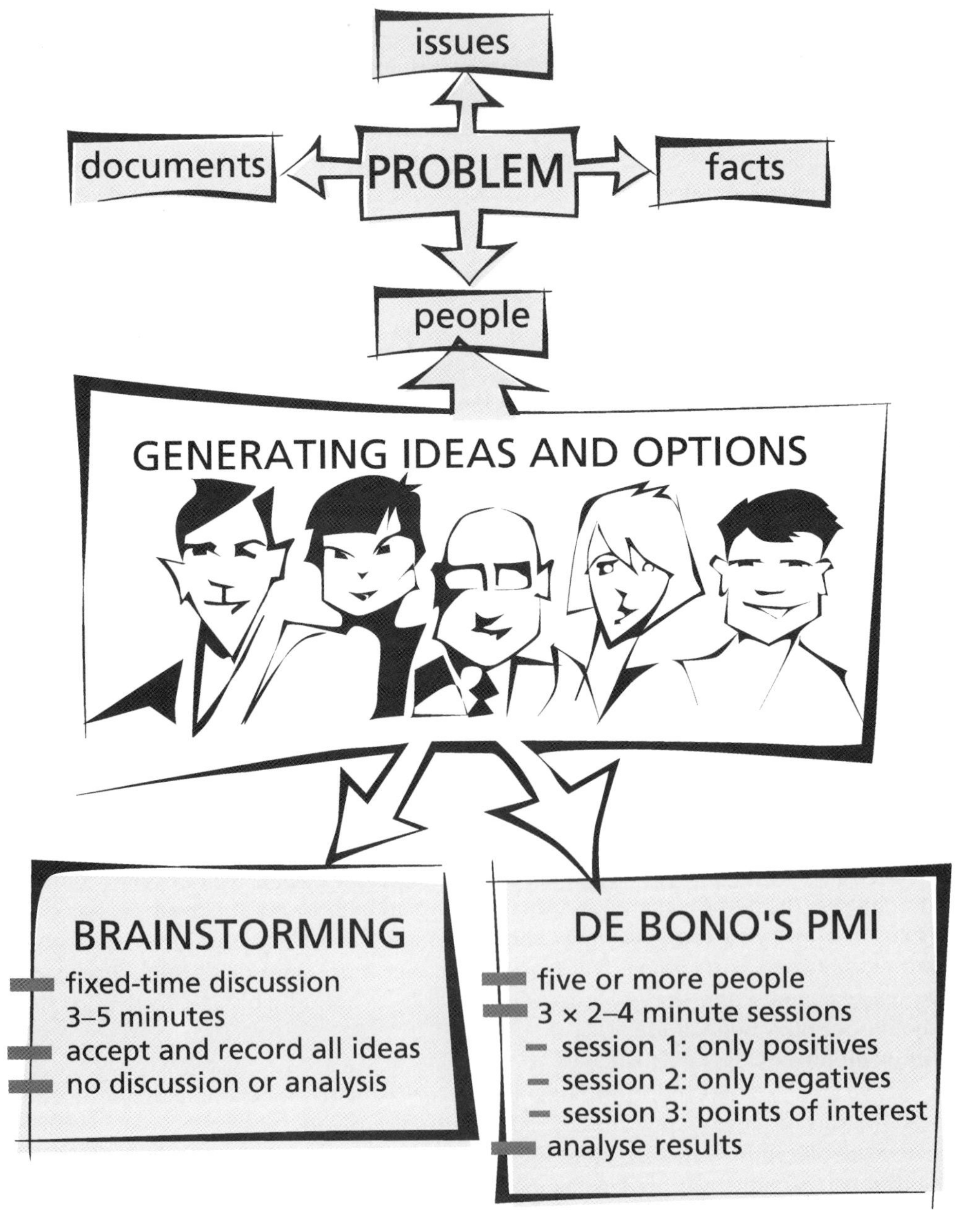

During the negotiation

Start the negotiation by clarifying the issue. It is essential that the parties be clear about this, and that they are all addressing the same issue. The goals of each party may be different but the issue must be clearly stated at the start of the negotiation.

Get agreement on the process that will be used during the negotiation. All parties need to discuss and agree on the way that it will be conducted, which is the same as setting the agenda or the rules. Different processes can be used, depending on the goal of the negotiation.

Use the following as a checklist for the negotiation process:

- Be clear on the outcome and flexible on the route.
- Define needs instead of solutions.
- Deal with emotions first.
- Be soft on the person, hard on the problem.
- Work on the relationship independent of the problem.
- Use 'and' not 'but'.
- Be aware of who is behind the scenes.
- Stress common areas of agreement.
- Is it fair? Can you find an objective yardstick?
- Develop a smorgasbord of options.
- Help each other save face.
- Choose solutions that recognise the on-going relationship.
- Make it easy for the other person to say 'yes'.

A solution comprises a mutually accepted objective and the means for achieving it. You might negotiate the sale of a product but until all the means for concluding the sale are fully understood and agreed upon, you do not have a sale.

Get agreement on criteria for a successful outcome. Criteria also indicate the issues that are important to the parties. **Establishing criteria for the outcome means identifying the factors against which the decision will be assessed.** Agreeing on criteria is often a difficult process and cannot always be achieved at the start of a negotiation, especially if the issue to be discussed has produced strong and divided feelings on both sides. But it is an essential step towards a successful outcome and so should be taken as early as possible in the negotiation.

Imagine a situation where the development team has asked for a change in the implementation schedule of a network to try to relieve the pressures that arise when there are delays in the preparation of training material. As part of the negotiation, it could be agreed that any solution should not increase overall costs as a result of a delay in implementation. This then gives the negotiators a benchmark for testing the viability of any proposals.

Follow-up processes

At the end of the negotiation process, check if:

- all parties have really chosen their agreement
- the agreement resolves or manages the 'problem'
- both parties can really fulfil their promises
- the agreement is specific enough about when, where, how, who and how much
- it is balanced, that is, that both sides share responsibility for making it work
- there are steps you can take if either party cannot keep to the contract
- a follow-up or review time is built into the plan.

EVALUATING THE EFFECTIVENESS OF THE NEGOTIATION

- **Confirm areas of agreement.** This provides an opportunity for each party to publicly state a clear understanding and acceptance of the negotiated outcome.
- **Check viability.** Confirm that the proposed solution satisfies the criteria you established at the start of the negotiation.
- **Record the agreement.** Record and circulate the details of the decision:
  —what was agreed to
  —processes for implementing the agreement
  —processes for monitoring the implementation.
- **Decide on follow-up action.** Plan what action has to be taken to ensure the outcome is achieved. Write down each action and the name of the person responsible for each action.

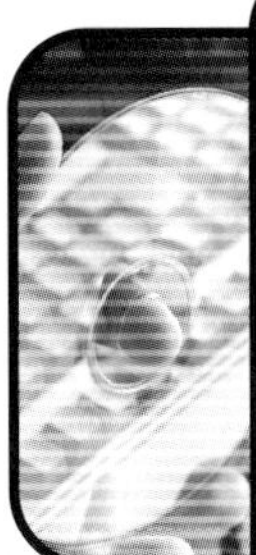

Case study 2.6

Negotiation

Prepare a negotiation plan to resolve an issue in your workplace. Choose an issue that is relevant to you and where you would have a role in the negotiation. If you do not have a suitable workplace issue, complete the activity by using the following scenario.

Database administrator

You work as a Database Administrator for a company which supplies networking, database implementation, training and support, and programming services to clients. You have quoted an incorrect price to an important customer for implementing a database system. You verbally quoted them $5750, but the correct price is $7990.

You have called the client to arrange a meeting. At this meeting you want to tell them the correct price, as well as any alternatives you might be able to offer in order to keep the contract. The aim is to negotiate a suitable price with the client.

Case study activities

1. Identify the problem and the key players.
2. What are the goals for the main participants?
3. List the key information relevant to the negotiation.
4. Map the negotiation using a similar map to that shown in Figure 2.5.
5. List and evaluate possible options to solve the problem

Option	Advantages	Disadvantages

6. Decide on the best option and give reasons for your decision.

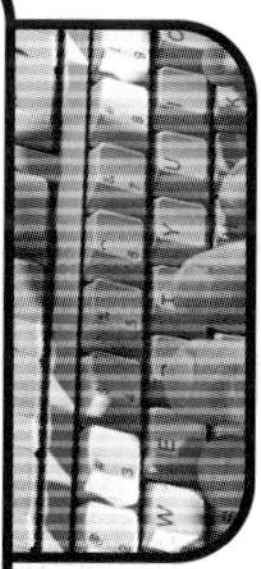

Checklist 2.1

Negotiation

Use this checklist to identify which planning steps have been addressed in your solutions to Case study 2.6. Missing any of the steps may affect the outcome.

Were you clear about what outcome/s you wished to achieve?

Was this negotiation a cooperative or a confrontational process? How did this show?

Did you talk about everyone's needs?

Did you separate emotions from the problem?

Did you look at a number of solutions?

Did you reach an agreement that was fair to all concerned?

Did you focus on areas of agreement as much as on areas of disagreements? How did you do this?

Did you take into account any objections to the solutions? How?

Were you assertive about explaining your views? Did you show respect for the other person's self esteem? How?

What do you still need to do to solve the problem?

ACTION POINTS

- Stop: take a deep breath and count to three before reacting to an 'attack'.
- Ask yourself: 'What is the problem?', 'What do I want to get out of this?' and 'What does the other person want to get out of this?'.
- Ask yourself if there is a better time and place to deal with the conflict.
- Concentrate on 'hearing' the other person.
- Ask questions, get information: use these to defuse the situation.
- Use 'I' statements. Avoid escalating the situation with 'You' statements.
- If you see a conflict coming, spend five minutes planning.
- Write things down. Brainstorm issues, information, options and scripts.
- Check your body language and non-verbal signals in conflict situations.
- Use neutral responses such as, 'that's interesting' to deflect anger.
- Check understanding: 'Now what I hear you saying is ...'
- Record outcomes and follow-up.
- Plan your communication—be aware of the needs and wants of all involved in the communication.

- Consider and evaluate as wide a range as possible of likely outcomes.
- Use the appropriate negotiating tools.
- Make sure time, location, furniture and seating are appropriate to the negotiation situation.
- Aim for a principled outcome.
- Close the negotiation effectively and follow up the outcomes by checking areas of agreement and recording the negotiated outcome and the specific details of the decision.

SUMMARY

Conflict occurs as a result of poor communication when two or more people are attempting to have differing needs met, resulting in discomfort and negative reactions. Conflicting expectations, misunderstanding, aggression and uncertainty play a role in the occurrence of conflict. The signs range from discomfort and impaired work performance on the part of individuals through to lower morale and industrial disputes at the organisational level.

Conflict can escalate through several stages resulting in a full-blown crisis. The longer a conflict is allowed to develop, the harder it is to identify the real problem and deal with the conflict effectively. The behaviour of individuals, as well as factors in the environment, influence the development of conflict. People's needs, self-concept, past experience of conflicts, and health affect their performance.

Many people find it hard to manage conflict situations. Typical responses include denial that a conflict exists, hiding from conflict situations, smoothing things over at all costs, and aggression. Those who approach conflict positively use a cooperative, people-centred and problem-solving style.

Effective communication through all aspects of the situation is essential and depends on following a number of simple rules:

1. Identify the problem.
2. Plan.
3. Communicate effectively.
4. Use an effective close.
5. Follow up the outcomes.

Being an active listener and tuning in to people's non-verbal signals as well as to their words when they are communicating their rights and feelings are the keys to handling conflict effectively. To do this you need to have empathy and a strong self-concept. Open assertion also plays a role but all aspects of effective communication need to be practised and adapted to each particular conflict situation.

Brainstorming a range of possible outcomes is useful in any negotiation plan. It is also useful to find a balance between goals and relationships, identify factors such as cost and deadlines, and map the negotiation using empathy. You should analyse the non-verbal environment including timing, location, practical needs and team members.

To start the negotiation successfully, you need to explain the importance of identifying the issue, deciding on a process for the negotiation and agreeing on the criteria for judging the outcome. Effective responding and listening techniques are important, including the use of 'I' statements. The needs and wants of all parties, and options to satisfy those needs, must be addressed.

Processes that escalate and de-escalate conflict are important during negotiation, and ways to manage conflict also need to be employed. Checking the agreement and viability, and confirming and recording the agreement are important when finalising the negotiation.

TRAINING LOG

Attitudes to conflict

1. This is the table you completed at the beginning of this chapter in Activity 2.2. Now that you have learned more about conflict and negotiation complete the table again.

Statement	T/F	Reason
Conflict at work means that the team and/or the organisation is not functioning properly.		
Conflict is caused by poor communication between people.		
If avoided conflict will eventually go away.		
All conflicts can be resolved.		
Conflict always results in a winner and a loser.		

2. Compare your two sets of responses.
3. Describe the three most important issues about conflict in the workplace for you.

Action plan

1. What will you now do to:
   (a) handle other people's anger, threats or distress?
   (b) be assertive in conflict situations?
   (c) deal with the issues resulting from the conflict in your workplace that you identified in Activity 2.5?
2. List the problem or conflict situations you are involved in which could be resolved by establishing a negotiation process.

WORKING IN TEAMS

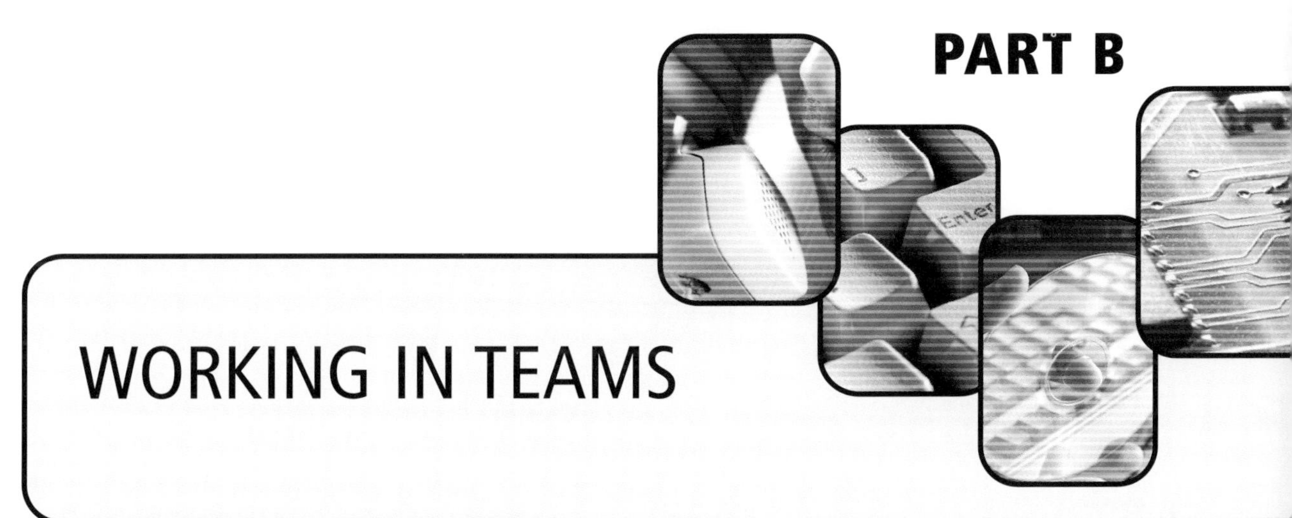

3 CHAPTER 3

PARTICIPATING IN AND LEADING WORK TEAMS

COMPETENCIES

This chapter is linked to elements contained in the following competencies which are in the Information Technology Training Package.
1. Participate in a Team and Individually to Achieve Organisational Goals ICAITTW011B
2. Coordinate and Maintain Teams ICAITTW026B
3. Apply Skills in Human Resources Management BSX154L406
4. Guide Application of Human Resources Management BSX154L506
5. Manage Human Resources BSX154L606

This aim of this chapter is to help you develop communication skills for working effectively in teams. It examines individual and group strategies for working together, planning work, and skills for communicating effectively when managing a work team. It looks at why we need teams, the nature of effective teams, planning to achieve team goals, team leadership, and evaluating the team.

In particular it will help you answer questions such as these:

- How strongly should I express my opinions in a team meeting?
- How can I help to keep the team focused on our task?
- How do I integrate my work with everyone else's?
- How do we ensure that everyone understands and contributes to our project?
- What if we just cannot work together?
- How can teams be used to improve organisational performance?
- Is there a simple way to look at how teams are established, developed and how they achieve their goals?
- How does a team move from a plan to action?
- What is a leader?
- Are leaders born rather than made?

TOPICS DISCUSSED

- What is a work team?
- Models of team development
- Team roles
- Team meetings
- Planning
- Decision making in teams
- Evaluating team progress and outcomes
- Leadership

INTRODUCTION

Many of the individual tasks that make up the work in the IT industry are complex. A diverse range of people with different skills is required to deal with issues such as:

- designing new software and hardware
- providing network and user support systems
- maintaining systems
- developing new projects
- providing training.

To do this, an IT organisation has to be able to gather and manage complex data, analyse problems, plan effectively, implement plans, and evaluate outcomes. The key to success in this environment is people working in teams all sharing ideas, energy and resources.

WHAT IS A WORK TEAM?

Work teams have been around for some time and it is likely that you work in a team in your organisation.

What is the difference between a group and a team? A work team is a group of people who work together to achieve a common goal. The team shares a common purpose and has a specific role in the organisation.

A work team deals with the day-to-day tasks of the organisation so it can respond more readily to changes in work practices. The members of the team should therefore be more capable of assuming the responsibility to decide and implement appropriate changes.

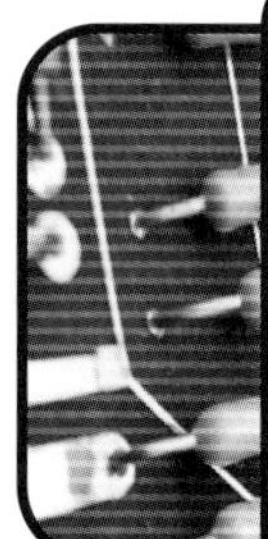

Activity 3.1

Personal experiences in a team

This activity allows you to examine your experiences in teams.

1. What groups/teams have you been involved in? Think of work-related teams, sporting teams, hobby groups, etc. Next to each one decide whether it was an effective team, an ineffective team or something in between.

Group/team	Effective	Ineffective

2. If you enjoyed the group/team, what aspects of your involvement did you enjoy?
3. If the group/team had experienced any problems, what kind of problem/s did you have?
4. List the qualities that you think make a team effective in your workplace/industry.
5. List the teams that operate in your workplace. You will not be a member of them all but the list will help you to understand the priorities and structure of your workplace.

Qualities of effective teams

The process to make a team effective is complex and influenced by many factors. Here is a list of qualities often associated with effective teams. In your workplace/industry there may be other important features. Does your list from Activity 3.1 look similar?

Effective teams:

- value and respect each other
- complete tasks efficiently
- clarify goals and tasks
- develop new visions/goals collaboratively
- are a safe place to express feelings and ideas
- listen to and consult each other about matters which affect them
- respect diversity within the group (age, gender, culture, etc.)
- are committed to resolving problems
- develop and train members in new skills
- contribute to defining the organisation's goals
- have fun together.

It does not 'just happen' that a team develops these qualities. It takes quite a bit of effort, patience and persistence to help move the team in a positive direction. The better the communication, the more successful the group will be.

If team members accept their strengths and weaknesses and blend them with the talents and strengths of others, the result can be a powerful, effective and cooperative team.

MODELS OF TEAM DEVELOPMENT

A number of models of team development talk about 'stages' that teams go through as they develop. A useful model is one developed by Kormanski and Mozenter (1987) and based on the work of Tuckman (1965). This model describes five stages that groups go through.

Table 3.1
Five-stage model of team development

Stage	Theme*	Task outcome†	Relationship outcome‡
1	Awareness	Commitment	Acceptance
2	Conflict	Clarification	Belonging
3	Cooperation	Involvement	Support
4	Productivity	Recognition	Satisfaction
5	Separation	Recognition	Satisfaction

* The label that can be applied to the stage.

† The kinds of outcomes produced by the actions of team members.

‡ The kinds of feelings likely to be experienced by team members during each of the stages.

Experience has shown that each stage requires specific inputs and is characterised by identifiable features.

In Stage 1, for example, team members need to develop an *awareness* of each other, the environment in which the team operates, its purpose and its goals. It results in team members feeling committed to the team and this will lead to acceptance of individual team

Figure 3.1
Qualities of effective team members

members. Without these conditions, it is difficult to successfully move to the *conflict* stage (Stage 2) where team members start to challenge the process as information emerges and people begin to work on team tasks.

Once the conflict stage (often called the 'storming' stage) has been effectively managed, and team members are clear about directions and their role, it is possible to start work on things that will achieve *cooperation* (Stage 3). This stage produces a sense of involvement, with team members showing support for each other. **The role of the leader is to ensure individuals have the skills, resources and opportunities to work cooperatively.**

Productivity (Stage 4) occurs when the cooperation has been successful. If the planning has been done well, the team will know what the goals are and recognise them when they are achieved. Feedback and rewards are critical at this stage. **The leader and team members must know how to give and receive feedback as well as give each other rewards for work done well.**

With the work done, *separation* (Stage 5) becomes an issue. If team members feel as though the whole process has been worthwhile; they are more inclined to feel OK about working with each other in the future, and will be more likely to respect the skills of the leader in other team situations.

This and other formal models of team development can help you do all of the following.

1. Plan the development of a team.
2. Analyse the causes of problems with the way a team is functioning.
3. Identify activities for building team cohesion.

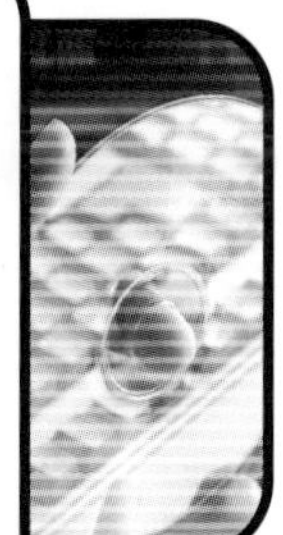

Case study 3.1

SYSDAN specification problem

The new product development team at SYSDAN has been working on designs for customer information software for a national retail chain. Over the last three days, the team has been dealing with a conflict arising from mistakes made by a team member. Peter, one of the design engineers, is responsible for developing the specifications from data supplied by the client. He has misinterpreted some of the data, which means that at least two weeks of work has been wasted.

The deadline for the product is looming and penalty clauses in the contract mean the company could lose money on the job. To add to the problems, the team is due to start work on another contract on the date scheduled for completion of this one. Most team members are very angry about the situation and tensions between some of them are very high.

Jill, the project team leader, has kept in close touch with management throughout the project and has been able to argue that the stakes are high enough to do something special. Her view is that if money is to be lost on the project, it is better spent getting the project done on time, rather than being hit with the penalty clauses, because that would damage relations with the client.

Jill has arranged for the team to work for four days at a local resort with Monday set aside for relaxation. She has also convinced the client to send one of their marketing managers along to the sessions to help with the issues.

> The time has been planned so that team members could achieve a tangible result in the three days. In addition to planning the work program, Jill has spent time with individual team members, enlisting their help with rebuilding ongoing relationships between team members.
>
> **Case study activities**
> 1. How can Jill best manage the team as well as plan the activities for the 'retreat'? Would it help to use a team development model to analyse the situation?
> 2. If yes, what stage of development do you think the team has reached?
> 3. What kinds of activities would help the team maintain its progress and achieve its goals?
> 4. How should the team and/or Jill deal with Peter?
> 5. Discuss any other useful follow-up actions which would lower the chances of these situations recurring.

Even the best teams have periods when they lose focus and the facilitator or leader has to go through steps to refocus the team. This requires an understanding of the principles of team development which in turn makes it easier to utilise the tools described in this chapter.

TEAM ROLES

Teams are comprised of many different personalities that exhibit a variety of behaviours. There are many styles, behaviour patterns and fashions displayed in workplace communication.

The two broad roles within a team are task roles and maintenance roles.

Task roles

Task roles are roles that help get the job done. Team members take on a task role within the team if their contribution focuses on getting the 'job' completed. These roles include:
- **Initiating.** For example, someone who suggests or proposes a new procedure to log common problems at the help desk for a new software product.
- **Summarising.** For example, someone who lists all the pros and cons of purchasing a particular piece of new hardware on the whiteboard at a team meeting.
- **Clarifying.** For example, someone who asks questions about the specifications of a piece of equipment or the requirements for purchasing a new computer.
- **Information giving and/or seeking.** For example, someone who researches and presents information about the progress on software solutions for a particular problem.
- **Opinion giving and/or seeking.** For example, someone who offers their reason for selection of a particular hardware component.

Activity 3.2

Identifying task roles

In your work team:
1. Who makes suggestions for solving problems?
2. If people go off on tangents in the discussion who brings the focus back on the topic?
3. Who provides information about issues?

Maintenance roles

Maintenance roles are roles that promote the relationships within the team. Team members who take on maintenance roles are contributing to team cohesion and relationships. These roles include:

- **Encouraging.** For example, someone who asks, 'What do you think about this idea?', or a person who keeps the lines of communication open.
- **Calmer.** For example, someone who tries to resolve differences They ask questions and use the conflict resolution skills described in Chapter 2.
- **Observer.** For example, someone who offers comments on the process: 'We seem to be getting bogged down! Some of us seem confused. Could we look at the procedure again?'.
- **Joker.** For example, someone who relieves tension with appropriate humour.

Activity 3.3

Identifying maintenance roles

In your work team:
1. Who helps to include members of the team in a discussion?
2. How does the team reject ideas? Who are the key players in this process?
3. Who helps to resolve conflict in the team?
4. How would you describe your role in your work teams?

TEAM MEETINGS

Teams need to meet regularly. The meetings may be run formally or informally. A more detailed look at meetings can be found in Chapter 4.

Much of your time at work can include meeting with other workers to discuss issues and make decisions. Some of these meetings may be regular and some may occur in response to a problem. Team members will feel meetings have value to them if they understand the reason for the meeting. Teams meet to:

- share information about work issues
- plan and organise work activities
- make decisions

- provide a forum for discussion and feedback
- contribute towards team building
- support each other
- catch-up on news with friends and relations
- respond to requests for workplace improvement
- review work practices
- undergo training.

Can you think of any other reasons within your workplace why teams may meet?

The role of team leaders in meetings

Leadership may be shared among team members but commonly there is an official 'leader'. Effective teams recognise that leadership is a complex set of attributes that is shared by many members of the team. These skills are used when the circumstances demand. Team leadership will be discussed in more detail later in this chapter.

Once a meeting starts, team leaders need to assume many roles. They should:

- promote and stimulate discussion, but keep it to the point
- maintain an even distribution of discussion—control the overenthusiastic talker and encourage more reticent members to have their say
- restrict private discussion, and stop any 'ganging up' against individuals
- encourage lively discussion, but guard against it becoming too heated
- assist members to express their ideas, but do not do their thinking for them
- ask questions to provoke discussion and stimulate interest.

Questions from leaders help to keep the discussion on track and can reduce the time taken to reach a decision.

The role of team members in a meeting

Each member should go into a meeting with a positive attitude. Ask yourself: 'What can I contribute to the group process?'. To participate in the meeting each member needs to develop an approach that includes:

- showing respect for other group members and their opinions
- understanding the forces at work when people meet in a group
- speaking clearly and to the point
- active listening
- thinking logically and analysing ideas as they are presented
- a willingness to share speaking time with others and to help others reach agreement
- keeping discussion on the right track and encouraging good ideas.

PLANNING

The old saying that 'those who fail to plan, plan to fail' represents the key to approaching the task. **The role of the plan is to focus the team's thinking, ensure that a wide range of information is used to make decisions, and help monitor progress.**

The planning process

At the simplest level, a practical approach follows the formula for effective problem solving. Steps in the planning process are as follows:

1. Identify the problem.
2. Get agreement on the goal to aim for.
3. Establish criteria for successful achievement of the goal.
4. Identify issues, factors and information that affect the situation.
5. Identify resources available to address the problem.
6. Develop options for addressing the problem.
7. Decide on the preferred strategy.
8. Plan the action to be taken.
9. Set up feedback processes.

Identify the problem

It is essential to describe the problem and not just the obvious symptoms. To do this you need to analyse these symptoms to uncover the reason or underlying problem. Falling sales for a particular piece of software, for example, may be caused by some or all of the following factors:

- demographic changes
- product-line changes
- the behaviour of sales staff.

A low sales figure is usually only the symptom, and focusing on it exclusively may cause you to be distracted from the real problem. Some of the questions the team should address include:

- Is what is being considered the whole problem or is it only part of a group of connected problems?
- What is the central cause of the problem?

Whatever the problem is or how it is described, once it has been identified it is then possible to turn it into a positive goal.

Get agreement on the goal to aim for

Vague goals, although capable of being achieved, are impossible to measure and it is hard to know when they have been achieved.

Establish criteria for successful achievement of the goal

In the case of a team set up to manage the design of a new software product, criteria would have to cover things like:

- a timetable for completing each stage
- standards for each aspect of the design process
- standards for reports.

Having clear criteria is also an important aspect of performance management.

Identify issues, factors and information that affect the situation

Ask the team these questions:

- Who and what is affected by the problem?
- How are they being affected?
- How reliable is the available data?

Examples of issues include:

- limits on expenditure/budget restrictions

- limits on information (data on the problem may be restricted)
- time limits (how soon is a solution needed?)
- limited personal commitment (people may talk loudly about the need to act, but how much practical effort is each speaker willing to contribute?).

Consider the decision-making strategies outlined earlier in this chapter. The most useful outcomes arise from an ideas-generating process that is well planned and effectively managed.

Identify resources available to address the problem

People often think resources are tangible things like money, people or equipment. Modern thinking about management has begun to view non-tangibles, such as intellectual capital, data, goodwill and customers, as resources that can be quantified, managed and built into the accounting equation.

Develop options for addressing the problem

Collect as many options as possible; do not reject random ideas out of hand. Write each option on a board, card or screen and let everyone see what is on the menu. The best solutions are often 'synthesised' (built up from a mixture of several options), so the more possibilities, the better.

Discourage excessive competitiveness. Put a hold on discussion or criticism of options when they are first presented. Some members treat problem solving as a contest in which they try to be the first to come up with the 'winning solution'. They criticise everyone else's ideas, especially any that might be superior. Apart from the effect this has on clear thinking, such a spate of negative comments makes others wary of offering any suggestions at all.

Decide on the preferred strategy

Once all the options have been tabled, you need a method for helping people select the best one/s that will be supported. **Use decision-making approaches that allow each person's views to be valued**; decisions reached in this manner will have the commitment of team members.

Some of the questions that need to be addressed when discussing the options include the following:

- How well might any one option help the team reach its goal?
- What are the chances of success for any one option?
- How long will it take to get any one option going? (Would a slightly less popular solution produce a quicker result?)
- What is the 'marketability' of each option? Will people give an idea the support needed to make it work?
- What is the risk factor? (Is there a chance that implementing a solution will in turn create a new problem?)
- Will there be external effects on the environment, for instance, and the quality of life?

Plan the action to be taken

This is where you develop plans for making the decisions happen. **Even the best decisions need people to turn them into actions.** Groups often find this step the hardest of all. Many group decisions are never implemented and this is not necessarily due to lack of interest or commitment. Key supporters may be promoted or transferred. People who originally opposed the decision may not now be relied on to support it fully. Workloads may be increased, deadlines brought forward or priorities reordered due to changed work schedules. Therefore, without allowing the group to become too negative, look ahead. Now, in the planning stage, is the time to consider what might happen to block the solution and how these factors can be overcome, not when the problem occurs.

A clear time frame showing specified stages or 'stepping stones' enables group members to monitor progress and make adjustments to personnel or deadlines before the situation reaches crisis point.

A product development team for a software design company is given the task of improving two components of the office applications for a local desktop publishing company. Having gone through the planning steps they came up with the following list of key tasks:

- identify client requirements
- produce product specifications
- design Part A
- code Part A
- test Part A
- design Part B
- code Part B
- test Part B
- do final Quality Assurance testing.

Once the tasks were agreed on, an implementation chart was produced (see Table 3.2).

Table 3.2
An implementation chart

Product Improvement Project ALS98–7

23 Jul	6 Aug	20 Aug	3 Sept	17 Sept	1 Oct	15 Oct	29 Oct
Identify client requirements							
	Produce product specification						
			Design Part A	Code Part A	Test Part A		
					Design Part B	Code Part B	Test Part B
					Quality Assurance testing		

Set up feedback processes

Monitoring progress is one of the most important elements of a team's operation. Options for monitoring progress include simple checklists, observation, meetings, questionnaires and surveys. The choice of mechanisms will be determined by the purpose of the exercise and how high the stakes are.

Checklists are a means for keeping in touch with the way things are moving. They are not a substitute for a well-designed consultative process, but they do direct you to issues that may need attention.

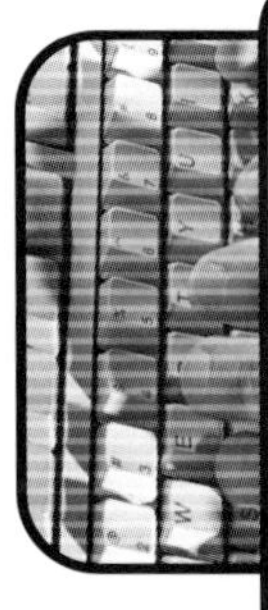

Checklist 3.1

Team progress

Complete this checklist as you work with a team. Any 'no' or 'not sure' responses suggest an area in which your team might be vulnerable. Do you have a plan to manage such problems?

	Yes	No	Not sure
Team members understand the tasks to be performed	☐	☐	☐
Each team member understands their role	☐	☐	☐
Activities of individuals foster cohesiveness, productivity, morale and communication	☐	☐	☐
Communication processes are operating effectively	☐	☐	☐
Operating procedures are working effectively	☐	☐	☐
Project milestones are being achieved on time and within resource constraints	☐	☐	☐
Conflict is managed effectively	☐	☐	☐
Communications with stakeholders are effective	☐	☐	☐

DECISION MAKING IN A TEAM

One of the most important skills for a member of a work team is to be able to solve work-related problems. There are a number of ways for workplace teams to meet and make decisions. These ways will be influenced by such things as the:

- size of the work team
- management or supervision style in the workplace
- experience or training among the team members
- opportunities for all team members to gather together.

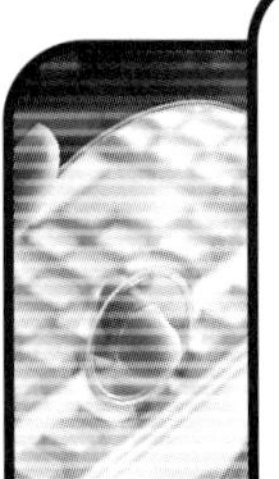

Case study 3.2

Decision making in a team

Select one of the following scenarios and work in teams of four or five people to decide on a solution to the problem.

Software selection

Your group has been asked to work on a software solution for a client. The client is a large insurance company that sells policies on the internet. Their current software does not link well to the website and customers are experiencing problems when using the website. At this stage the team has to reach agreement on what they will recommend to the managers meeting next week.

Furnish the office

The purpose of this exercise is to create the kind of tension that may occur in work teams when organisations restructure or reorganise. In your group choose one of the work teams listed below.

Team A consists of:	**Team B** consists of:
Janine, team leader with the company for 5 years.	*Leslie*, acting team leader after the departure of the previous team leader, has been with the company for 3 years.
Terry, member of the team for 1 year.	*Greg*, with the team for 2 years and a specialist in software design.
Lee, with the team for 2 years but has 10 years industry experience.	*Max*, a technical support team member for 3 years.
Kim, expert in preparing software training packages and a new member of the team for 1 month.	*Joe*, with the team for 1 year after completing a tertiary course.
Len, has been with the company for 8 years and was retrained for the position as technical support after a previous restructure.	*Sam*, recently returned from a leave of absence after travelling for a year, has 5 years industry experience but is brand new to the team.

The company has relocated and the team is moving into new premises. Their task is to furnish the new office using the plan provided and according to the requirements of individual team members. They need to decide on the placement of both equipment and people.

Office plan

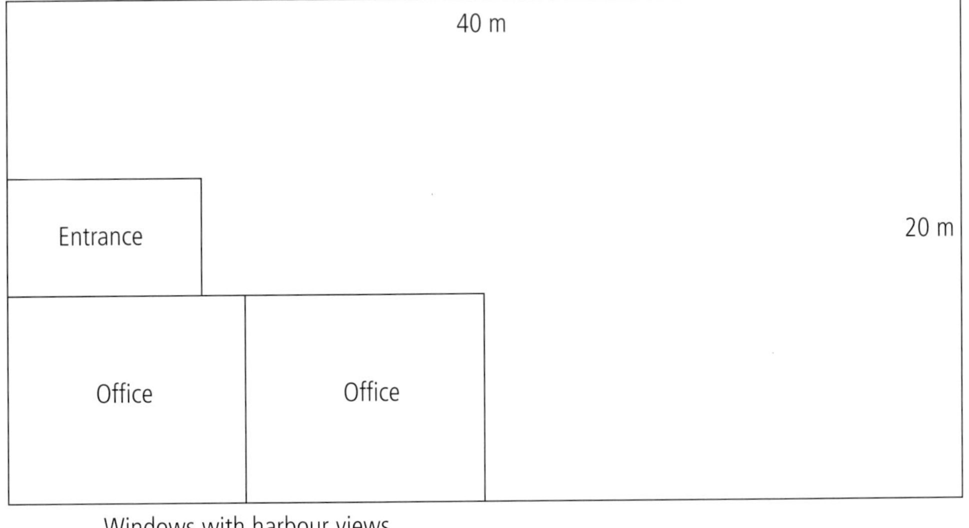

Case study activities

Using the nine-step planning process mentioned earlier in the chapter, plan the approach the group should take to solve this problem. Your task is not to find the solution but to present management with a strategy or plan that would enable the group to decide on a solution.

Activity 3.4

Evaluation of group processes

Consider the last team meeting you attended and answer the following questions. You may choose to use the group activity from Case study 3.2.
1. What decisions were made?
2. How did the group make decisions?
3. Was there a leader/facilitator? How was this determined?
4. Was there equal participation by all people in the process? Why/why not?
5. What communication problems did your team experience?
6. Did you contribute actively and communicate effectively?
7. What helped the group to function?

Decision-making strategies

Good communication and high morale go hand in hand. Probably the most important of all group communication concerns is the way people deal (or fail to deal) with problems; 'problem solving' and 'decision making' are joint activities. Groups that solve their problems effectively have high morale and work better.

It is important to establish an atmosphere in which all parties can share ideas, information and feelings openly and comfortably. For teams to function cohesively, everyone needs to understand clearly the team's purpose and how it relates to the primary aim of the company (often expressed as a 'mission statement').

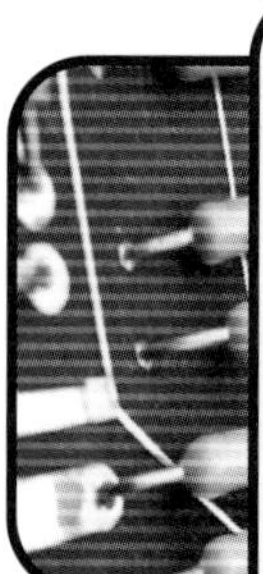

Activity 3.5

Decision-making strategies

There are many ways to make decisions. A few common methods are listed in the following table. List the advantages and disadvantages of each for your work group in the space provided.

Strategy	Advantages	Disadvantages
Informal discussion. Bouncing ideas around the group and discussing advantages and disadvantages as you go.		

Strategy	Advantages	Disadvantages
Brainstorming. Listing all suggestions quickly without evaluating. Evaluating the options after all suggestions have been made.		
Criteria for selection. Developing a set of criteria which is used to rate/rank the various options.		
Consensus. Discussion continues until all participants agree on an option.		
Voting. The option with the highest number of votes wins.		
Weighing against consequences for the organisation. Rank each option against cost, risks to team, objectives of the organisation, effect on members etc.		
Combination of any of the above. This is the typical process used. A combination of two or more of the above processes often takes place during decision making.		

Activity 3.6

Team activity

In teams, test out different strategies for making decisions. Your task is to develop a plan of action to solve the problem/issue. You do not need to design or develop the software or database. Try a different method for each of the following problems:

- a work-related issue relevant to you or another member of your group
- developing PC specifications for a contract writer of teaching and learning material (not in the IT industry) for a tertiary institution
- developing a website for a car spare parts company
- designing a new client-record database for an insurance company
- developing a training manual for accounting software.

  For each of the problems listed above:

1. Which decision-making strategies would you use?
2. Explain why you think these strategies would be most useful.
3. What difficulties would you expect to encounter?
4. What would you do to overcome these difficulties?

EVALUATING TEAM PROGRESS AND OUTCOMES

The capacity of systems to survive is often closely linked to the extent that they are able to process feedback on their performance and adapt accordingly. Without appropriate feedback and a willingness to respond to it, teams run the risk of eventually being out of touch with where the organisation is headed.

The message here is that it is no good having access to information about how the team is functioning unless the mechanisms for managing that feedback are in place and people are comfortable using them. Examples of situations where feedback is very important include:

- discipline interviews
- team-performance appraisals
- customer surveys of service quality.

Sound evaluation processes also save time and effort by ensuring lessons from earlier work are integrated with what is happening now.

Consulting the team

Although people are notoriously inefficient at soliciting and using data about themselves, they respond well to information that comes as a result of processes they understand and trust. The best way to develop these is to get the team to do the work.

Step 1: Develop rules about the information

Get the group to develop a set of rules that should be applied to any feedback information that is obtained. These might include rules like the following:

- The aspect of group behaviour being discussed should be specific and clarified through examples.
- The information must be confined to matters that the group has the power to deal with.

Step 2: Work out the sorts of things on which feedback will be sought

At this point the team decides on the sorts of things that are likely to yield useful information. The team leader should ensure there is a spread covering areas such as team dynamics, external perceptions, organisational perceptions and objective performance data. Some examples include:

- communication patterns within the group
- goals of the group (implicit and explicit)
- customer perceptions of performance
- performance on a range of agreed measures.

Step 3: Develop mechanisms for collecting information

You need a clear idea of how you plan to use the information because that will determine how much you need and how detailed it has to be. Many of the more comprehensive texts on teams in organisations provide models for collecting information on performance. Examples of sources of information include production statistics, customer surveys and management.

The simplest systems are often the best. Sometimes we introduce very sophisticated systems for providing feedback to make up for long periods of neglect, when simply spending a short amount of time with each team member each week would have been adequate.

Here are some ideas for gathering and processing information.

1. Ask members of the group to fill out reaction forms at predetermined stages.
2. Videotape interactions with clients (with their permission, of course).
3. Ask individuals to act as observers of meetings, team activities or day-to-day activities.
4. Conduct formal surveys.
5. Ask team members to keep a journal, focusing on specific areas.
6. Share information.

Information that is not used is a wasted resource. Examples of how to use the information that you have collected include:

- reward individuals for a job done well (this could be as simple as praising someone)
- train individuals or the group in processes that need strengthening
- guide behaviour
- celebrate achievements
- sell the team to the organisation or clients.

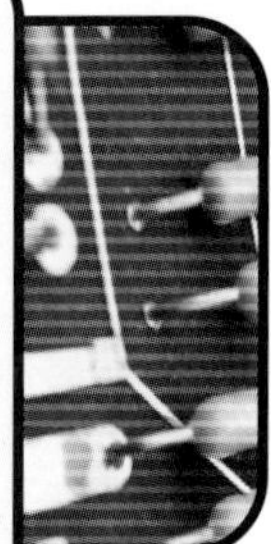

Activity 3.7

Feedback mechanisms

Look back at the SYSDAN scenario in Case study 3.1.
1. How could feedback mechanisms have been used to avoid the problem?
2. How should the team use them from now on?
3. Think about a team of which you are a part. What feedback mechanisms are used? Can they be improved? How?

LEADERSHIP

Up to this point we have examined things that work towards helping a team achieve its goals. These do not just happen—it's the actions of individuals that make them happen.

What is leadership?

Leadership is, in fact, one of the most elusive aspects of organisational behaviour and has occupied writers and researchers throughout history. **When a team experiences effective leadership, it is characterised by stability and a sense of purpose.** Without leadership a team will be characterised by instability, conflict and an apparent lack of purpose or focus.

When the leadership roles are working effectively, you would expect to see the following team characteristics:

- effective communication
- behaviours that show people feel OK about themselves and each other
- team-building activities
- appropriate use of rewards and praise, and constructive criticism
- convincing presentations, on behalf of the group, to management and clients
- fair delegation of tasks and roles
- appropriate responses to stress and conflict

- effective meetings
- access to orientation and training
- constructive management of conflict
- use of appropriate problem-solving techniques
- effective decision-making processes
- effective performance monitoring processes.

'Leadership' should not be confused with 'management'. A team may have an appointed 'manager' who does all the things a good manager does (such as making sure deadlines are met, materials are ordered, staff are deployed appropriately and so on). This works well in stable situations, particularly when others on the team are fulfilling the leadership roles as needed. It breaks down, however, when the team is operating in a climate of change or when events are hard to predict or control. A manager may also be a leader, but if he or she does not or cannot fulfil this role, someone else on the team needs to emerge as the perceived 'leader'.

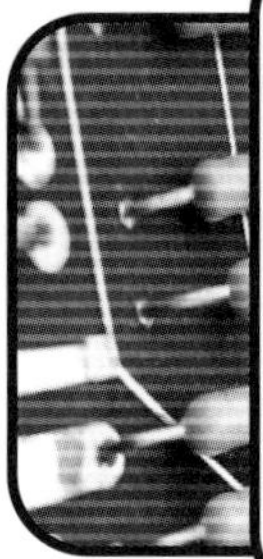

Activity 3.8

Managers and leaders

Have a look at some teams with which you are familiar, for example your current work team. Is the 'manager' also the 'leader'? This involves observing others on the team to see if the actual manager is seen as a leader and/or if team members look for leadership in other members.

Theories of leadership

Three major approaches have been used to explain leadership: the trait approach, the styles of leadership approach, and the contextual approach.

Trait approach

This assumes that leaders are born, not made. People who possess the appropriate traits will automatically emerge as leaders of a group or organisation. Research has, however, been unable to uncover any pattern of inherent personality traits that can be used to explain leadership or identify natural leaders.

Styles of leadership

Research into leadership in organisational settings investigated whether there was a particular style of leadership that worked better than others. Some of the styles identified included authoritarian, democratic, laissez-faire (hands off) and participatory. Initial studies indicated that the democratic or participative style seemed to produce the best results, but subsequent results have shown that all styles of leadership can be effective in the appropriate situation.

Contextual approach

The most satisfactory explanation of leadership says that it emerges from a complex relationship between:

- the nature of the team and/or organisation
- the context in which it operates
- the purpose of the team
- the way individuals on the team interact professionally and socially.

While an individual's leadership traits have been shown to be important, experience has shown that **leadership skills can be acquired** and the role can be taken on by people who would not at first glance be seen as likely leaders.

Activity 3.9

Approaches to leadership

Think about teams in which you are involved.
1. How was the leader chosen?
2. How would you describe the leadership style?
3. What leadership skills do you have?
4. What leadership skills would you like to acquire?

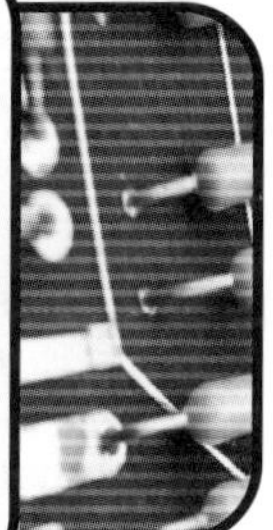

What is a leader?

If leadership is all the things that contribute to providing a team with energy and direction, then a leader is someone who either gives the team these things or ensures that someone else does. For this to happen, certain attributes or qualities are needed by a leader that enable team members to trust the leader and feel confident that they can get on with their delegated roles or tasks knowing that they will be effectively supported and managed.

Activity 3.10

Qualities of a leader

1. List one leader that you admire in each of the following areas:
   (a) sport
   (b) politics
   (c) the IT industry.
2. Use the answers from question 1 to complete the following table.

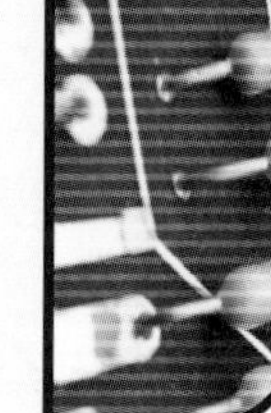

Leader's name	What leadership qualities do they have?	Why did you choose this person?	What leadership qualities do they have that you believe you also have or would like to have?

3. Make a list of the qualities of effective leaders.

The two key attributes are a commitment to the team, and a commitment to appropriate team processes. Commitment to the goals of the team and the team itself is essential for a leader. This requires being prepared to do the following, although you may be able to add more:

- do the work
- make personal sacrifices
- do the necessary homework
- make other people feel important
- always speak positively about the team
- represent the interests of the team rather than the self
- know and relate to the people on the team.

An effective leader is someone committed to team processes. Among characteristics you may have seen an effective leader:

- values communication
- encourages team-building activities
- values the sharing of tasks and roles.

An effective leader does not exploit power.

How to be a more effective leader

There are several group processes which help the team develop trust, confidence and cohesion. The team leader plays a critical role in all these processes.

Some of the processes that a leader must have the skills to implement and manage are:

- developing a group identity through the use of inclusive language (a 'we' rather than 'I' approach)
- holding events and ceremonies that build up the team's identity and traditions
- focusing on teamwork rather than the achievement of 'stars'
- teaching team members to give recognition to each other for work done well
- setting clear, attainable, short-term team goals to which all team members can relate
- arranging for team rewards such as letters of commendation to the team, dinners and social events that reinforce the role of the team in achieving outcomes
- treating people as individuals rather than machines through recognition of their unique needs.

These skills can by developed through practice.

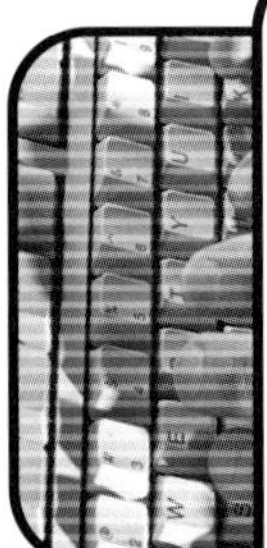

Checklist 3.2

Group processes

Complete the following checklist using your current work team or experiences of work teams in general.

Group process	Yes	No	Sometimes
Does the team leader facilitate effective communication to ensure people have the information they need to get the job done?	☐	☐	☐
Is there a group identity through the use of inclusive language (a 'we' rather than 'I' approach)?	☐	☐	☐

Group process	Yes	No	Sometimes
Does your team leader plan and/or encourage events that build up the team's identity and traditions?	☐	☐	☐
Is there a focus on teamwork rather than the achievement of 'stars'?	☐	☐	☐
Do individual team members give informal recognition to each other for work done well?	☐	☐	☐
Does the team leader set clear, attainable short-term team goals, to which all team members can relate?	☐	☐	☐
Are there formal team rewards such as letters of commendation to the team, dinners and social events that reinforce the role of the team in achieving outcomes?	☐	☐	☐
Does the team leader acknowledge the skills of all team members and provide opportunities to apply them?	☐	☐	☐
Does the team leader delegate tasks and roles so that the full potential of each team member is utilised?	☐	☐	☐
Does the team leader orient new team members well?	☐	☐	☐
Does the team leader give and receive constructive feedback?	☐	☐	☐
Can the team leader represent the team effectively to management?	☐	☐	☐
Does the team leader manage conflict to reduce its negative impact and help the team grow?	☐	☐	☐
Does the team leader facilitate effective meetings to solve problems, make decisions and share information?	☐	☐	☐
Does the team leader involve the team in decision making when it affects the effectiveness of the team?	☐	☐	☐
Does the team leader monitor the performance of team members to ensure people have the support they need, when they need it?	☐	☐	☐

Look at the skills in the above table and list which areas you need to work on to improve your skills as a team leader. These will contribute to your action plan to develop your leadership skills.

Case study 3.3

Effective leadership

There is a team that is part of a consultancy firm specialising in PC and network support. Currently there are five team members working on a large contract for a major client. The team also provides support and training for other clients and runs an online telephone support service.

There are problems within the team. The team leader has received an email from the manager stating that from now on each team will have to justify their existence or it will be disbanded and members moved to different teams. The leader has been

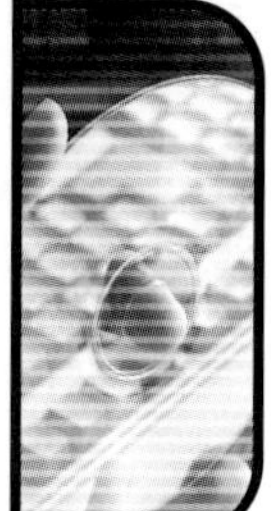

asked to draw up a proposal to say why the team should continue and describe how the team will solve its current problems.

The team consists of:

Kelvin, the team leader. Although Kelvin is quite sociable, he expects all workers to be as committed as himself. He expects people to stay late or work extra days when there is work to be done. He feels pressure from above to complete projects quickly. On occasions he feels he has been forced to complete a program without enough time to 'debug' it first. This has led to some complaints from clients and considerable work for the team. Kelvin tends to take on the burden of responsibility by checking the work of others regularly.

Phillip. An experienced programmer with many years in this firm, Phillip feels he has been overlooked for promotion to the role of team leader. Although a competent programmer he is very shy and prefers to work on his own rather than be involved in group situations such as meetings. If you give Phillip a problem he will work on his own to solve it rather than ask for any help. However, other team members may, on occasions, misinterpret this as arrogance. He is good with clients and is able to explain issues in simple terms to users.

Wendy. Wendy is a new programmer who topped her class at TAFE. She spends most of her spare time with her home computer and seems to be aware of all the latest products. She is keen to get ahead and is constantly demanding that you give her more responsibility. Wendy feels that she is more up-to-date than Phillip. When she is on duty for the telephone support line she often assumes too much and gives a quick solution.

Terri. An IT trainee who is completing her course at TAFE, Terri has limited understanding of some of the programming issues due to her lack of experience. However, she is good with clients and can get to the main problems of a client quickly due to good listening and questioning skills.

Chris. Chris is the most senior programmer in the organisation. He has a lot of knowledge but seems unwilling to share because he has seen so many people take his ideas and claim them as their own. He would prefer the good old days when sales staff saw clients and technical people did technical things only.

Case study activities

Using the information in this chapter as a guide, complete the following tasks in groups of four to five people.

1. **Identify issues and strategies** to help solve any problems.
2. Draw up a list of **objectives** for the team.
3. Prepare the proposal.

ACTION POINTS

You will be effective in a work team if you consider all of the following points.

> Tolerate differences in communication style and understand how diversity broadens your team's options.

> Contribute to a clear, collective understanding of the team goals.

- Understand that caring for and maintaining the dynamism and integrity of the team is as important as focusing on the task.
- Accept your share of the workload and meet your deadlines.
- Offer honest, constructive feedback on individual and team progress.
- Ask for support when you need it and accept constructive feedback on your performance.
- Find out about the context of the team—do you understand its history, purpose and goals?
- Become familiar with the people on the team—ask yourself: 'Do I know who they are, where they are coming from and what they want to get out of being on the team?'.
- Ask yourself: 'What do I want to get out of working with this team?'.
- Understand how teams develop and operate—become familiar with at least one model of team development.
- Spend time on the planning process.
- Be clear about the goals of the team.
- Involve team members in all stages of the planning process.
- Use open and consultative approaches to decision making.
- Follow up on all decisions.
- Foster cooperation among team members.
- Monitor and manage conflict situations.
- Use a blend of tools to monitor progress of the team and provide feedback.
- Develop trust and cohesion through the effective management of group processes.
- Be aware of your leadership strengths and weaknesses.
- Develop skills in the use of leadership tools and techniques.
- Use effective communication tools to convey information, share ideas and get feedback.

A team may be defined as 'a group of people committed to working towards a common goal, using accepted rules and procedures to undertake identifiable tasks and roles aimed at achieving the goal'. An effective team is characterised by a common goal or purpose, clear strategies, appropriate rules and procedures, effective leadership, rewards, and feedback mechanisms. In order to be effective team members, people need a wide range of skills, such as commitment, participation skills and conflict management skills.

In many organisations work teams are established by management to deal with particular problems or focus on a specific task. The purpose of the work team needs to be clearly stated and if possible related to the mission statement of the company. The work team needs to identify its specific goals and the role of the team in the organisation.

Teams operate effectively when basic meeting procedures are followed. The most traditional problem-solving formula uses a step-by-step, analytical format to keep the group on track. It incorporates defining the problem, defining the end goal, defining limits on solutions, brainstorming alternatives for action, and selecting the best solution. Team members need to share the gathering of information from various sources. They also need to allocate tasks related to presenting their report in the workplace.

Important forces that influence team processes in today's organisations include client demands for quality products and service, and pressure to offer quality customer service. Consequently, effective planning involves successful implementation of the nine steps of the planning process.

1. Identify the problem.
2. Get agreement on the goal to aim for.
3. Establish criteria for successful achievement of that goal.
4. Identify issues, factors and information that impinge on the situation.
5. Identify resources available to address the problem.
6. Develop options for addressing the problem.
7. Decide on the preferred strategy.
8. Plan the action to be taken.
9. Set up feedback processes.

Involve the team in all aspects of the planning process.

For a plan to have any chance of succeeding, you must meet the needs of team members, use effective decision-making and problem-solving processes, foster a climate of cooperation, and manage uncertainty, stress and conflict. Effective team outcomes, therefore, depend on effective feedback and evaluation processes. These help keep the team on track and provide opportunities to reward team members.

Effective leadership is the key to developing a team that is dynamic, cohesive and successful; it is the sum of actions that gives the team a sense of purpose and security, enabling team members to work confidently towards the team's goals. Leadership emerges from a complex interplay between the nature of the team, the context in which it operates, the purpose of the team, and how individuals on the team interact professionally and socially. An effective leader has a strong commitment to the team and team processes.

Simply telling people to cooperate, or just setting up the structures, has never been enough to get teams functioning effectively. Cooperation involves a high degree of commitment and a preparedness to work with other people. This in turn needs each person to be clear about the organisation's goals and their role in that organisation.

Even more important is team members' perception of the degree to which management is committed to the process. Most people are only convinced that management is serious when they see evidence of management modelling what employees are being asked to do, and then making sure that people have the resources to do what is asked of them.

Team skills

The activities in this chapter have asked you to participate
in a number of teams, review your contribution to teams you already belong to or
evaluate the team skills of others.

For this entry in your Training Log you will need to ask another member of a team
you have participated in to evaluate your team skills. This person may be a member
of:

* a work team
* a sporting team or hobby group as listed in Activity 3.1
* one of the teams you have participated in to complete the activities.

Ask your team member to review your contribution to the team by completing the
following checklist:

	Often	Sometimes	Rarely
Did you initiate and contribute ideas?	☐	☐	☐
Did you listen to others?	☐	☐	☐
Did you ask others for their ideas?	☐	☐	☐
Did you encourage others to speak?	☐	☐	☐
Did you provide feedback on the contributions of others?	☐	☐	☐
Did you stay focused on the issues?	☐	☐	☐
Did you wait your turn to speak?	☐	☐	☐
Did you manage time effectively?	☐	☐	☐
If you disagreed with an idea did you use assertive behaviour to give your ideas?	☐	☐	☐
Did you assist the team to achieve the organisation's goals?	☐	☐	☐
Did you use effective problem-solving strategies?	☐	☐	☐

Action plan

List three things you mean to do as part of your personal action plan to develop your
team skills further.

4 CHAPTER 4

MEETINGS

COMPETENCIES

This chapter is linked to elements contained in the following competencies which are in the Information Technology Training Package.
- Communicate in the Workplace ICAITTW002B
- Interact with Clients ICAITS009B
- Determine Client Business Expectations and Needs ICAITAD041A
- Determine Client Computing Problems and Action ICAITS022B
- Establish and Maintain Client Liaison ICAITS102A
- Apply Problem-solving Techniques to Achieve Organisational Goals ICAITS010B
- Participate in a Team and Individually to Achieve Organisational Goals ICAITTW011B
- Coordinate and Maintain Teams ICAITTW026B
- Apply Skills in Human Resources Management BSX154L406
- Guide Application of Human Resources Management BSX154L506
- Manage Human Resources BSX154L606

The aim of this chapter is to help you develop skills and knowledge to organise, lead and participate in the different kinds of meetings you will be involved in at your workplace. This will include both formal and informal meetings.

You will be involved in meetings to interact with clients, make decisions that affect a work team, provide information to clients about products, develop client-focused solutions to information technology issues, and for many other purposes. You may be asked to lead or facilitate many of these as well.

This chapter will help answer such questions as the following:

- Why are meetings important?
- When do you need to have a meeting?
- What kind of meeting should you have?
- How can you successfully plan a meeting?
- How can you focus the discussion and involve the participants?
- What records should you keep?
- How do you organise follow-up action?
- What do you use to evaluate the meeting?

TOPICS DISCUSSED

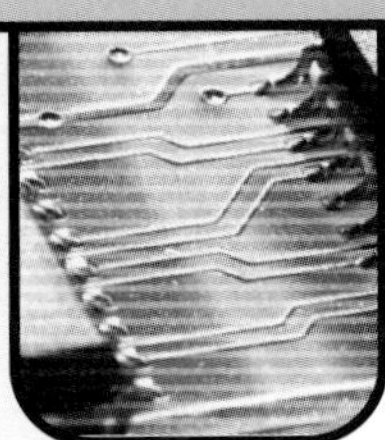

- Reasons for meetings
- Types of meetings
- Meeting structures and leadership
- Participating in a meeting
- Organising a meeting
- Conducting a meeting
- Recording
- Following-up meeting outcomes

INTRODUCTION

Depending on your job, you may be involved in meetings once a week or several times a day. Teams may use meetings for various reasons including:

- helping coordinate activities for the development of a software project
- negotiating sales of technology
- investigating problems with networks and systems
- planing implementation of large networks and hardware changes
- discussing technical service agreements with clients
- developing new procedures.

The skills needed to be effective in meetings are not purely organisational. Effective interpersonal skills such as active listening, questioning, non-verbal communication and cultural awareness will increase your effectiveness as an organiser/leader/chair and as a participant.

How many times have you heard people say 'Not another meeting!'? It is a common enough complaint, one that is often justified because their experiences with meetings have left them thinking they are a waste of time. If you take a step back, however, and ask why a particular meeting left you with a negative impression, you will probably find some simple causes. Most of these causes can be grouped under three headings—*purpose*, *planning* and *participants*.

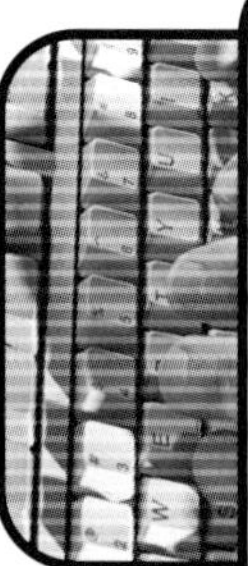

Checklist 4.1

Evaluating meetings

Think of a meeting you have attended. It might be work related or one you have attended in your community. Evaluate the success of this meeting by completing the checklist below.

	Yes	No
Was the purpose clear?	☐	☐
Were you informed about what was to be discussed?	☐	☐
Did it follow a plan?	☐	☐
Was the leader prepared?	☐	☐
Was everybody involved?	☐	☐
Did it finish on time?	☐	☐
Was there a clear follow-up action plan?	☐	☐

What was your overall impression of the meeting? Did it achieve anything?

____

____

____

____

Effective meetings:

- have a clear **purpose**
- are well **planned**
- involve the **participants**
- result in **action**.

REASONS FOR MEETINGS

Meetings offer many benefits to an organisation and its members. **A well-run meeting encourages coordination—people can keep up-to-date with developments and changes. This means better planning and cooperation between sections.** Meetings can give people an opportunity to share ideas and help develop team spirit. Other benefits of well-managed meetings include greater organisational consensus resulting from collaboration, and more effective problem solving.

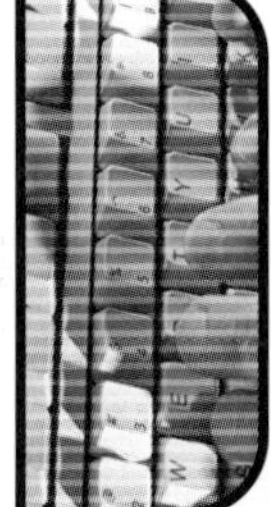

Checklist 4.2

Identifying meetings

Think of the last meeting you attended. What were the benefits? Look at the list below describing times when people get together at work. Which of these do you consider to be a meeting in your workplace?

Situation	Yes	No
Lunchroom discussion about a social function on the weekend	☐	☐
Talking to a group of clients about new hardware products	☐	☐
Section/work team briefing problems arising from new software applications	☐	☐
One-to-one instructional session with a clerical assistant on a new software product	☐	☐
Weekly address to staff by the section manager	☐	☐
Social Club session for planning the office Christmas party	☐	☐
A group chatting at the coffee machine about the new CEO appointee	☐	☐
A teleconference about a proposed merger with another computer company	☐	☐

Meetings will vary according to your workplace. What is considered to be a meeting in one workplace may not be considered so in another. The nature of the workplace will also determine whether meetings are mostly formal or informal.

TYPES OF MEETINGS

Different situations require different kinds of meetings depending on the problem to be solved, the type of business to be transacted, and the nature of the group and leadership style.

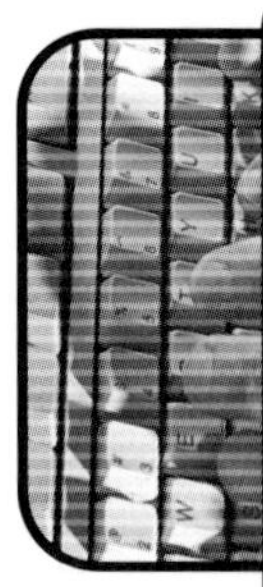

Checklist 4.3

Types of meetings

Which of the following types of meetings do you attend in your workplace? Indicate if you were a leader or a participant and add any others not mentioned to the bottom of the list.

Types of meetings	Yes	No	Leader	Participant
Committee meetings	☐	☐	☐	☐
Conferences	☐	☐	☐	☐
Client consultations	☐	☐	☐	☐
Informal decision-making sessions	☐	☐	☐	☐
Conventions	☐	☐	☐	☐
General staff meetings	☐	☐	☐	☐
Formal board meetings	☐	☐	☐	☐
Meetings to give instructions	☐	☐	☐	☐
Training sessions	☐	☐	☐	☐
Teleconferences	☐	☐	☐	☐
Breakfast/lunchtime meetings	☐	☐	☐	☐

Formal meetings

People think that a formal meeting follows 'meeting procedure'. Meeting procedure is just a set of guidelines and established codes of behaviour designed to:

- allow one person only to speak at one time, yet give everyone a chance to be heard
- allow the person in control to maintain order and direct the flow of business during the meeting
- formulate ideas as motions, which are discussed and voted on in a democratic fashion.

It is quite acceptable for a meeting to discuss matters without a motion being proposed. However, when following discussion of items on an agenda it is often appropriate to make decisions relating to that item.

The chairperson is responsible for controlling the meeting and can request a member to move a motion. The member proposes the motion (a formal proposal), which is seconded by someone else. The chairperson then asks the meeting if anyone would like to discuss the motion and if no one does, the chairperson asks the meeting to vote on the motion. The chairperson asks the secretary or minute taker to read the motion to the meeting so that members know what they are voting for. The decision is then recorded by the minute taker.

Formal meetings that stick strictly to 'the book' are rare these days, since they seldom provide the fair and democratic procedure intended. In reality, many such meetings are controlled by whoever knows the most about the rules and can turn this knowledge to their advantage. Also, there are a number of different authorities on meeting procedures, so the outcome may depend more on who is relying on which book than on any democratic process.

Informal meetings

Most of the meetings you will attend in your workplace are more likely to be informal meetings rather than formal meetings that run to a strict meeting procedure. Informal does not mean disorganised. Informal meetings must still be planned, organised and run efficiently, and achieve their purpose and result in action. People do not like to feel that their time has been wasted.

Most workplace meetings do not need to be strictly controlled (in the fashion of parliamentary procedure) or to have just one person in the chair, but formal measures do become necessary if proceedings are heated or if a minority group attempts to force its views on the rest. For this reason, participants in even the most informal meetings should know how to:

- formally bring an unruly meeting to order
- participate in a formal meeting
- control a hostile meeting from the chair.

However, everyday meetings, in which one or several leaders encourage participation while still maintaining informal control, are likely to be more productive for business purposes. Provided all its members are skilled in facilitating a group and managing a meeting, a panel of two or three people (representing, for example, both sexes) in the chair will help a meeting function more effectively than an individual leader.

Activity 4.1

Informal meetings

Look at the list of meetings in Checklist 4.3. List those that you think would be more effective if conducted informally.

____

____

____

Video- and teleconference meetings

Many organisations have discovered that bringing people together physically for meetings can be costly and disruptive. This is especially true for organisations that have a number of branches or offices, or where sales staff are either interstate or on the road a great deal. One approach used to address this problem is to use video or telephone links. Conducting meetings in this way saves travel time and costs, and allows proceedings to be recorded. Figure 4.1 shows some ways meetings may be held over a distance.

Conducting videoconference or teleconference meetings poses a number of challenges for participants and the chairperson or convenor, for instance:

- in most cases, only one person can talk at a time
- participants in a teleconference cannot see each other (except of course where there is more than one person at a site)
- videoconference sessions usually have to finish at a set time because of line-booking constraints
- it is not possible to pass things around for people to read or look at (in videoconference sessions where someone has access to a graphics camera, people can be shown objects and documents)
- Picture or sound quality may be poor which means participants have to watch or listen more carefully.

Despite the limitations, video- and teleconference meetings and online forums are a very cost-effective and efficient way of getting people to work together and/or share information. A one-hour videoconference meeting connecting one site in each state (i.e. a seven-site hook-up) with, for example, four to seven people at each site, can cost as little as $2000. Getting twenty-five people physically together from around Australia can cost well in excess of $25 000 (which does not include the cost of time spent away from their workplace).

Once you have mastered the use of tele- and videoconference meetings and online discussions, you will have access to an efficient and flexible tool for getting widely dispersed people to collaborate and achieve results that are not possible using traditional approaches.

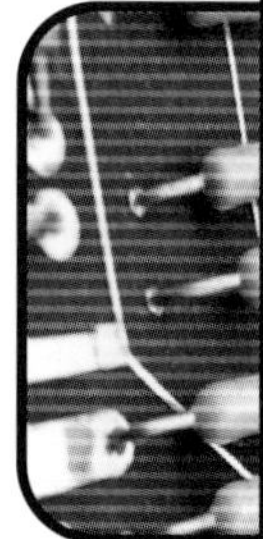

Activity 4.2

Meetings over a distance

1. List the videoconference, teleconference and online meetings in which you have participated. Were they beneficial?
2. In the table below, add three advantages and three limitations of these types of meetings. The first has been done for you.

Advantages	Limitations
➢ Cost effective	➢ Written material can't be shared

Figure 4.1
Meetings do not always have to be conducted face-to-face

MEETING STRUCTURES AND LEADERSHIP

In Table 4.1, meetings are classified according to their purpose. Notice, however, that as the meeting's goals vary, so too does its structure. Leadership in these meetings ranges between chairing, telling, selling, joining, consulting, participating and combinations of these styles.

Table 4.1
Structure and leadership can vary according to the meeting's purpose

Purpose	Structure and leadership
Getting agreement with minimal discussion	1. Leaders 'tell' the group what to agree on and how to agree. 2. Direct influence is exerted by those who hold the most power. 3. Rules and traditional procedures are used to restrict who speaks.
Getting agreement by majority vote	1. Analysis of facts and discussion is allowed, but only of 'approved' agenda items. 2. Discussion may be restricted by use of personal power, authority, formality, manipulation, pressure and other ways. This can be particularly true if there is time pressure to reach a decision. 3. Leaders 'direct' or 'chair' discussion. Resulting vote may not always be truly 'democratic'.
Reaching decisions and solving problems using a consultative format	1. Open discussion is held, with unrestricted presentation of problems, facts and opinions, followed by open debate. 2. Leaders can vary the level of control to help encourage or limit discussion. 3. Leaders 'join' the group as participative members.
Getting approval for decisions already made that need the team's full support if the project is to succeed	1. Members put forward ideas and suggestions. This is where a consensus is most likely to be achieved. 2. Leaders 'sell' the idea of teamwork and cooperation, but allow the group to play a part in deciding how the decision will be implemented.
Developing new ideas, encouraging creative thinking, planning, consulting and investigating	1. Open and informal discussions have few constraints other than time limits. 2. Leaders 'consult' with the rest of the group. Leaders do need to work hard to make sure the group sticks to the topic.
Organising, getting the job done, delegating tasks	1. There is limited discussion, but wide opportunity for questions and answers on details. 2. Those with the highest level of responsibility for results tend to control the discussion. 3. Leaders 'tell' or 'sell', according to the type of project.
Developing team spirit and goal setting	1. Open and informal discussion centres on what the group should be aiming for. 2. Leadership is still needed, but leaders should participate rather than dominate.

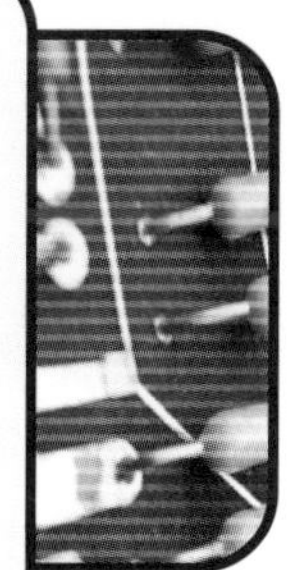

Activity 4.3

Meeting structures and purpose

1. For each meeting purpose listed in Table 4.1, list an example from your workplace and explain your role.
2. Consider what you have learned about the reasons for having a meeting and the different types of meetings that occur in workplaces. Look back over the lists of meetings in Checklist 4.3. Do the following situations require a meeting? If so, what type of meeting do you think would be most effective?

Purpose	Type of meeting
You want to explain a new network and intranet system for a client	
It is time for the team's session on the budget for new hardware	
You want to outline the new procedures for the staff in your section regarding recording help desk problems	
It is your section's turn to organise the office Christmas party	
You want to explain your company's software products to a prospective client	
You want to discuss a new company product with the regional staff	
There is going to be a restructure of work teams	

Case study 4.1

Staff meeting

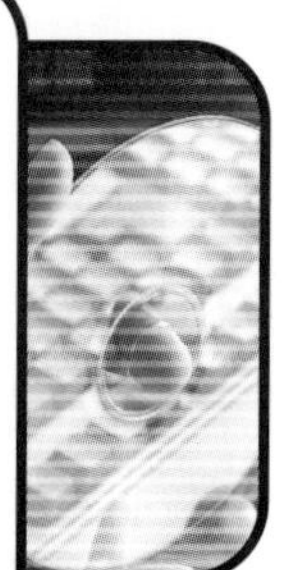

A leading daily newspaper has just conducted a review of services offered by local computer businesses. Part of the review involved someone acting as a customer/client and visiting selected businesses in search of advice and assistance for home computing systems for high school and university students.

Your workplace received a very low rating as a result of poor service, higher prices and inappropriate advice on the specifications required for the situation. The day after the article was published, Kim, the manager, calls an after-hours meeting of all staff to 'fix' the problem. It does not take long for the meeting to degenerate, with everyone trying to shift the blame onto someone else. After about an hour of rambling discussion and, at times, heated argument, Michael, one of the senior consultants, gets up to leave, saying he is already late collecting his children. At that point Kim (who is chairing the meeting) terminates the meeting and tells everyone they will have to lift their game or people's jobs will be on the line. Kim then informs everybody that they will have to attend a meeting after work every Monday to review progress and 'fix' any problems until everything is back on track.

Three days later Michael resigns.

Case study activities

1. Read the case study. List five problems and make some suggestions for possible improvements to the staff meeting.
2. Regardless of who or what was to blame, would this meeting have helped resolve the problems?
3. What problems did Kim create in the way the meeting was organised and run?
4. Suggest some reasons for the arguments occurring.

PARTICIPATING IN A MEETING

In many organisations work teams are established by management to deal with particular problems or focus on a specific task. Therefore the group may meet informally to discuss a work-related issue. For the team to operate effectively certain basic meeting procedures need to be followed.

Problems that cannot be handled by any other method may be solved through a work team meeting, as it often takes a team to penetrate the core of a problem that exists across the whole organisation. What seems to be a large and universal issue may in fact be made up of many smaller ones, not all of which were previously evident.

Each member should go into a meeting with a positive attitude. Ask yourself: 'What can I contribute to the group process?'.

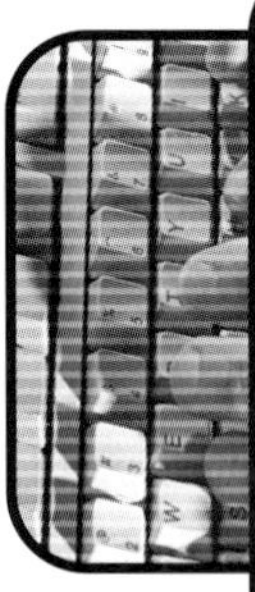

Checklist 4.4

Self-evaluation

Think of the last meeting you attended as a participant.

Did you:	Yes	No
have a positive attitude?	☐	☐
show respect for other group members and their opinions?	☐	☐
show an understanding of group dynamics?	☐	☐
speak clearly and to the point?	☐	☐
listen actively?	☐	☐
think logically and analyse ideas as they were presented?	☐	☐
share speaking time with others and help reach agreement?	☐	☐
keep your discussion on the right track?	☐	☐

ORGANISING A MEETING

Team members with responsibilities for action need to organise further meetings if required. Review the task and maintenance roles in Chapter 3, 'Participating in and leading work teams', pages 70–1.

There are five key steps that must be managed in order to get the most from meetings.

1. Plan the meeting.
2. Conduct the meeting.
3. Record meeting outcomes.
4. Organise follow-up action.
5. Plan a follow-up meeting if necessary.

Figure 4.2
Key steps to organising a meeting

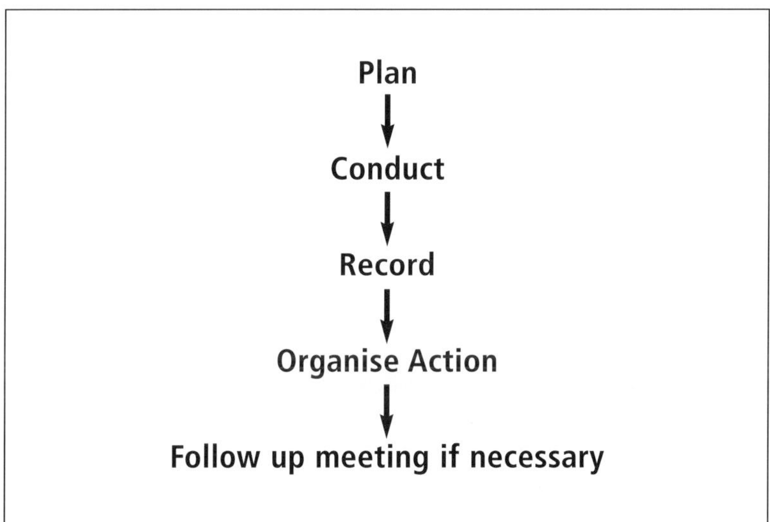

Meetings seldom happen in isolation. Any given meeting is usually one of a series, as is the case for project meetings, work-team meetings or meetings dealing with quality or safety issues. This means that the outcomes of one meeting usually influence the agenda for the next meeting.

Planning the meeting

This is one of the most important tasks. As with any task, **good planning pays off through increased satisfaction with the process and outcomes**. The four steps for planning an effective meeting are usually the responsibility of the chairperson and/or secretary.

1. Determine the purpose of the meeting (do you really need it?).
2. Organise the venue, refreshments, furniture, presentation aids and so on.
3. Circulate a preliminary notification of date, time, place and purpose.
4. Prepare and circulate the detailed agenda and supporting documentation.

The purpose of the meeting

You should be able to **tell people what will be achieved by having the meeting**. Always try to complete the statement, 'The purpose of the meeting is to ...' with an active or outcomes-oriented statement. For example:

- **Vague.** The purpose of the meeting is to *discuss problems* in the network.
- **Active.** The purpose of the meeting is to *produce a plan* for improving the time taken to access and add information to the database using the network.
- **Vague.** The purpose of the meeting is to *look at* complaints.
- **Active.** The purpose of the meeting is to identify the common causes of downtime with the database and *recommend an action plan* to solve the problem.

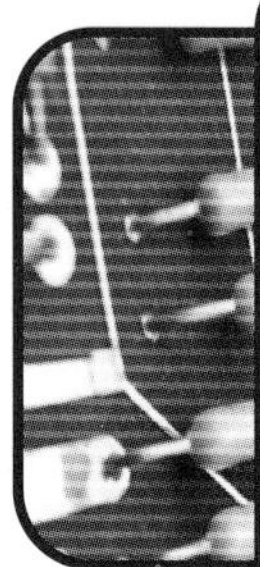

Activity 4.4

Purpose statements

Change the following vague purpose statements to active outcomes-oriented statements.

1. The purpose of the meeting is to examine the problems we are having with GST collection.
2. The purpose of the meeting is to consider the options we have regarding the purchase of new office software.

The venue

The room chosen should be quiet, and big enough for you to use charts and audiovisual equipment without anyone having to move in order to see them. Do not assume the room will be available; book the room well in advance. Rooms, tables, chairs, screens, recorders, computer equipment, players and videos for use during discussions need to be organised. Test-run all equipment: it must work effectively. Preview all videos. Remember also that pens, pencils and notepaper are equally important. Run off extra copies of handouts and agendas (some people are sure to arrive without them). On the day, display signs directing the participants to the venue. Make sure the room is accessible for people with special needs.

Planning the room layout

Plan the positioning of tables and chairs, and physical resources. A neat, symmetrical layout looks efficient, but people relax more and contribute better if the surroundings are informal and they can move furniture around to suit themselves. The worst arrangement is something that resembles a classroom. Figure 4.3 shows a variety of meeting room layouts.

Layouts which help to build effective communication depend on the number of people, the purpose of the meeting and the degree of formality. The best layout will encourage interaction and reduce physical barriers such as distance and sightlines.

Preparing name tags and cards

Name cards set around a large table enable you to place key individuals where you want them, and to separate people known to be either very friendly or unfriendly towards one another. For example, put antagonists where they will find it hardest to look directly at one another.

Figure 4.3
Meeting room layouts

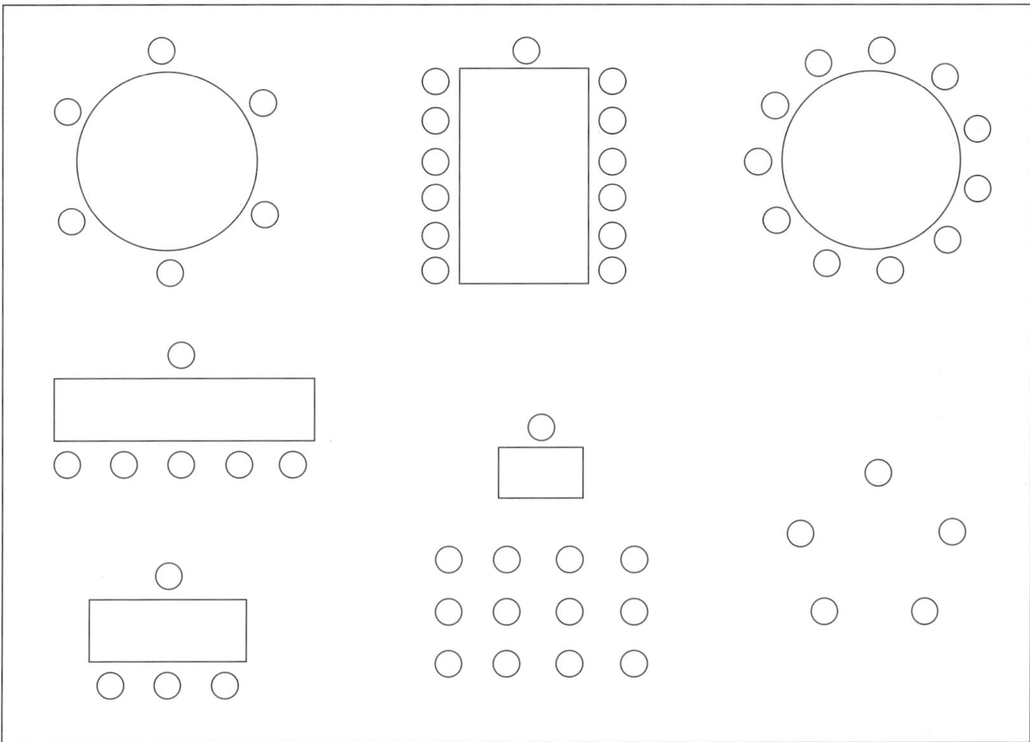

Food and drink

Where you intend providing beverages (such as tea, coffee, iced water or other cool drinks) or light food (such as nuts or mints), they should be available at all times. Encourage people to help themselves whenever they wish, rather than to wait for breaks. If the meeting extends through a meal period, have food brought in (preferably nutritious rather than high-kilojoule items). Sandwiches—or anything that can be held in the hand—are better than food that requires plates and cutlery. The whole climate of the meeting and valuable discussion time are lost if the group splits up and leaves the room to eat elsewhere. (Consumption of alcohol during outside lunches does nothing to help the process.)

Informing the participants

Set the meeting time well in advance and check that the key stakeholders are available at that time. (Remember the problems Kim had in Case Study 4.1.) As soon as the time has been fixed, telephone everyone concerned. Follow this with a notice of meeting (in writing as a letter, fax, memo or email) and, if specific topics are already known, a draft agenda. Otherwise invite participants to submit items for an agenda, which will be sent out closer to the meeting time.

Make sure each person knows why they are being invited. This allows them to prepare their thoughts in advance.

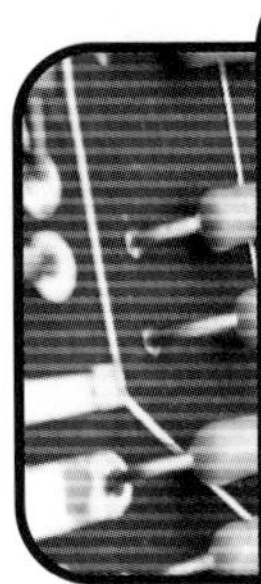

Activity 4.5

Organising a venue

You have been asked to facilitate or chair one of the meetings listed in Activity 4.3. Make a list of what you would need to do to organise the venue.

Meeting: ____

Room/furniture/equipment	Participants	Refreshments

The agenda

An **agenda** helps the chairperson to structure the meeting and the secretary or minute taker to keep track of what is being discussed. It needs to include the most important items and be sent out in advance. This allows the participants to research any agenda items before the meeting. An agenda can be just a list of items to be discussed at the meeting or may include more information advising the members on action related to the topics. The type of advice could be for **discussion**, **information**, or **recommendation**.

An agenda can be considerably enhanced by providing an explanatory note (1–4 sentences) with each new or important item. Some chairpersons/facilitators insist that each agenda item be accompanied by a motion or formal proposal. This ensures that whoever is putting the item forward is clear about the purpose of the item. It also **provides a focus for discussion and makes it easier for the chairperson to manage the discussion and judge when it is appropriate to move to a decision.**

Pro forma for an agenda

The agenda usually follows a structure and lists standard items.

1. Welcome to any special visitors.
2. Apologies for absence.
3. Special event (to allow guest speaker to address the meeting and then leave if necessary).
4. Confirmation of minutes of the previous meeting.
5. Business arising out of minutes (chairperson reviews action list from the previous meeting).
6. Correspondence sent and received (to be summarised by the chairperson—only articles important to the group should be read).
7. Reports (any which include a recommendation can be dealt with or discussed in general business).
8. Adjourned business (any items carried over from a previous meeting—to be dealt with before new business).

9. General business (meeting should approve priority of order of items of general business, especially if members have contributed agenda items).
10. Any other business.
11. Close of meeting (details of next meeting and official close of meeting).

The agenda must list a realistic number of items for discussion and give an appropriate time for each one. These items should be prioritised and ordered according to their urgency and importance. However, the ordering of controversial items needs careful consideration. It is useless to overload an agenda if there is not enough time for discussion. Whoever sets the agenda (usually the chairperson or secretary) should indicate a realistic timeframe for discussion next to each item. Items should be numbered and have clear headings with any necessary details following.

Figure 4.4
Example of a formal agenda

AGENDA

Logical Solutions Software Development Committee
Meeting to be held in the committee room at head office

Wednesday, 4 December 2002
10.00 am to 12.30 pm

Chairperson: Chris Silverton

1.	**Apologies:** Mike Smith	
2.	**Confirmation of agenda**	(5 mins)
3.	**Confirmation of minutes of 27 October 2002**	(5 mins)
4.	**Business arising from minutes of 27 October 2002**	(10 mins)
	4.1 Plan for launch of SD line	(Sue)
5.	Agenda items	
	5.1 Budget for 2003–4	(30 mins) (Mary)
	5.2 Implementation of trial program	(15 mins) (Richard)
	5.3 Graphic design contract	(15 mins) (Jane)
	5.4 Market survey data	(15 mins) (Di)
6.	**Reports**	(30 mins)
	6.1 Current status of trial implementation	(Nathan)
	6.2 Problems identified	(Paul)
	6.3 Possible solutions	(John)
	6.4 Preparation of *Training Manual*	(Richard)
7.	**Any other business**	(15 mins)
8.	**Forward agenda items**	(10 mins)
9.	Next meeting	

Figure 4.5
Example of an informal agenda

Logical Solutions Project Team—4/12/02

Meeting in training room 3rd floor 10.00 am to 12.30 pm

1. Identify implementation problems of new hardware at BZT Industries.

2. List key issues.

3. Discuss reasons.

4. Decide on action plan.

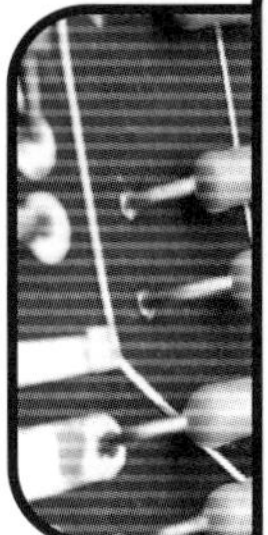

Activity 4.6

Writing an informal agenda

Use the pro forma on pages 104–5 to write an informal agenda for a meeting you are to attend in your workplace or a meeting listed earlier in this chapter.

Questions to ask before the meeting

Remember, good planning on your part, particularly attention to administrative details, gives participants the feeling that the meeting is important and that the work they will do is being taken seriously. The following questions will guide you through the planning process but remember also to leave yourself enough time to complete all the necessary arrangements beforehand and not at the last minute.

1. What is the purpose of the meeting?
2. What is the best format for the meeting? (short presentation, free discussion, formal procedures)
3. Who should attend?
4. What is the best time and place for the meeting?
5. What background information and preparation do participants need?
6. What physical arrangements need to be made? (audiovisual equipment, refreshments, ventilation, heating, seating, etc.)
7. How will proceedings be recorded?
8. Who will prepare and circulate the agenda?
9. Who will chair/lead the meeting?

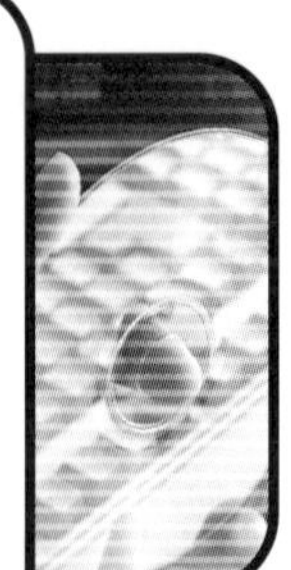

Case study 4.2

Organising a meeting

1. You have been working on a review of network and access procedures in your workplace. You have written a report that has a number of recommendations for change. Your line manager has accepted your report and has asked you to organise a meeting with the rest of the staff. Use these details and any other information that you need to answer the nine questions you should ask before a meeting.
2. Use either the formal or informal pro forma to prepare the agenda for this meeting.

CONDUCTING A MEETING

Formal or informal

Do not use formal parliamentary procedure for ordinary meetings. It is slow-moving and restricts the free flow of ideas. However, if a discussion gets out of hand or a minority group attempt to take over a meeting, it is comforting to be able to move quickly into formal mode and restore order.

The following are some of the times when formal meeting rules can help achieve agreement:

- in a meeting attended by over fifty people
- when time is limited—for instance, if key members have to leave a meeting and important decisions *must* be made
- when very controversial matters (such as dismissal of a key figure, legal action or a financial crisis) have to be resolved and the decision noted in formal minutes
- when a decision must be recorded as having been passed by a formal resolution (for instance, in company matters)
- when a group is polarised into opposing factions
- if a group is being troubled by 'bush lawyers' or 'rule-book wavers'—people who are more concerned with showing their knowledge of the rules than helping to resolve issues informally and amicably.

Videoconferences, teleconferences and online forums

These can be formal or informal in tone but always need to be well-managed and have a clear structure. **Here are some hints for running these meetings more effectively.**

Produce a printed guide for use by the participants which includes information about:

- how to make the connection
- what to do in case of problems with the line or equipment
- protocols for participating in the meeting
- guidelines for presenting verbal and graphical information.

The role of facilitator is much more critical in these settings, especially if participants are not familiar with the environment. Here are some of the things you can do to improve the quality of participation and outcomes:

- ensure everyone has the information they need beforehand and that they understand the purpose and agenda for the meeting
- get everyone to introduce themselves
- ask questions to help people get their ideas across more effectively
- use images and metaphors to clarify what is being said and help others understand
- paraphrase information
- regularly check that people understand what is happening
- ensure everyone states their name each time they start speaking (online discussion software identifies who is speaking for you)
- keep a record of who has contributed so that no one gets left out of the discussion, particularly for online discussions where some people can be left out if they cannot type quickly.

In the case of videoconference meetings:

- plan how different visual resources such as videotapes, audiotapes, graphics and slides will be integrated
- ensure that graphics conform to guidelines for effective transmission
  —use pastel coloured, not white paper
  —keep messages simple
  —use typeface larger than 24 pt
  —display text material long enough for a slow reader to read
  —display non-text material (e.g. a cartoon or photograph)
  —keep images/text within the display frame (this usually means using 3–4 cm margins)
- encourage speakers to look at the camera.

Avoid:

- referring to documents and graphics that cannot be seen by everyone
- letting anyone talk for more than ten continuous minutes
- making sharp or frequent movements in front of the camera
- having too much white in the background for videoconference sessions
- wearing stripes or busy patterns during videoconference meetings
- noises made by tapping a pen or rustling paper because these sounds are often amplified by microphones.

Meeting management roles

All meetings need a leader or leaders if they are to achieve their purpose. The type of meeting will determine what kind of leader or management style is most

appropriate. Below are descriptions of different types of management roles and some advice as to when their use is most appropriate.

1. **The convenor or chairperson.** The convenor or chairperson convenes the meeting by adopting the appropriate procedures for conducting a structured meeting. Their responsibilities are to check that there is a quorum (minimum number to hold a particular meeting), then call the meeting to order and proceed by following the agenda. Finally it is the convenor who adjourns the meeting at the appropriate time.

   - By guiding the group in discussion, the chairperson assists the group in recognising the concerns and needs of individual members. Every proposition is entitled to a fair hearing, so only one member should speak at a time. However, in more informal meetings the convenor could allow two speakers to engage in debate if it seems to be an efficient way of dealing with the problem-solving process.

   - If members are obstructive, putting forward motions that are deliberately frivolous, then the convenor needs to rule them out of order. This balancing of group and individual needs is a difficult task, especially when group members' behaviour is often focused on meeting personal goals. Chapter 3 discusses strategies for effective leadership of a team; these same strategies apply to the role of chairperson or team leader in a meeting.

2. **The discussion facilitator.** An effective facilitator will be able to help the group identify its common goal, analyse it and then work with the group to reach this goal. An effective facilitator leads the group discussion but then steps back from the leadership role and allows the group discussion to continue until it requires drawing together or summing up. The facilitator can then return to the role of group leader and refocus the group on the task.

   In a formal meeting the designated leader is the chairperson, who also facilitates discussion. This person should not express personal opinions on the merits of ideas proposed and should remain impartial. **The chairperson facilitates discussion by making sure that all points of view get a hearing and then assists the group in summarising arguments and the general feeling of the group on particular issues.** This role also requires the facilitator/chairperson to listen for the sense of what is being said and, if this is not clear, to ask speakers to explain their proposals.

Suggestions for convenors

- Establish a friendly climate in the meeting room.
- Schedule meetings at a regular time so that members can plan ahead.
- Stress that the task and the final output are the group's responsibility.
- Encourage every member to bring up ideas, confident that they will be treated with respect.
- Tell members why they were selected; they will then know what, how and why they are expected to contribute.
- Share responsibility—identify specialists among members, or make each person responsible for carrying out specific jobs.

Introductions

If you are the convenor, then welcome people as they arrive. Hand out name tags and introduce members to one another using first names. At the start of the first session, welcome everyone again. Mention special individuals or guests by name, calling attention to the special skills that each is able to contribute.

Encourage all members to participate fully. Outline the broad objectives, but do not indicate limits or make specific predictions as to what conclusions you expect the meeting to reach.

Facilitating/leading the meeting

The facilitator/leader needs to take an active role to ensure the success of the meeting. As leader, you cannot assume the meeting will achieve its purpose without your active guidance and participation. Conducting a meeting is a lot like driving a car. Even on a straight road, just pointing the car and putting your foot on the accelerator will not guarantee safe arrival. You have to constantly monitor the car's progress, making small corrections (often instinctively), checking things inside and outside the car. Sometimes you have to apply the brakes, change direction slightly, or even go in reverse if you come to a barrier. The main point is that you have to consciously monitor what's happening, interpret the feedback and act accordingly. Review task and maintenance roles in the section 'Team roles' in Chapter 3.

Meetings require the same sort of effort in order to make the most of the time and work people put into them. This section looks at the seven steps for effective meetings:
1. Establish the purpose of the meeting.
2. Specify the outcomes.
3. Get agreement on the process and rules.
4. Facilitate participation.
5. Maintain focus.
6. Pull the issues and outcomes together.
7. Get agreement on action.

Once there is agreement on the purpose, clarify how you will know that the purpose has been achieved. In the case of a meeting to identify production problems, decide whether the meeting has to spell out exact steps for fixing the problems, or whether only general recommendations are required. Does agreement have to be unanimous, or is it enough that a majority agree? As with the purpose, it is worth spending up to five minutes on this issue (in the case of an informal workplace meeting).

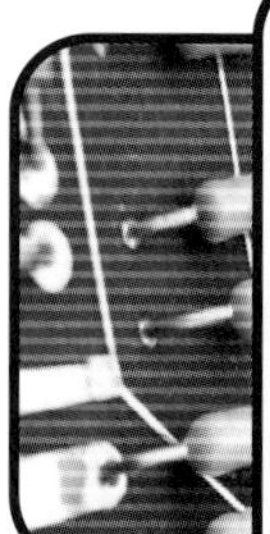

Activity 4.7

Purpose and outcomes of a meeting

Refer to Case study 4.1. Write down what Kim could have said at the beginning of the meeting to establish the purpose and specify outcomes.

In many cases, especially when the same group meets regularly, old habits, strong personalities and previous meeting experience determine how decisions are made. There may, however, be situations when it is necessary to address this. Examples include:

- when a decision has to be made quickly
- when the issue is a contentious one and you expect strong emotions or conflict
- when there are new members in the group and they are not familiar with the 'rules'
- when some other action or event is dependent on your meeting achieving its purpose
- when the meeting is addressing sensitive issues and it is important to get the outcome 'right' (e.g. the success of a contract negotiation is at stake).

Here are some examples of process issues on which agreement might be necessary:

- the amount of time for discussion on any/all issues
- how decisions will be made (e.g. voting, consensus or exhaustion)
- whether discussion should only proceed if there is a motion or proposal before the meeting
- how to manage strong disagreement.

Some people are quite happy to sit back and simply be there for the ride. Others feel as though their opinions are not valued, and then there are some who just cannot get a word in around the 'hogs'. Whatever the reason, unequal participation can leave some people feeling frustrated. Some options for dealing with this are to:

- invite individual participants to contribute, for example, 'Perhaps you would like to comment on the proposal, Lee'
- restrict the input of some members, for example, 'That's a good point, Vuong, but I would like to see whether anyone else wants to comment on the proposal'
- assign individual roles, such as record keeper or timekeeper to individual people to encourage them to become involved, however, be sure to discuss this with them first
- use a change in activity such as stretching or a short coffee break to provide some stimulation in longer meetings
- divide larger groups into smaller subgroups for some activities in other rooms nearby or in some cleared space in the main meeting room so that:
  —quieter members may be more encouraged to contribute
  —several people can be speaking simultaneously
  —dominant speakers cannot control the whole discussion.

Another way to maintain focus is to ask someone periodically to summarise the discussion so far and comment on progress in dealing with the agenda item. You can, of course, do this yourself, but sharing the task engages more people in the meeting and gives others responsibility for some of the meeting processes.

Avoid extending the meeting time—this makes it hard for people who have other commitments, and can be seen as bad management on your part.

Hidden agendas

Apart from the written or open agenda, which outlines the topics to be discussed, some people bring with them issues that make up their 'hidden agendas'. The term refers to issues raised in discussion that have no official place in the meeting but relate to private or individual goals. In such cases individuals try to push through decisions that will benefit some people, but not the whole group. Following is an example of how this might occur.

Power plays at Power Holdings

The management team at Power Holdings is meeting to plan its budget for the next twelve months. Everybody knows that the company must economise, and that the goal of the meeting is to produce a budget that will restrict spending by individual sections.

Despite this, Mike, who is responsible for advertising, has come to the meeting determined to obtain a bigger budget for his section. His efforts to achieve this will detract from the overall objective of the meeting. His agenda item must remain hidden, since if it becomes obvious to the group, it cannot succeed. While Mike is pushing his own goals, he cannot contribute fully to those of the meeting as a whole. He will be too busy watching for a chance to turn matters to his advantage.

Rae, from production, has recently been promoted and also has a hidden agenda. She wants to take every opportunity to impress Kem, the managing director. She will support everything Kem says, whether it is sound or not. So Rae will not be able to contribute fully to the meeting either. Her hidden agenda, although different from Mike's, is just as harmful.

Identifying hidden agendas

Hidden agendas are present in almost all meetings, but are hard to identify. The best defence against them is to be constantly aware of their possible existence and to keep a sharp eye out for any sign that somebody might be pushing one into the discussion. A number of verbal and non-verbal background signals can be useful indications:

- one person regularly interrupting others while they are speaking, or disrupting logical discussion in other ways
- two people supporting each other on every issue, especially if the support is personal rather than related to the topic under discussion
- attempts to debate people's characters rather than the ideas they put forward
- the amount of 'air time' commanded by one speaker—individuals who talk far more than they listen, see themselves as more important than others (a hidden agenda in itself), or may be trying to stop others having their say.

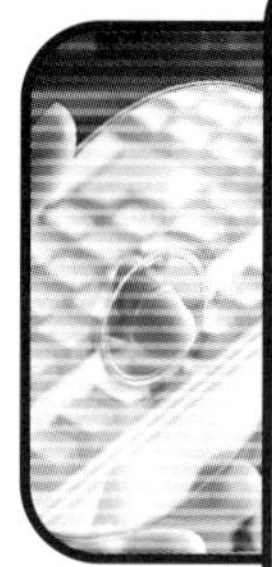

Case study 4.3

Jai the organiser

Jai is a very confident person who likes to keep things moving. Jai is always on top of everything that is going on. In other words Jai is 'a mover and a shaker'.

Meetings are Jai's specialty. Everything is organised to the last detail. Jai's chairing skills are second to none. Her motto is 'Action! Action! Action!'. She makes sure everyone knows what has to be done, how and by when. After meetings Jai follows up on everything, making sure people do what was allocated to them.

Case study activities

Consider what you have learned about meetings in this chapter and your experiences of meetings in your workplace.

1. How do you think most people would react to this style of meeting management?
2. Would Jai's style fit with the sort of meetings you attend?

RECORDING

Getting agreement on actions

Most meetings take place in order to produce some sort of outcome—to get **action**—which means getting agreement on what has to be done, who by, how and when. This means the convenor must be skilled in problem-solving techniques and guiding the group towards making a decision. The convenor needs to take the initiative in drawing the discussion to a close so as to guide the meeting towards achieving its aims.

Any decision on action should address the four elements of an action outcome, **what**, **who**, **how** and **when**.

If the outcomes have been summarised effectively, this step can be relatively simple. Where decisions have been made progressively, you would summarise the agreements and confirm the actions arising from those agreements. In meetings where there has not been a formal decision, you would draw conclusions from what has been discussed and then summarise what you see as the next step using the elements of an action outcome.

Minutes

Minutes of a meeting are the agreed record of discussion and decisions made. That's why they always have to be accepted at the next meeting. **The purpose of minutes is to record permanently the proceedings of a meeting, as well as to provide a basis for action.** There are a variety of ways of recording the proceedings of a meeting; it is optional whether you record the main points of discussion or the names of members who moved and seconded motions. However, it is essential to record the name of the organisation, date, attendees, decisions and actions. An action list indicates the person who will implement the decision made at the meeting, allocating tasks and indicating who will do what, by when.

Taking minutes

It is usually an assistant's job to take notes in the meeting and then write them up as the minutes. If there is no secretary, then the chairperson either appoints a minute taker or calls for a volunteer from the meeting. It is not possible for the chairperson to be the minute taker, but it can be helpful if the two sit together so that recording of discussions can be more accurate.

If you are the minute taker, then you are recording the meeting for those present and absent, and as a historical record of resolutions, decisions and actions. Be tactful and do not mention members by name who may have been very vocal about certain issues. It is better to record, 'a member expressed grave concerns over relocating to new premises' than 'Angela raved on about how she wouldn't move again'. Minority points of view should be recorded in the discussion if they were the source of debate, as these opinions affect the decision. Sometimes previous minutes are consulted to understand the reason for certain decisions. Do not include too much detail as the minutes should be clear and concise.

Your minutes should be a summary of what happened at the meeting, listed in the order of the agenda. You should always record items such as the minutes of the previous meeting being approved or corrected. You must be exact in the wording of each motion and the recording of the result—was it carried or lost? You also have the responsibility of recording the reason for decisions so that those who did not attend can understand the rationale for such decisions.

Figure 4.6
Sample minutes

MINUTES
Quick Solve Computing—Technical Support Team/OH&S Committee

1 December 2001

Present: A Pearce, D Thomas, P Hirosam, M Wu, S Moshtar, D Adams
Apologies: S Kelty, Y London

1. **Minutes of meeting held on 13 October**
   Minutes of the previous meeting were accepted.
   Moved D Thomas, seconded P Hirosam
   The motion relating to item 3, RCD installation had been omitted—this will be corrected in the official record.

2. **Business arising**
   (a) RCD installation. M Wu will contact the supplier and arrange for a compliance certificate to be issued by 15 December. P Hirosam reported that a certificate of compliance needs to be issued. The legal implications of not having a certificate were addressed.
   (b) Emergency procedures—technical team room. D Thomas will draft a new set of procedures and circulate them to committee members for comment by 8 December.
   It was noted that the procedures had not been reviewed. Changes to work practices and physical layout meant that existing procedures did not cover the new arrangements.

3. **Emergency control team**
   It was agreed that a formal allocation of funds for emergency-control team training will be made in the 2002 budget.
   Moved S Moshtar, seconded D Adams
   D Adams will present a detailed training plan and recommended budget allocation to the next meeting.
   The committee noted the report on training for emergency-control team members. It was agreed that a budget allocation would be made for this activity in the 2002 budget.

4. **Next meeting**
   The next meeting will be held on Wednesday, 12 January 2002 in the conference room.

Minutes pro forma

Some organisations use a pro forma for all minutes to help the minute taker and make sure all important details are recorded. You may decide to use the one shown here or adapt it to your local needs.

Figure 4.7
Minutes pro forma

Topic/title	
Purpose of the meeting	
Date/time/location	
Present	
Apologies	
Discussion items and decision/action	Key points of discussion (who/what/when)

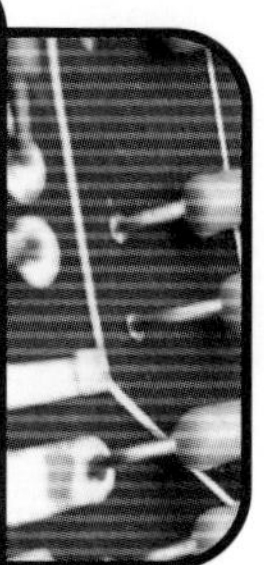

Activity 4.8

Minutes

1. Locate a set of minutes from a meeting you have attended. Be sure that you maintain the privacy of the organisation. Assess the effectiveness of the minutes according to the criteria above. Is it clear what has to be done, who by and when?
2. Read the sample minutes in Figure 4.6. Make a list of four important points of action that have to be completed before the next meeting.
3. Rewrite the sample minutes as action points (what, who, how and when) using the following form.

Minutes of meeting:
Technical Support Team

Quick Solve Computing

File:

Date: Time: Location:

Chairperson:

Documents tabled:

Present:

Apologies:

Agenda Item	Key Points	Action	By Whom	When	Communication Strategy
1	• • • • • • • • • •				

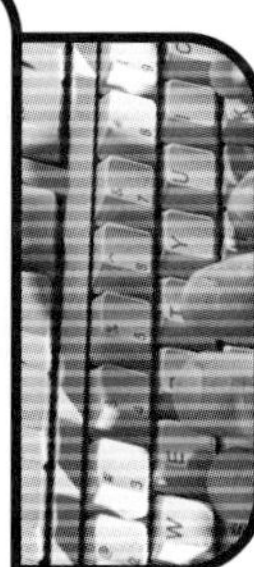

Checklist 4.5

Taking the minutes

Do you complete all minute-taker tasks? Complete this checklist after a meeting to identify any gaps. Ask the chairperson to complete it as well.

I have:	3 Good	2 Fair	1 Improve
positioned myself so that I could hear all participants			
written clearly and succinctly			
used tact in describing personal opinions			
referred to the agenda when keeping minutes			
noted name, place, time and date of meeting			
recorded attendance			
recorded apologies			
recorded confirmation of minutes			
taken notes on key points of discussion			
accurately recorded motions			
checked with the chairperson for exact wording			
listed names of mover and seconder of motions			
recorded all decisions			
prepared an action list			
distributed the minutes			

Total: _______________________

If you scored below 30 you would benefit from reviewing the notes and activities in this chapter and practising your skills in your workplace.

FOLLOWING UP MEETING OUTCOMES

During the meeting you would have identified who is responsible for what as decisions were made. It is useful, at the end of the meeting, to summarise the actions that have been agreed to and then check that everyone understands what they have agreed to do.

The effectiveness of your follow-up is what really decides the effectiveness of the meeting. It is a good idea to contact participants a little before their deadlines to check on how they are progressing with their tasks.

Avoid the 'Jai approach' or sounding too critical if people have not made the progress you expected. One approach is to say 'Hi, James. I'm calling to see how things are going with the policy papers you were collecting for the next meeting—is there anything I can do to help with the task?'. Checking before the deadline gives James the chance to respond to the reminder. Calling *after* the deadline generally results in panic, excuses and guilt.

Another way is to circulate a note that summarises what people have agreed to do.

ACTION POINTS

▶ Make sure the reason for the meeting justifies the time and effort people give.

▶ Determine the purpose of the meeting.

▶ Produce an agenda that clearly states what will be addressed during the meeting.

▶ Prepare the location for the meeting—do not forget refreshments where appropriate.

▶ Begin on time, in a positive and businesslike manner.

▶ Encourage involvement by all participants.

▶ Get agreement on meeting processes and decision making.

▶ Keep notes to help with checking the minutes.

▶ Summarise progress at strategic points in the meeting.

▶ Ensure all decisions state what has to be done, who by, when by, and how.

▶ Check minutes and documents before they are distributed.

▶ Follow up all outcomes and decisions.

SUMMARY

Organisations should hold regular general meetings of all staff. These improve morale and help to encourage teamwork. Both meeting structure and style of leadership should vary to suit the conditions and purpose of a meeting. Careful planning will improve the effectiveness of meetings. Follow the four key steps in the section 'Planning the meeting'.

Not everyone enjoys meetings. A mixture of different communication styles will be present in any meeting room. Be tolerant, and try to help everyone to benefit. An agenda should give, in advance, as much information as possible about the topic to be discussed, the time and length of the meeting, and other details, to enable participants to prepare. Large meetings may work better if at various stages members split into subgroups for discussions and subsequently report their views to the full meeting.

Meetings work best if you follow the seven steps for effective meetings in the section 'Facilitating/leading the meeting'. Facilitators and convenors assume many roles. They promote, lead, direct, inform, interpret, encourage, stimulate, referee, judge, moderate and conciliate, and do anything else necessary for the group to achieve its aims.

Items of hidden agendas are personal goals (not on the open agenda) which individuals (or subgroups) bring with them to a meeting. Hidden agenda issues are necessarily self-centred. Leaders who suspect such an issue is being raised should try to bring it out into the open.

Minutes of a meeting are the agreed record of decisions made. Each motion must be accurately recorded. An effective minute taker summarises what happened at the meeting in the order set by the agenda.

Teleconference and videoconference meetings are an efficient and flexible tool for getting widely dispersed people to collaborate and achieve results that are not possible using traditional approaches. Online forums are increasingly being used.

The meeting has not really achieved its purpose until the decisions have been implemented. It is the role of the convenor to follow up meeting outcomes.

Facilitating and participating in meetings

1. Record all the meetings you have attended in the last month.
2. What kind of meeting facilitator or participant were you?
3. How could you improve your facilitation/participation skills?

Action plan

Complete this checklist after you have facilitated a meeting, or have someone else complete it for you during the meeting. Use the results as a guide to areas you need to work on.

Did you:	3 Good	2 Fair	1 Improve
prepare or assist with the agenda and circulate it before the meeting			
prepare or assist with background material needed for the meeting			
follow the agenda and time limits for each item			
keep the discussion focused on the item			
maintain the group			
limit the development of splinter group discussions			
handle disruptive and obstructive behaviour by members			
use problem-solving strategies to reach decisions			
discourage irrelevant or frivolous discussion			
encourage participation by all members			
start and finish the meeting on time			

Total:_______________________________

If you scored below 20 points you would benefit from revising the notes and activities presented earlier in the chapter.

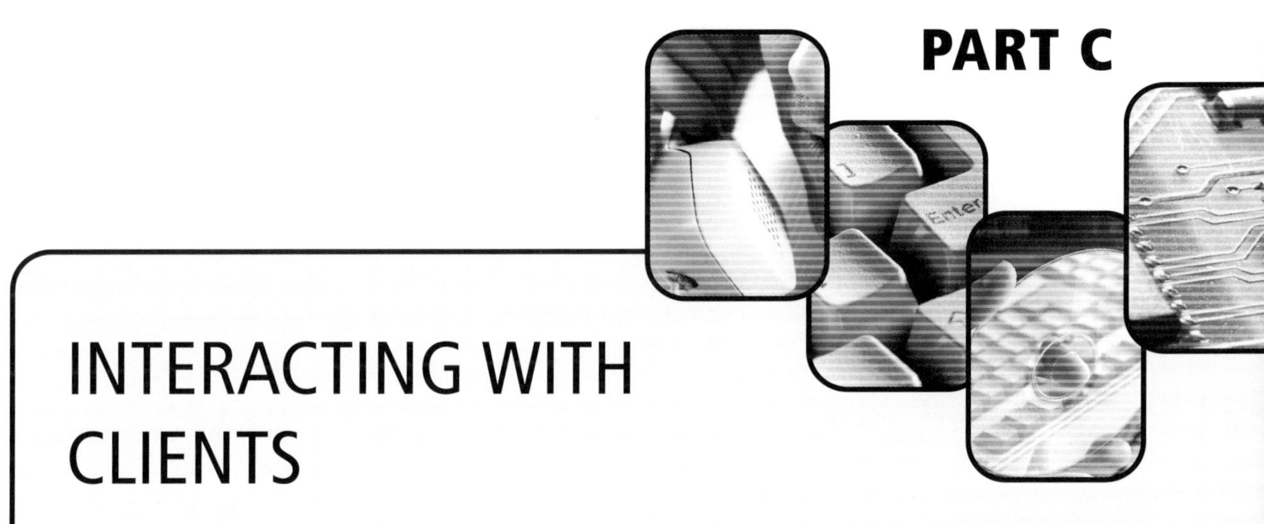

INTERACTING WITH CLIENTS

5 CHAPTER 5

COMMUNICATING WITH CLIENTS

COMPETENCIES

This chapter is linked to elements contained in the following competencies which are in the Information Technology Training Package.

- Interact with Clients ICAITS009B
- Provide Advice to Clients ICAITS031B
- Relate to Clients on a Business Level ICAITTW027B
- Work Effectively in an Information Technology Environment ICAITTW001B
- Determine Client Business Expectations and Needs ICAITAD041A
- Confirm Client Business Needs ICAITAD042A
- Establish and Maintain Client User Liaison ICAITS102A
- Establish and Maintain Client User Liaison During Support Activity ICAITS103A
- Record Client Support Requirements ICAITS016B
- Determine Client Computing Problems and Action ICAITS022B
- Provide One on One Instruction ICAITS023B
- Assist with Policy Development for Client Support Procedures ICAITS033B

The aim of this chapter is to help you develop your skills in establishing and maintaining successful relationships with customers and clients. It deals with important questions about building mutually satisfying relationships with your customers and giving them the highest possible levels of service. These include:

- What is the most personable and professional way to greet my customers?
- How can I anticipate what my customers would like from me?
- Which method will give me the most useful feedback?
- How do I manage speedy, efficient service and keep the personal touch?
- What do I do when a customer gets stroppy?
- How can I communicate well with my customers over the telephone?

Generally customers are people who purchase or receive goods, i.e. they pay for the product. Clients are people who use services provided by individuals or organisations. They may be internal to the business, e.g. financial support from the accounts staff, or external such as a supplier. In this book both terms are used.

TOPICS DISCUSSED

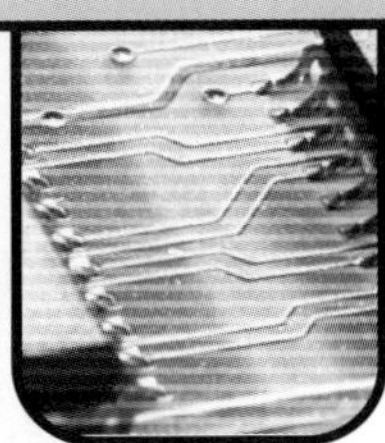

- Who your clients are
- Communication skills in customer service
- Greeting clients
- Consulting with clients to solve problems
- Identifying and responding to client needs
- How stereotypes affect service
- Using the telephone effectively
- Extending your relationship with clients

INTRODUCTION

Interacting with clients means establishing and developing positive relationships between all clients and representatives of an organisation. Delivering quality service, from the client's first approaches to the satisfactory closing of the deal, ensures that you stay in business.

All levels of an organisation must be committed to giving external and internal clients optimal service.

Clients are **all** the people you have a business relationship with whether:

- you work for a private company or a government organisation
- they pay for your services or not
- they purchase goods that you produce or to which you add value.

If you want business you need clients. Essential skills for successful client interaction are described throughout this book. For example, Chapter 1 deals with active listening, questioning techniques, feedback, understanding and empathy, while strategies for dealing with conflict and negotiation skills are covered in Chapter 2.

This chapter focuses on two complementary elements in building successful working relationships with customers. It looks at organisational policy behind effective customer service and at the communication skills needed to put this policy into practice.

Most businesses are very dependent on technology, and IT services are critical to business survival. Individuals' knowledge about technical issues varies greatly and the way we deal with client problems has to reflect this. The range of issues that we communicate about include:

- determining both hardware and software requirements
- training needs
- implementing and training in new procedures
- negotiating support and service agreements
- complaints about technology.

Personal experiences as a customer

It has been estimated that for every disgruntled customer who has a complaint, about forty people get to hear about it either first or second hand. How many times have you avoided using a business because you heard about someone who had a bad experience with them? With the growth of so many Information Technology businesses competition is fierce and many businesses will not survive for long if they do not attract and keep their clients.

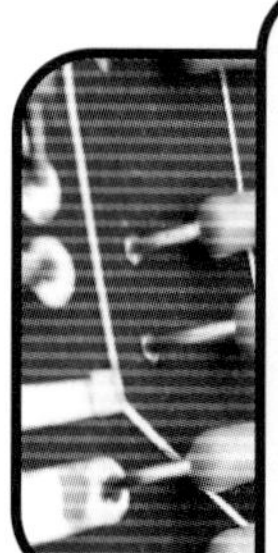

Activity 5.1

Customer service

1. Think of a situation when you were on the receiving end of poor customer service. List the behaviour of the person that made you feel that the service was poor.
2. Did you tell anyone about your experience?
3. Did you buy the product or service you requested?
4. List four things that the person serving you could have done to improve the exchange.

Figure 5.1
Elements in customer service

WHO ARE YOUR CLIENTS?

Your clients include anyone to whom you provide a product or service. This includes people within your organisation and external customers.

If you are a network administrator you will have mainly internal clients because you are supporting the provision of the network to all employees of the company. If you are a software designer you may have a mixture of internal and external clients. The internal clients include anyone who you provide advice or software to in your company. Your external clients include people who purchase your software and training.

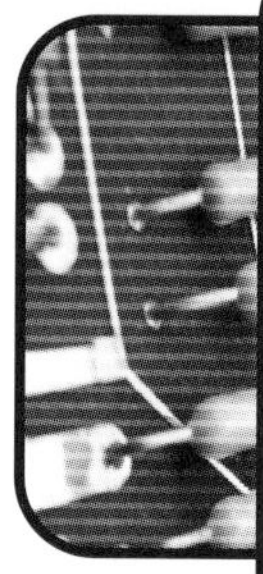

Activity 5.2

Identifying clients

1. List the possible internal and external clients of the following people:
   (a) a Help Desk attendant
   (b) the store person in your company
   (c) a technician who repairs the computers
   (d) a computer sales person
   (e) the accounts clerk
   (f) a software designer.
2. Make a list of your customers and clients.

COMMUNICATION SKILLS IN CUSTOMER SERVICE

Every satisfied client has the potential to bring other new clients. Quality service is appreciated and clients' satisfaction advertises a successful business. Therefore business expands and your career prospects grow.

Accomplished providers of customer service are adept at the following skills. They know how to:

- greet clients
- identify and respond to their needs
- solve problems by consulting with clients.

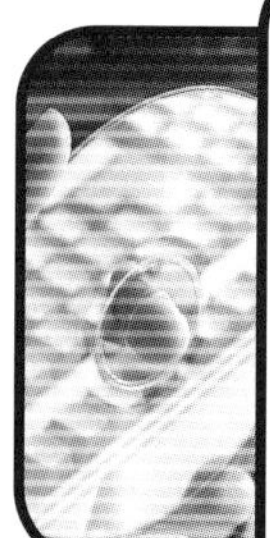

Case study 5.1

Toning up customer service

Maria's printer needed a service and some minor repairs. She rang two potential repairers to find out approximate costs and timeframes for the work. The first company, Print Fix, kept Maria waiting for two minutes before transferring her call to an unidentified 'technician'. He would not discuss the repairs over the phone and seemed very keen to sell Maria a new printer. The technician assured her that the $30 quotation fee would be absorbed into the purchase cost of the new machine. He was not able to estimate the repair period but said it would probably take 'about a week'.

When Maria called the second company, Tone Up, she was promptly transferred to Miles, a technician who asked her specific questions about the problems with her machine before concluding that he could not help her over the phone. Tone Up's quotation fee was $40 and Miles assured her that the printer would be repaired within forty-eight hours of delivery to Tone Up's offices. Although Tone Up's fee was higher and they were thirty minutes further away from her house than Print Fix, Maria decided to take her printer to Tone Up.

Tone Up operate from a factory unit at the back of an industrial complex. Maria found it difficult to find them as there was no obvious signage on the building's street front and she had not received any directions when she rang the company. No one was at the reception desk when she arrived and there was no bell or buzzer to alert staff to her presence. After waiting a minute, Maria called out 'Hello' and a receptionist appeared with a coffee cup in one hand and a cigarette in the other. The woman took the printer but insisted that Maria keep the connection cords after telling her, 'Look love, the techies are hopeless—they lose everything, leave those here and you'll never see them again!'. The receptionist then tore off a sheet of coffee-stained scribble-pad for Maria to write down her name, number and a note about the printer's problems.

Although Maria's confidence in Tone Up's efficiency was a bit shaken by the encounter with their receptionist, her initial confidence was restored when she received a call from Miles the next afternoon telling her that the printer was ready for collection. He explained the $130 charge in detail so Maria knew exactly what she was paying for. The cost breakdown was also detailed on the invoice enclosed with the printer when Maria collected it at 7 o'clock the next morning.

Case study activities

1. Which elements in customer service led to Maria choosing Tone Up over Print Fix? Complete the table below.

Positive customer service of Tone-up	Negative customer service of Print Fix

2. How could Tone Up further improve their customer service?

GREETING CLIENTS

Clients' lasting impressions of you and your organisation are formed as soon as they enter your premises. Greet your customers by smiling and offering your assistance. Make them feel special by approaching them in a friendly and professional manner. Most customers react badly to pushy or overbearing service. If you cannot attend to their needs immediately, always acknowledge their presence and advise them that you will be with them soon.

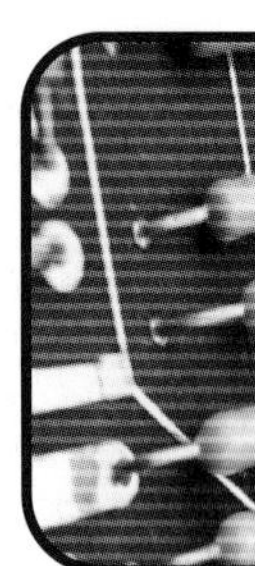

Activity 5.3

Timeliness

One of the most annoying aspects of customer service is waiting to be served.

1. Answer the following questions individually then compare answers in small groups.
   (a) A client walks into a computer sales area. There are three people waiting and two people attending to the clients. How long should they wait before they need to be acknowledged? What would you regard as an acceptable strategy to deal with this type of situation?
   (b) A client has waited for twenty minutes to be served and looks like they are about to walk away. What should you do?
   (c) A client emails for sales advice on new hardware. How long before you reply? Do you also telephone?
2. In pairs look at situations (a) and (b). Prepare an appropriate greeting response and demonstrate how you would deal with the situation.

IDENTIFYING AND RESPONDING TO CLIENT NEEDS

Once your client feels welcome and assured of your attention, listen carefully to find out how you can *best* meet their needs. Know your company's services and products thoroughly and keep abreast of changes and updates. This enables you to ask questions to focus clients on services you can provide. Listening to their responses helps you further assist clients in deciding on what service best suits their needs by understanding the extent of the use of IT in the client's user area with details of applications, operating systems, hardware, networks etc.

Active listening and questioning skills (see Chapter 1) are essential in dealing with clients to convey and clarify complex information. You need to check that what you are providing is what the client wants. As the focus of client service is giving customers what they want, open questions are appropriate. You would need to establish such things as:

- how critical the IT is to the client
- what support services are required
- the physical requirements of the system, taking into account the current system's functionality, geography, environment, client user and cost constraints.

Reflective questioning techniques allow you to restate the client's demand and check your understanding. The reflective question also lets the speaker know that you have been actively listening and are checking your understanding. Your tone should be tentative as you are asking for clarification, not stating a fact. Examples of reflective questions are: 'You found the warranty conditions very confusing, is that what you mean?' and 'So you feel very annoyed by the late delivery of your training manuals—in other words you are dissatisfied with our service?'. This technique will allow you to understand both the message and the feeling expressed by the client. It is particularly important with clients who may not have extensive knowledge of IT systems.

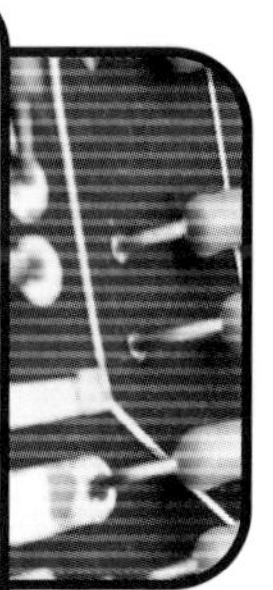

Activity 5.4

Communication role play

In pairs, consider the following scenarios. Write down a set of responses from the staff member for each example in a way that centres on the customer's need. In pairs role play the parts of the customer and staff member OR write out the conversation using the communication skills described in this book.

1. **Customer.** You have started a computer business specialising in design software for architects and engineers. You go to a new wholesale computer hardware distributor to open an account. Think of the likely things you would require and the quantities involved. Consider how you would like to arrange the payment for your supplies.

   Staff member. Greet the customer and identify their needs using active listening skills. Remember that your company has a policy of only opening accounts with customers who purchase over $2000 worth of supplies per month.

2. **Customer.** You enter a computer shop looking for the ideal anniversary gift for your partner. You are not sure what you want. You know he recently purchased a digital camera and needs some software for his computer. You only have this lunchbreak available to choose the gift.

   Staff member. It is a busy lunchtime with two customers entering the shop in quick succession. You serve this customer. The customer is not sure what they want and you are conscious of the second waiting customer. Use active listening skills to identify the needs of the first customer.

3. **Customer.** You require information about a home computer. Approach a staff member to make your enquiries.

   Staff member. A customer approaches you wanting to make enquiries about a product. There are several possible products to suit their needs although they have different features. Use active listening skills to identify the needs of the customer.

CONSULTING WITH CLIENTS TO SOLVE PROBLEMS

When a customer approaches you with a problem, you need to do the following.

1. Gather all the facts by using open questions to encourage detail.
2. Listen to the client. Use active listening to interpret what is said by listening for meaning and sense, rather than just the words. Empathise by restating the facts and using positive body language to reinforce your concern. Once the client sees you as empathetic, cooperative and genuinely interested in finding a solution, tension levels will drop.
3. Summarise your understanding of the problem and check with the client for agreement or changes. Always be flexible; do not impose your views on the client.
4. Avoid being drawn into slanging matches about who is to blame, and concentrate on gently but firmly getting the details of the problem.
5. Be prepared to negotiate so that you both achieve a positive outcome. Take action to resolve the problem and keep the client informed at all stages of the process. If further action is required inform the client and take the necessary steps to implement another solution.

Customer complaints should be seen as opportunities to fix problems and improve your product or service.

Dealing with complaints is a good test of your customer service. If you handle complaints well, clients will probably stay with your company. However, dissatisfied clients whose problems were not resolved will leave you and tell many other people of your bad service.

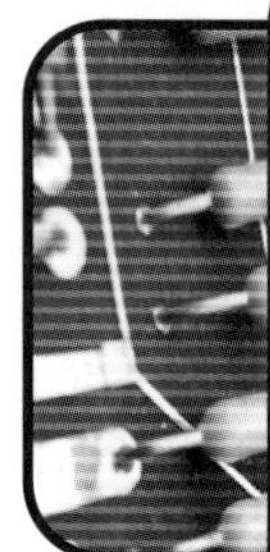

Activity 5.5

Unexpected problems

In pairs develop strategies to deal with the following problems and prepare a short role play. To try and resolve the problems you should:
- clarify exactly what the client needs
- use effective communication skills
- develop a strategy that maintains client goodwill as well as meeting their needs.

1. A customer has ordered a new scanner through your company. After a delay of a week the scanner has finally arrived. You ring the customer and they tell you they will be coming around in the next half-hour. You check the scanner and discover that it is a different model to the one the customer ordered. The customer has just walked through the door. What are you going to say and how are you going to deal with the situation?

2. A regular customer rings you up to ask you to put aside a particular bit of computer hardware. You are sure that there are plenty of these items in store so you agree to put one aside. It will be collected at lunchtime. When you finish the call you attend to some other tasks before going into the storeroom to get the requested item. There is no stock of this item left. You try to ring the customer but are told they are on the way to see you. The customer arrives about ten minutes after this call. What are you going to say and how are you going to deal with the situation?

3. You have booked a client into a software training course at a conference centre located about an hour's drive away. The client rings you from the training centre and tells you that the trainers have no record of the reservation and say they are fully booked. What are you going to say and how are you going to deal with the situation?

4. A customer rings you about a systems failure. It is obvious from your conversation that the customer has incorrect information but is insisting that they are right. The customer is now showing signs of frustration.

Dealing with difficult customers

Unfortunately not all people are easy to deal with. Even with the best intentions some customers are awkward. Customers need to:
- feel welcome
- receive prompt service
- feel that they have been heard
- be understood
- feel valued
- be treated respectfully
- be given accurate and reliable information and advice
- have their problem/s solved.

Be aware that your customer needs attention. When a customer approaches, remember to:
- stop what you are doing, look at them, smile and ask how you can help

- send a positive attitude through your body language
- stay focused on their needs
- look for signs that they need attention
- acknowledge them when they have to wait:
    —non-verbally by a smile or gesture which tells them they have been noticed
    —by excusing yourself from your current customer briefly to let the new person know how long you will be
    —by developing a queuing system if waiting is common in your organisation.

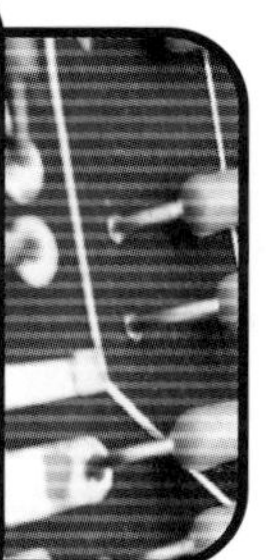

Activity 5.6

Difficult customers

1. What behaviour in customers do you find difficult?
2. What sort of things do they do which make it difficult for you?
3. In small groups list some ideas to help deal with the situations you have identified. Try to identify the approaches that are required to deal with these people. You can review the strategies discussed in Chapter 2.

HOW STEREOTYPES AFFECT SERVICE

Australia is a multicultural society, meaning that it is made up of people from many countries and cultures. It is important to be sensitive to cultural differences in communication as well as be sensitive in dealing with people who have limited English-language skills.

Stereotyping occurs when we assume we know something about a person because of their cultural background, what they look like, how they dress, etc. Stereotyping can lead to pre-judging, inaccurate assumptions and prejudice.

Stereotyping can affect service because instead of relating to people as individuals, we judge their appearance or behaviour on the basis of the stereotype we have of their cultural group. This can easily lead to misunderstandings.

When communicating in your workplace with customers, clients or colleagues, remember to treat each person as an individual, listen actively to what they have to say, and respond using inclusive language to foster mutual understanding.

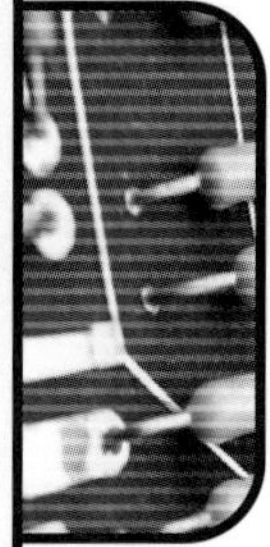

Activity 5.7

Identifying cultural barriers in customer service

Identify the barriers to customer service in the following scenarios and develop more appropriate responses.

1. A customer approaches a salesperson and begins to explain what she wants. The customer has a strong accent. The salesperson interrupts before she can finish and calls for another staff member, saying loudly, 'Phillip, can you talk to this woman? She doesn't speak English. You can explain in Chinese'. The customer is not from China and speaks a different language.

2. A man walks into a computer repair centre with a damaged computer. His 10-year-old daughter accompanies him. He attempts to explain the problem but has great difficulty making himself understood in English. The assistant looks at the daughter and explains quickly that they will investigate the problem and asks them to come back in a week to pick up the computer. The assistant then takes the computer and leaves them looking confused.

Tips for speaking across language barriers

- Use words that are simple, common English—avoid slang and jargon. This is very hard when talking about computers! If you must use jargon, check if the customer understands.
- Choose the most simple and direct forms of expressing your ideas.
- Organise your thoughts before you speak—focus on the essential information and avoid overloading the person.
- Speak at a suitable pace.
- Speak clearly.
- Allow pauses between sentences.
- Do not complete their sentences.
- Do not yell.
- Do not condescend or patronise.

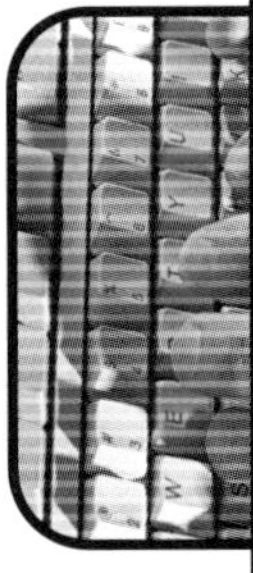

Checklist 5.1

Establishing relationships with clients

Think about the way you deal with customers, and choose the option that best describes your skills.

I can:	Yes	No	Not sure
greet customers in a friendly, professional manner	☐	☐	☐
establish quickly if they want help or want to look around unaided	☐	☐	☐
use my extensive and current product knowledge to meet customers' needs best	☐	☐	☐
ask open and reflective questions to find out exactly how to help the customer	☐	☐	☐
find their desired information and/or product efficiently	☐	☐	☐
calm upset customers by empathising with their distress while focusing on the problem	☐	☐	☐
use my organisation's systems for resolving customer complaints quickly and efficiently	☐	☐	☐
close the interaction in a friendly, interested manner designed to encourage future business	☐	☐	☐

USING THE TELEPHONE EFFECTIVELY

The telephone is your organisation's 'front line'. It provides many potential customers with their first impression of your business and how it is run. A well-managed system should meet the needs of people at the other end of the phone as well as your own. Two significant factors can undermine telephone effectiveness:

1. You cannot see the other person. In ordinary conversation your spoken words are reinforced by non-verbal signals such as body movement. Over the phone the only non-verbal support comes from the tone of your voice, and that can be distorted.
2. Both sender and receiver have difficulties remembering details of the conversation. People tend to hear what they want to hear. Over time, details of the call become distorted and, unless both parties record the call in writing, memories about what was said will vary.

Making calls

A phone conversation between two strangers works best after they have been 'introduced'. A little extra effort at the start will make the 'introduction barrier' disappear. A good introduction establishes the names, status and mood of both parties and states the reason for the call.

1. **Introduce yourself in a polite yet friendly way.** This encourages the other person to respond the same way.
2. **If calling a stranger, identify yourself immediately.** 'Hello. Paul Martin here. I'm trying to get in touch with ...' Failure to identify yourself at the start is a non-verbal signal that worries many people.
3. **Explain how you obtained the number.** If the listener does not know you, this will establish your credibility and connect you to them. Was it advertised? Did you get it through a personal contact? If the contact is a mutual friend or colleague, mention that person's name: 'This is Angelo Perez from Software Solutions. Tran gave me your name and suggested I call you about ...'
4. **Put the listener at ease.** Add a further remark in a friendly, personal tone to show you are relaxed and looking forward to communicating. Your introduction should say (verbally and non-verbally), 'I'm happy to meet you'.
5. **Add to the listener's picture.** After your name, add other details to help the listener develop a clear mental picture; for example, the name of your firm, your department or your location, and your reason for calling: 'Hello. I'm Wendy Chan from Blitz Computing in Bairnsdale. I phoned to ask about your ...'
6. **Refer to previous discussions or activities.** Fill in possible gaps in your listener's memory: 'Is that Kel Blakie? It's Anna Samos. I'm the graduate who flew over from Perth last week to see you about a job as a project officer'.

Answering calls

Answer the phone no later than the third or fourth ring. Once you have greeted the customer, direct the conversation towards meeting their needs in a personalised and efficient manner.

Identify your organisation and give your name

'Kel's Communications, Rani Ratnam speaking. How can I help you?'. Mentioning your section or unit can also help to focus the caller's attention. Even on a call transferred from a switchboard, it pays to open with a similar identification, to assure callers they have reached the correct extension.

Figure 5.2
Communicating using the telephone

Identify the caller

You should know the name and the business of the person you are talking to. If this is not given after your introduction, ask for it:

- 'Could I please have your name?'
- 'Who am I talking to, please?'
- 'Can I ask who's calling (speaking)?', or 'May I say who's calling?' if you are going to transfer the call.

Listen actively

It is easy to miss or misinterpret information over the phone. This is especially true if the caller is agitated, nervous or vague about why they are phoning. Listen carefully and indicate that you are paying close attention by commenting on the message and confirming information. Check your understanding by asking for feedback: 'The cursor freezes when you select options on the tool bar. Have I got it right?'. This makes it easier for the listener to acknowledge the possibility of a misunderstanding.

Tell the caller what happens next

If you need to leave the phone to find information, tell the caller what's happening—'I'll just get my screen up on this ...'—and give them the option of waiting or having you return their call. If you are transferring the call, give the name and number of the person who will deal with the inquiry so that the caller can contact them directly, if this call is not connected.

Record the message

Keep a notepad and (*a functioning*) pen next to the phone. Write down the caller's name and contact details and a summary of their message. If you are transferring the information to someone else, tell the caller that you have recorded the details. Saying 'I'll put the message on her desk ...' or 'I'll see that he gets the message ...' reassures them that the message is likely to reach the right person.

Close the call courteously

Confirm any action you and the caller will take as a result of the conversation and, if appropriate, show that you anticipate further contacts with the caller: 'So we'll see you on Friday when you pick up the printer. Thanks for calling'.

Activity 5.8

Telephone scripts

Write telephone scripts for the four scenarios listed, recording what you would say to fulfil each of the following guidelines.

- start with a pleasant greeting
- introduce yourself clearly
- explain why you are making the call or, if you are answering a call, ask their reason for calling
- ask for the name of the person you are speaking to and write the name down so you can use their name during the call
- listen carefully and actively to the other person, providing feedback
- finish the call pleasantly.

1. Freda Sanderson is the local florist. She asks you to call her regarding pricing on desktop publishing packages for her business.
2. Minh Nguyen is a manager of accounts. She calls you to ask for some information about the new network procedures.
3. Kerry Thomas has left a message asking you to call back regarding his complaint about a recent upgrade that you provided.
4. A client contacts the help desk. The cursor freezes when he attempts certain functions.

Improving your telephone technique

It takes extra effort and empathy to share positive feelings (liking, trust, respect, enthusiasm) over the phone, yet when you express negative feelings (dislike, distrust, boredom, anger), the message seems to travel very easily. Take extra care about what you say and how you say it. Despite the visual handicap it is possible to send positive messages about your feelings.

- Learn to 'smile' over the phone. You will *sound* as though you are smiling if your face muscles are formed into a smile as you speak.
- Monitor your tone of voice and non-verbal expression. Learn how to tell the difference between a positive tone and tones that make you sound negative when perhaps you are just unhappy or tired.
- Practise using clear, distinct speech (a 'microphone' voice).

- Put yourself in the receiver's position. Be friendly and show that you care. People who are happy and relaxed on the phone will also be feeling cooperative. Try to create this atmosphere for both of you. Use active listening.
- Repeat the other person's first name during the call.
- Plan phone calls in advance. This saves time and helps you clarify your ideas before you ring. Choose a time to ring that you know will suit the other person as well as yourself.
- Keep business calls as short as possible. There may be other callers waiting to get through to both of you.
- Listen for clues. A sudden pause or change in the conversation may be a signal that the other person is upset by something in your vocal tone, or that you might have used a phrase that gave the wrong impression. Check.
- Treat listeners as adults. You may be annoyed by a caller's attitude, but try not to 'talk down' to anyone. If you become angry or adopt a tone of voice signalling a superior (parent to child) attitude, you will send negative signals that reduce your chance of gaining agreement over the phone.

Handling difficult situations on the telephone

You cannot avoid difficult phone calls. Angry words on the phone are easily mis-interpreted, and trying to persuade people to cooperate when they are angry does not work anywhere, especially not on the phone. Sometimes you receive difficult calls without warning. If possible, however, prepare for them beforehand. Work out what you want to say and what responses you might expect.

- **Relate to the caller.** If the call is about an overdue account, do not launch straight into money matters without some relationship building first.
- **Get information.** First find out as much as you can about the problem, concentrating on facts rather than feelings. If the other person involved is angry, try to find out why. For instance, use open-ended questions, with the key words 'how', 'why', 'when', 'where', 'who', 'what' and 'would you'.
- **Exchange information.** It is easier for both parties to remain logical and unemotional if you centre the discussion on cold, hard facts.
- **Paint the picture as clearly as you can.** Discuss what action is to be taken, where and when it will be taken, and who will take it.
- **Persuade, point by point.** Deal with one thing at a time. Once agreement is reached on one point, make a note, read it back, have it confirmed. Recap and summarise regularly.
- **Agree on an acceptable solution.** Ask for (or give) a specific commitment. Advise the caller that you will be sending a written message confirming the agreement.

EXTENDING YOUR RELATIONSHIPS WITH CLIENTS

Repeat business is the lifeblood of most organisations. Once you have attracted clients to your business, you want to maintain their patronage by continuing to fulfil their needs and expectations and providing 'value-added' products and services. You can do this by:

- keeping up to date
- following up your service
- giving information freely
- rewarding customer loyalty

- anticipating and learning from your mistakes
- promoting your products and services.

Getting client feedback

The best way to evaluate a service is to ask the clients if what you are delivering meets their needs. Research indicates that only one dissatisfied customer out of every twenty actually complains. If you want to access this information, as well as find out what your clients like best about your service, you will have to find a way to collect it.

You can of course collect feedback informally by talking to customers when they visit your business. This is a really good way to build up your knowledge about particular client preferences while letting them know that you are genuinely interested in their opinions and experiences.

Some more formal methods include:

- Asking the front-line staff for feedback on common issues raised by clients. For example, if a computer trainer decides to offer a course in Word Perfect but the booking clerk says that she has only received inquiries about courses in Microsoft Word, then the organisation should listen to the clients' needs.
- Focus groups, where you invite your clients to join you to discuss mutually important issues. For example, a company deciding on establishing a one-stop help desk might set up a focus group. This group would determine the need for the desk and discuss what services should be provided.
- Surveys or questionnaires can check and monitor the success of your service and canvass changes and improvements. For instance, a company has had many suggestions about establishing a new product line in computer games. Normally this company only sells educational software and does not want to risk investing in stock that might not sell. Therefore a questionnaire could be designed to find out if existing clients would also purchase games. Be aware that writing questionnaires is a specialised skill. There are reference books available to advise you.

Following up your service

Keep up-to-date client records

List your clients' contact details and details of products and services you have provided to them. Do this with the clients' permission and support by talking to them to confirm and extend your records and assuring them of the confidentiality of the information.

Check that your client is satisfied

You could phone them or write a closing letter to let them know that a transaction has been settled and you look forward to continuing the business relationship in the future. Always be alert to ways of renewing contact with the client.

Record and assess handling of complaints

Once you have dealt with a customer complaint, a record of the decision needs to be filed and then reviewed at a later date, to assess whether the decision was effective.

Maintain your after-sales service

If you buy a car and are phoned a month later by the salesperson and asked if you are pleased with the purchase, then you are more likely to have a positive attitude towards the company.

Send out checklists

This will help you determine if the product or service provided could be improved. Questions based on value, reliability and quality are usually included with a rating grid ranging from poor to excellent. This is often followed up with a further checklist a few months later that thanks the 'valued' client for their feedback and seeks to further improve the product or service. **Reinforce** that they are welcome to phone you for information or advice on new products.

Rewarding customer loyalty

Clients need to feel valued by your organisation and there are many ways of promoting this. Some companies use newsletters to keep the clients up-to-date with new products or services and any special discounts or benefits available to 'valued' clients. Other rewards include:

- issuing bonus points that can eventually be cashed in for a discount on a new product
- offering gold memberships to longstanding clients, entitling them to attend special events
- sending clients gifts at Christmas bearing the company logo.

Anticipating and learning from your mistakes

Another way of promoting customer satisfaction is to have a recognised system for minimising complaints. This helps everyone anticipate difficulties and learn from individual and collective mistakes. Here are some strategies for this system:

- give greater attention to resolving customer complaints quickly
- attend regularly to problem files
- analyse customer complaints for maximum information
- inform everyone involved in the problem-solving process of the negotiated solution
- support solutions that are consistent with organisational goals
- remain flexible
- use complaints to improve quality
- involve front-line staff in suggesting changes to improve customer service
- improve standards and implement best practice
- implement Quality Management.

Promoting your products and services

Advertising is concerned with informing buyers about products and services. Effective advertising is based on analysing and researching your market, and determining which options will serve you best. Different strategies work in different situations, so you must decide whether you want to:

- develop general awareness or knowledge of a product or service
- alter existing customer attitudes
- achieve sales of a specific product.

Checklist 5.2

Extending relationships with clients

Look at the way the organisation you work for manages its relationships with clients, and choose the option that best describes that relationship.

My organisation:	Yes	No	Not sure
maintains accurate client records	☐	☐	☐
gathers feedback from staff and clients both formally and informally	☐	☐	☐
chooses advertising strategies to fit our product and services	☐	☐	☐
has a practical system for managing complaints which is supported by the staff	☐	☐	☐
recognises and rewards customer loyalty	☐	☐	☐
checks levels of customer satisfaction with specific products and services	☐	☐	☐
looks for innovative ways to renew and extend contact with our clients	☐	☐	☐
offers excellent after-sales service	☐	☐	☐

Activity 5.9

Extending relationships with clients

1. What methods does your organisation use to follow up clients and check on satisfaction with the services or products they have purchased?
2. Read a variety of IT publications, e.g. magazines, ezines, brochures and websites. List five different types of incentives that companies offer to attract and maintain customers.
3. Design a questionnaire for distribution to current clients of your company. The purpose is to find out what they are doing now and how much they feel your products/services helped them.
4. Design a client-record form for your own computer sales and service business.
5. List the issues you think are important for a client service policy.
6. Contact two other organisations similar to your own or ones that you may be interested to work in and outline their client policies.

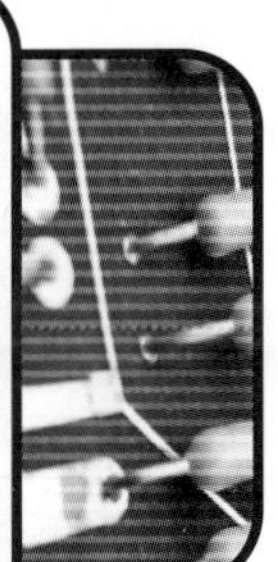

ACTION POINTS

You will become adept at customer service if you:

> work for an organisation that views effective customer service as everyone's right and responsibility

> are able to support your organisation's goals and ethos

- are sufficiently confident and professional to deal with *all* your customers in an empathetic and helpful manner
- can use extensive product knowledge to best fulfil your customers' needs
- ask the right questions to establish customer needs and expectations
- stay calm and focused on the issues when resolving disputes with customers
- are familiar and comfortable with your organisation's systems for resolving problems and dealing with complaints
- talk openly to customers about their views on your products and services
- contribute your knowledge of customer satisfaction as constructive feedback to improve performance
- enjoy working with your customers and take a genuine interest in their dealings with your organisation.

SUMMARY

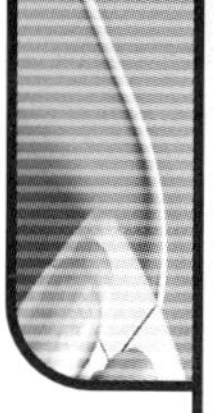

Client (or customer) service involves an organisation-wide policy that puts people first and does not distinguish between internal and external customers. Effective customer service balances speed and efficiency with friendly, personalised attention.

Every successful company has a procedure for dealing with customer complaints which staff understand and accept, and which involves consultation with clients. When a customer approaches you with a problem, you need to stay calm and gather all the facts by using open and reflective questions.

Overcome the visual barrier in telephone communication by:

- introducing yourself
- offering information to help listeners state their requests clearly
- smiling over the phone
- planning difficult calls
- giving positive feedback throughout the call
- confirming your understanding of the message
- stating clearly what will happen as a result of the call
- noting the details of the message.

Businesses can improve their service to clients by encouraging feedback through a range of informal and formal sources. Clients need to feel valued by the organisation and there are many ways of promoting this, including keeping customer records updated, rewarding customer loyalty, and maintaining after-sales service. Worthwhile advertising depends on matching the type of promotion to your marketing aims, determined by your clients' needs.

Communicating with clients

TRAINING LOG

1. Use the following checklist to evaluate:
    (a) yourself answering a business call
    (b) a person you make a business call to in the next week.

Did the receiver of the call:	You	Other caller
pick up the receiver promptly	☐	☐
identify the organisation and gave its name	☐	☐
offer assistance in a friendly, professional way	☐	☐
note the caller's name and organisation	☐	☐
listen carefully and confirm the information/reasons for the call	☐	☐
use the caller's name	☐	☐
explain what would happen as a result of the call	☐	☐
indicate if the information is being recorded in some way	☐	☐
close the call on a friendly, active note	☐	☐

2. Think back to a workplace situation where you had to deal with a difficult client or situation. Describe the steps you followed to deal with the problem. How effective were they? If a similar situation occurred, would you do anything differently?

Action plan

1. Outline three important issues that are stressed in the client service policy in your workplace.
2. Identify one area in the client service area that you feel should be addressed. Give your suggestions on how service in this area could be improved.
3. List the particular aspects of communicating with clients you plan to concentrate on over the next month. Explain how you propose to do this.

6 CHAPTER 6

PRESENTATION SKILLS

COMPETENCIES

This chapter is linked to elements contained in the following competencies which are in the Information Technology Training Package.

- Interact with Clients ICAITS009B
- Provide One on One Instruction ICAITS023B
- Provide Advice to Clients ICAITS031B
- Work Effectively in an Information Technology Environment ICAITTW001B
- Relate to Clients on a Business Level ICAITTW027B
- Participate in a Team and Individually to Achieve Organisational Goals ICAITTW011B
- Coordinate and Maintain Teams ICAITTW026B

The aim of this chapter is to develop your speaking skills so that you can plan and present talks to a range of audiences, including clients and colleagues.

The amount of information and the rate at which it changes within the IT industry means that you will be required to present information on a regular basis to all your clients and customers (both internal and external). Sometimes you may need to present to a group while at other times it may be to individuals. In all cases, the skills in this chapter will assist you in making sure your presentation is effective.

In particular it will help you answer questions such as these:

- How can I overcome any feelings of nervousness about public speaking?
- How can I appear confident when I really feel nervous?
- How do I begin my talk?
- How much information should I include in a talk?
- How can I keep my audience's attention and interest?
- How do I finish my talk?
- What if my audience is hostile?
- How do I deal with questions and interjections?
- What do I do about visual support for my talk?

TOPICS DISCUSSED

- Types of presentations
- Qualities of an effective presenter
- The purpose of your presentation
- Analysing your audience
- Preparing your presentation
- Giving your presentation

INTRODUCTION

Most positions in the IT industry involve providing technical information to a wide range of people with diverse experience and understanding of the information. Whether you present to an audience of one or one hundred, the steps in planning and preparing appropriate information are essential in ensuring you are an effective presenter. You may also find it useful to refer to the basics of good communication discussed in Chapter 1 and the specific skills for participating in formal meetings, which are covered in Chapter 4.

As part of your work in the IT industry you may be required to:

- gather and communicate product information to groups of internal and external clients or colleagues
- provide one to one instruction to work colleagues or clients
- facilitate groups to gain consensus on concepts
- deliver oral briefings and advice
- report to colleagues on workplace procedures.

Most of us fear speaking in public. If the prospect of giving a presentation horrifies you, have a good look at the reasons for your discomfort.

If a group asks you to talk to them it is because they want to hear from you. You are probably already regarded as a credible speaker with valuable expertise and experience to offer them. However they will not necessarily accept everything you say. One-way lectures to a silent and 'captive' audience are increasingly rare in any business. It is far more likely that you will need to manage discussion and dissent in workplace presentations just as you do in conversations with friends and colleagues. This calls for empathy, flexibility and (occasionally) crowd control. To meet the challenge of an interactive presentation, you need to be well organised and clear about your aims. However, you are rewarded with immediate feedback and valuable audience input on your topic.

Communication styles differ from person to person and from situation to situation. You may be a member of a work team presenting a report to management or giving an oral presentation of your own research. You may be giving instructions for using equipment, or welcoming a new staff member at morning tea. A team leader adopts a friendly and open style while explaining the job to a newcomer but is more formal and forceful when requesting funding from management. Two programmers adopt a serious style while working on a computer system, but switch to happy informal communication over lunch. **Maintain your natural communication style but adapt your approach to fit the type of audience and presentation.**

TYPES OF PRESENTATIONS

The type of presentation you give will depend on a number of factors. Will you be presenting to one person, a few people or many? Is your audience a client, management, your work team or a service provider? Is your purpose to inform, persuade or instruct? The answers to these questions will help you decide the type of presentation to give.

In the IT workplace you may be asked to give different types of presentations including:

- one on one training
- demonstrations and explanations of new products to client groups
- team meeting reports

- project proposals to management
- promotion of your organisation's services.

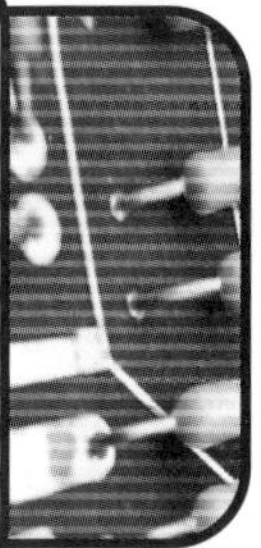

Activity 6.1

Presentation types

Make a list of the different types of presentations that you have given in the last month. These may be in your workplace or community.

QUALITIES OF AN EFFECTIVE PRESENTER

We have all had to sit and listen to speakers. Sometimes they are so boring that by the end of the talk it is hard to remember what they said. At other times we are really excited by the time the speaker reaches the end of the presentation.

Activity 6.2

Effective presentations

Think about presenters that you have heard. What do they do that makes the presentation effective/ineffective? Complete the following table.

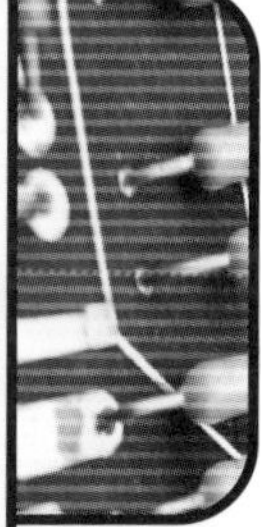

Effective	Ineffective

The following is a list of some of the common features of effective presenters. Your list from Activity 6.2 may have additional features. Effective speakers:

- are knowledgeable on the topic
- are well prepared
- give an overview of the content at the beginning, including the purpose of the presentation
- present information clearly and logically
- give examples to explain or support the information
- sound enthusiastic
- involve the audience
- use a variety of methods in the presentation
- look at the audience
- allow for questions from the audience.

Figure 6.1
Some different types of presentations

Steps in planning a presentation

In order to be an effective presenter it is essential to plan what you are going to say. This following model is useful to guide the planning process.

- What is the purpose of the presentation?
  —To inform?
  —To provide instruction on new procedures?
  —To promote an idea or change in policy?
  —To help make a decision?
  —Something else?
- Who is the audience?
  —Who are they?
  —How many are there?
  —What do they know about the topic?
  —What do they want to know?
  —What opinions do they have about the issue?
  —What else should you know about the audience?
- Preparing the presentation
  —How do I organise and present the information to suit the audience?
  —What visual aids do I need?
  —Is the room I am using suitable or do I need to modify or change it for the presentation?
  —What equipment do I need?
- Giving the presentation
  —How do I control my nerves?
  —How do I relate to and involve the audience?
  —How do I manage the time?

THE PURPOSE OF YOUR PRESENTATION

First work out your *principal goal.* What do you want your talk to achieve? For example, you may be:

- presenting a five-minute oral report to a work group to update them on a piece of equipment
- copresenting a job-related report to management to persuade them to implement a change in procedures
- delivering an oral presentation based on a new client project
- presenting a solution to a common problem from clients at the help desk
- running a training session in a new piece of software
- demonstrating a new computer application to a potential buyer to promote its advantages over an existing product
- explaining a new network procedure to persuade staff to accept the changed arrangement.

Write down your central theme in one short sentence. If you want to motivate staff to accept change, for instance, the central theme could be 'to explain the reasons for the change and outline the benefits for staff'.

Specific aims

Establish specific objectives; they represent the steps your talk will follow in support of the central theme. To persuade people to support the change rather than just accept it, your objectives might include:

- informing clients of the advantages of this new application
- explaining the advantages and demonstrating the features
- testing the use of the application using specific standards/tasks for the clients to complete.

The central theme and specific aims tie the talk together. Outline the central theme as part of your introductory remarks, discuss each aim as a specific topic in the body of the talk, and conclude by focusing on the action needed.

Activity 6.3

Presentation aims

Write down the central and specific aims for a presentation to a potential client about a software application that you want to promote. Choose something relevant to your area of expertise. Focus on the following points:

- Who? (audience)
- What? (content)
- Why? (purpose, for example, explaining, instructing and selling)
- When or where? (context, venue and time)
- How? (best means of delivery)

ANALYSING YOUR AUDIENCE

Thinking about your audience is important. Be aware of the powerful relationship that can and should exist between you and your audience. Finding out about their special needs and likely attitudes to your topic is a crucial first step to a successful presentation. It is better to talk *with* people rather than at them, and for this you need to know their experience of your subject and where it fits in their professional or personal expertise.

You may 'talk down' to an audience unintentionally if you fail to learn in advance the age and education level represented. Similarly, in the IT industry, you could easily 'talk up' to your audience if an individual client or group did not have the same technical expertise or experience as you. Remember that people are not always comfortable asking questions or requesting that things be repeated. Some will simply leave. Analysing your audience in advance helps you to decide what to say and how to say it.

You need to know:

- Who is the audience?
- What do they know about the subject?
- How large is the audience?

Sitting in the listener's chair

If you expect opposition, look closely at the issue from an opponent's point of view. What questions may be asked? What kind of arguments might be raised in opposition to yours? Forewarned is forearmed. Keep the focus squarely on the issues and avoid personalising the argument.

Be aware of the different ways in which members of your audience receive and process information. Some people remember *verbally*, but just as many think and remember *visually*, using mental images. A third type thinks in a *tactile* way; these people remember best by doing.

Think back to when you were first learning to use a new computer or piece of software. Which of the following did you learn by?

* reading a manual
* listening to an explanation
* watching someone using the equipment
* trying it out for yourself.

You may have learned through some or all of the above, or even through some other technique. **It is likely that you will need to use all of these approaches at various times, so build all methods into your presentation.**

PREPARING THE PRESENTATION

Many people try to answer the question of how to prepare for a presentation first. This is a trap for the unwary. If you have answered the questions 'what is my purpose?' and 'who is my audience?', then deciding on the content and format should follow logically.

How do I organise and present the information to suit the audience?

Draw up a written outline or a short list showing just the main features and key ideas. The following outline (based on the RIPPA formula in Chapter 7) is for a sales presentation on a new software application. The audience will be a group of twelve purchasers from a large organisation who could become major buyers. Because an outline is so much briefer than your actual speaking notes, it gives you a quick overall view and helps you to see if you have missed any important points.

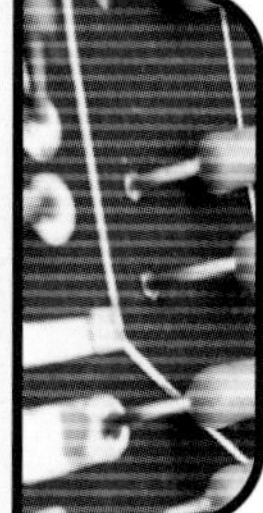

Activity 6.4

Preparing a presentation

Prepare an outline of a presentation relevant to your workplace. It could be a new product, a training session or anything relevant to your workplace's procedures, for example customer service policy or telephone protocol. Use the RIPPA formula in Chapter 7 to prepare the outline. You need to consider the audience before you write the outline. This could be internal or external clients, or work colleagues.

Phases of a presentation

A well-organised talk has three phases: the introduction, body and action ending.

Introduction

The introduction captures the audience's attention and gives an overview of your presentation. It tells the audience:

* what you want to achieve—the central theme (*why you are talking to them*)

- how long your talk will be (*in total and for key segments*)
- the specific themes (*linking them to the audience's experience and needs*).

Your first task is to create a bridge between you and each individual in the audience. Rarely will everyone's attention be focused on you at the start. You can get their attention in various ways. **Telling a humorous story or issuing a serious challenge are two useful strategies for capturing your audience's interest.** If you choose to use humour be very careful that you do not offend or alienate your audience.

Figure 6.2
Outline of a sales presentation for a new software application

MAIN AIM	1. To promote the benefits of the application, leading to sales.
OTHER AIMS	2. To build stronger personal relationships with the individual buyer/s.
	3. To arrange follow-up meetings to maintain client user liaison.

MAIN IDEA	**KEY POINTS**
Introduction	
Trigger or hook to listen	1. Breakthrough in features, e.g. links directly to web page, database, helps keep accounts section up-to-date.
	2. Your firm will be a leader in the use of this program.
	3. More efficient for tax purposes
Relationship	1. Builds our relationship with this market
Body	
Inform	1. Show new application.
	2. Demonstrate the major tasks.
	3. Give clients a common task to practise themselves
	4. List advantages in handouts, promotional material etc.
	5. Explain implementation requirements and cost.
Point-by-point persuasion	1. Only product with these features.
	2. New on market.
	3. Discount offer.
Paint picture	4. Projected efficiency measures, e.g. less time to process customer accounts.
Action	
Accept an order	1. Order signed within a week.
	2. Delivery installation in one month.
	3. Training to commence in three weeks.

Body

The body deals systematically with each of your specific themes. You can do some or all of the following.

- Provide your audience with facts, stories, jokes, demonstrations and visuals to explain your ideas and persuade them to use your product or service. The organisation of your material will depend on whether your presentation is a systems approach for workplace procedures or a technical demonstration.
- Involve your audience by using discussion, questions and participation in demonstrations.

- Use sequential (point-by-point) arguments. Make sure that your reasoning is clear, logical and easy to follow.
- Use specific examples rather than general statements. When you make a point, spend the next few minutes consolidating your meaning rather than moving on too quickly to the next one. This is particularly important in an IT environment where your presentation may have a high technical component.
- Check for feedback that your audience is still engaged and correctly understanding your meaning.
- Support and build on each key idea by talking about related topics and referring to the audience's existing understanding or knowledge.

Action ending

The action ending summarises your themes and informs the audience exactly what you and they need to do next. You can:

- signal the ending clearly to alert your audience to your request for action
- refocus attention with a memorable quote or story summarising the essence of your message (the last thing said is what people often remember first)
- ask if they have questions and tell them how to get additional information
- thank the audience for their time, attention and support.

Keep in mind the result you want to achieve and consider how persuasive you need to be to motivate your audience. Could you challenge them to accomplish a goal established during the presentation? Or restate the benefits of supporting your proposal? Reiterate the discussion points you used to get your message across. Highlight your main ideas and repeat the important arguments already proposed.

Make sure you know when to stop. A talk that seems to you to be too short is probably just right for everyone else.

The more you plan, organise and practise, the more easily you will achieve an energetic, natural-sounding presentation that flows well. It is vital to link your information to audience interests and experience and for your audience to appreciate why the topic is interesting and important to you. Do not be afraid to share appropriately personal perspectives and experience with your audience.

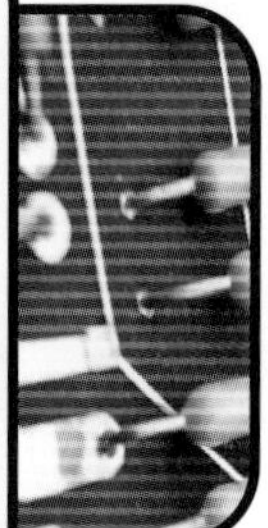

Activity 6.5

Preparing speaking notes

Expand your previous outline for a presentation to a group of twelve clients and write speaking notes for each section. Use the following questions and guidelines to help you.

Introduction

1. How will you explain your central and specific themes to the audience?
2. How will you link your themes to the audience's experience and interests?

Body

3. Plan to deal with these three specific themes in your talk:
    (a) the advantages and features of your specific computing equipment/software
    (b) how your product can be used and the differences between it and the other main competitors
    (c) how it can be implemented.
4. How will you support and develop each theme?
5. What sorts of visual and demonstration materials might you use?

Action ending

6. What specific action will you ask your audience to take?

7. How might you motivate and encourage them to act?

Practising and polishing

Practising should be as realistic as possible. If you can, use friends or family as a stand-in audience. A video camera or a tape recorder is also valuable as a practice aid because it gives you rapid and very honest (and unbiased) feedback in private: you can see and hear yourself as others do. This may come as a shock at first, but most speakers find that when they use a recorder regularly their choice of words, diction, tone, timing and style of delivery all improve rapidly, as does their confidence.

What visual aids do I need?

If you can give information in a way that people will receive it using more than one sense, it is more likely that the audience will remember the content. Figure 6.3 provides some guidelines on using support materials. Visual aids are useful because they:

- provide a logical order for the information
- prevent you from forgetting key points
- save time—a picture is worth a thousand words
- change the pace of the talk—helps keep the audience interested
- simplify complicated information
- assist the audience to remember the information.

In the IT industry, the type of information that you will be conveying to clients or colleagues is most likely highly technical and complex. You will need to think carefully about the types of visual aids (such as handouts, Microsoft PowerPoint presentations, OHTs and videos) that will help explain the purpose of your talk most clearly to your audience.

It is important to use visual aids effectively. How often have you seen poorly organised presenters show the audience material that is confusing or too small to read? If you are using equipment, make sure you know how it works. It can be quite embarrassing fumbling for the 'on' switch when you are in front of an audience. Test out your visual aid before using it in the presentation. If it is clear to you it is likely to be clear for the audience. Remember that some colours are easier to read than others.

Figure 6.3
Using support materials

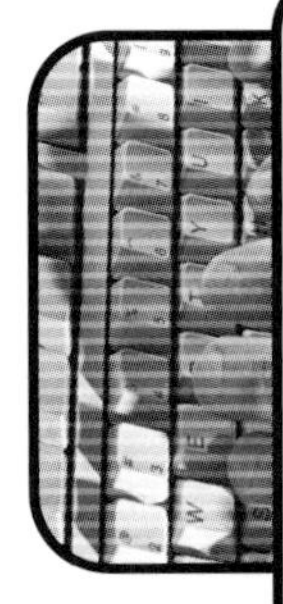

Checklist 6.1

Using visual aids

Use the following checklist to see if your use of visual aids is effective.

Did I:	Yes	No
check all equipment before the presentation?	☐	☐
introduce the material before it was shown?	☐	☐
explain what I wanted the audience to understand about the screen, graph, slide, chart, handout, etc.?	☐	☐
explain anything not obvious?	☐	☐
stand beside the visual (not in front of it)?	☐	☐
check that any writing or illustrations could be clearly seen from the back of the room?	☐	☐
leave the visual on view long enough for the audience to understand, ask questions or make notes?	☐	☐
provide a hard copy of the visual?	☐	☐
keep the information brief and in key points?	☐	☐
only provide relevant visual aids?	☐	☐

The venue

It is essential that you check the room before your presentation to see if you need to modify or change it. Ask yourself the following questions:

- Are there enough seats?
- Is the room comfortable for the amount of time we need?
- Is the room stuffy or well ventilated?
- Will everyone be able to see me and the visual aids well?
- Can all the equipment I need be plugged in and used in this room?
- Do I need to provide any refreshments?
- Is the room quiet?
- Is there a better room I could use?

If your audience is not comfortable they are unlikely to maintain their attention. The seating arrangements will affect the level of discussion and interaction in the session. A lecture-style arrangement will not encourage participation. Placing seats in a way that allows all participants to see each other will encourage discussion. Naturally if you are involved in computer training, allowing everyone access to a computer is essential.

Review the skills of a facilitator covered in Chapter 4 under the heading 'Facilitating/ leading the meeting'.

What equipment do I need?

Look at the kinds of visual aids you will be using. If you are using a lot of computers or other pieces of technology, allow yourself enough time to check that everything works before the participants arrive. It is very embarrassing for you to waste time at the beginning of a presentation sorting out equipment problems. It can make the audience feel that you are not credible.

Checklist 6.2

Planning presentations

Prepare a presentation on a topic relevant to your work and then complete the checklist below.

I have:	Yes	No	Not sure
identified my audience's interests, knowledge and expectations	☐	☐	☐
worked out my central and specific themes	☐	☐	☐
prepared an outline covering key points at each stage of the presentation	☐	☐	☐
researched credible information, including support materials to explain my ideas	☐	☐	☐
planned an attention-getting introduction giving an overview of the presentation	☐	☐	☐
organised the body to cover my specific themes in an interesting, logical way	☐	☐	☐
planned to finish by requesting specific action and motivating the audience by summarising the benefits of this action	☐	☐	☐
checked the venue for seating and equipment requirements	☐	☐	☐

GIVING YOUR PRESENTATION

The best way to build up your confidence is to practise the session so that you feel comfortable with the information and order of presentation. If possible ask someone else to listen to you prior to the actual session and give feedback.

Think about the issues and be prepared with answers to possible questions and concerns of the audience. If you have analysed your audience's needs well, you should be able to include the most appropriate information.

You need to be able to answer the following questions:

- How do I control my nerves?
- How do I relate to and involve the audience?
- How do I manage the time?

It is important to control your nerves but it is natural to be a little nervous before any presentation. If you have prepared and practised your presentation you will be more confident. Try a short relaxation exercise or visualisation if this helps you.

A bright, outgoing approach is a tremendous asset and will help you to overcome many speaking problems. Be positive, express enthusiasm, show enjoyment, and above all make it clear that you like your audience and care about them. You cannot expect your audience to be enthusiastic or interested if you do not appear to be.

Tips for controlling nerves

- You are more likely to build a favourable climate between you and your listeners if they see you as a credible communicator, so try to sound confident and authoritative.
- Maintain continuous contact with your audience: look at them and direct your talk to them rather than at them.

- Respect your audience. Perhaps you do know more than your listeners. If so, your task is to share your knowledge. Never criticise and never preach.
- Remember that the larger the space, the slower the pace! If you are addressing a large audience then phrasing is very important to allow your speech to be understood by everyone.
- Use inclusive language ('we', 'our', etc.) to 'signpost' your presentation by telling the audience when you have completed a section and are about to move on to your next point. Phrases such as 'now we will look at ...' or 'our next area is ...' help you stay focused while your listeners appreciate being directed and included.
- Vary your speaking style. An informal meeting, such as a work team presentation, needs less emphasis on 'speech making'. Informality is the key when you want to get through to people at work. Your vocal tone can add interest when you use inflection for a question or for emphasis. Monotone delivery is extremely boring.
- Smile and use open gestures; do not close yourself off from your audience or place a physical barrier in front of you (e.g. a desk or overhead projector). Use your natural gestures, but be aware that too much movement can distract from your ideas. Use gestures emphatically to highlight important points.
- Pause after you make an important point. The more important the point, the longer the pause should be. Give people time to think. Let your words sink in.
- Place your feet firmly and a little apart, moving slightly forward onto the balls of your feet, so that your weight is on the front of your feet. This prevents you from swaying and rocking back and forward. Standing slightly forward on your feet also presents a posture indicating enthusiasm.
- Be conscious of what your body is doing during the presentation. Many well-prepared and credible speakers are betrayed by unconscious body language revealing their tension and discomfort.
- Look around; maintain strong eye contact with as many people as you can. This gives people the feeling that you are speaking to them personally and increases the listeners' confidence in asking questions.
- If you feel nervous, then focus just above the heads of the audience.
- Do not try to bluff your way through answering a question—if you do not know, just say so. If the question is loaded (e.g., 'Why did you waste so much money on advertising?'), rephrase it. This is what politicians do all the time with the media. You could turn the question around by saying 'You'd like to look at the value of advertising?'.

Giving instructions

Use the following guidelines to help you give instructions successfully. These guidelines apply in particular to training in manual skills. However, the same points apply (perhaps with the exception of 'Ask for feedback') when giving almost any kind of order, instruction or direction at work.

Prepare people by putting them at ease

Spend time relaxing the listeners. If people are not at ease, they find it hard to pay attention.

Get people interested

Tell them why the task is important. Every job has a place in the overall plan. Explain how the one you are describing fits in.

Find out what people can do

You do not want to waste time teaching people something they already know, but you cannot assume they have skills or knowledge without first asking them. Make sure, also, that what a person knows is correct. Ask a specific question, for instance, 'Last time you used this application, how did you format the spreadsheet?'.

State the task

Describe each stage of the job clearly, in chronological sequence, and in sufficient detail for anyone to recognise what to do and what not to. Avoid statements such as 'Of course, you are familiar with the toolbar functions', 'I'm sure you know this', or 'I know you've done this before', implying that if the trainees do not have this knowledge they are at fault. Even if this is not so, they may be reluctant to admit to a lack of knowledge once you have shown you expected more of them.

Give full and complete directions

When giving directions, explain not only what you want done but also where, when, how and why. Only then will you be properly understood. Your instructions should include:

- why the job needs to be done
- when you want the work completed
- who is to be involved
- where it is to be done
- which machines or other equipment are to be used
- what not to do.

One of the best ways of clarifying any instruction is to put it on paper and include a diagram such as a flow chart. Nobody objects to this kind of clarification, even after you have explained something personally.

Ask for ideas or suggestions

No matter how interested they may be at the start, everyone's level of involvement in the job will increase if they feel they are able to contribute ideas as well as effort. Even the newest employee can have worthwhile ideas. If suggestions are not acceptable, explain why, avoiding outright rejection if possible.

Encourage questions

A good instructor knows how to stimulate questions. Do not talk all the time. Do not give the impression that you do not have time to answer questions. Good questions indicate that people are really thinking about the job.

Ask for feedback

Ask a trainee to show you what they have learned. Depending on the task, try to get either a verbal summary or a demonstration—or better still, a combination in which the trainee goes through the entire process in front of you, explaining what is being done and why. If you have given only general instructions, the feedback could be less detailed.

Follow-up

A wise instructor always checks progress a week or two after a training session. Even if you explained what, where, when, how and why, and you had sufficient feedback to be sure you were understood 'perfectly', situations can alter. Other people, with the best intentions, can give your trainee different instructions; the job itself may change. Even if everything is running smoothly, the trainee will appreciate your follow-up.

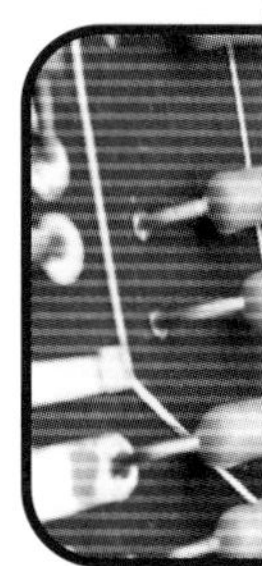

Activity 6.6

Instructing others

Choose a task relevant to your work suitable for instructing a novice. Do not choose a task that is too big. The session should last no more that twenty minutes. Examples include:

- how to do a mail merge
- how to organise your bookmarks
- creating a new folder
- providing an overview of the toolbar buttons on Netscape or Internet Explorer
- attaching a file or URL to email
- setting the properties for an application
- changing the look of a desktop
- adjusting the bios setting.

Prepare a session where you will train someone in the task you have selected. Use the information in this chapter to do the following.

1. Define the purpose of the session.
2. Analyse the needs of your trainee.
3. Prepare an outline for the session.
4. Present the instructions.
5. Evaluate the effectiveness of your session using Checklist 6.2.

ACTION POINTS

You will be a successful presenter if you:

- be yourself
- find out about your audience in advance
- plan a presentation that fits the timeframe
- link your information to the audience's interests and experience
- tell your audience exactly what to expect
- tell interesting stories and good jokes appropriate for your audience
- support your points in a logical, reasoned way
- finish by requesting specific action from your audience
- involve the audience in the presentation
- answer questions openly and honestly
- reduce hostility by staying focused on the issues
- use simple, well-integrated visuals to highlight key points.

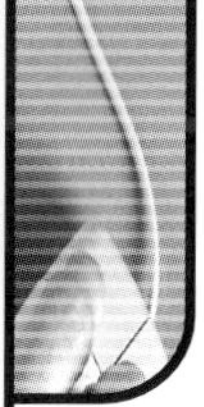

SUMMARY

Public speaking is a scary but rewarding activity that is hard to avoid in professional life. Audiences respond best to talks that fit their experience and expectations. Successful public speakers establish these things clearly before they present to a group, and provide the audience with both aural and visual information.

Time limits are crucial—prepare and practise your presentation to fit an allocated or appropriate timeframe. A talk that may seem too short to you is probably about right for your audience. Your message and its importance to you must be obvious to the audience. It is really difficult to convince anyone to accept something you do not believe in yourself.

All presentations are based on knowing the answers to these questions:

- Who will the audience be?
- What is my purpose or goal?
- What is the appropriate format for achieving my goal?

Verbal instructions describe each stage of the job clearly and check for understanding. Explanations combined with demonstrations by the audience in front of you help to ensure that the skill is absorbed.

In working out the shape and structure it is important that the information is clear, correct and logically organised so your ideas are easier to follow. Know what you are going to talk about, and when you will deal with each point. A well-organised talk has three phases: the introduction (say what you want to achieve), the body (support and explain your ideas), and the action ending (summarise, and say what needs to be done).

The most successful presentations are delivered with enthusiasm, making it clear that you like your audience and care about them. Audiences are rarely hostile but you can reduce hostility by dealing calmly with the issues and refusing to engage in personal attacks. Questions are an opportunity to win the audience over. Practising should be as realistic as possible, so try to use friends, family and recording equipment.

Presentations are supported by different forms of media. Simple items such as flip-charts, models, or actual pieces of equipment are all useful. They enhance your speech by highlighting, summarising and illustrating relationships between ideas. The most effective support materials are simply designed and integrated into your presentation.

TRAINING LOG

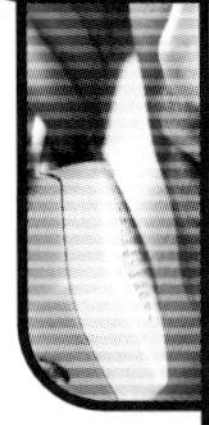

Workplace presentations

1. Interview a person in an IT-related role and list the kinds of workplace presentations they give to:
   (a) internal clients
   (b) external clients/customers.
2. Make a list of the workplace presentations that you have delivered in the last month. How satisfied were you with your delivery? What could you do to improve your presentation skills?

Action plan

1. Plan, prepare and deliver a presentation about an IT-related issue to a small group. It could be:
   (a) a monthly report in your regular work team meeting
   (b) a summary of an interview with a new client
   (c) instructions on new workplace procedures or a new product
   (d) an explanation on the different services/plans offered by a variety of internet service providers.

   Use the steps and guidelines presented in this chapter.
2. Ask a friend or colleague to evaluate your presentation according to the checklist below.

Did the speaker:	Yes	No	Not sure
show respect for the audience by giving them an overview of the content and timeframe?	☐	☐	☐
smile and make eye contact with the audience?	☐	☐	☐
speak naturally and confidently?	☐	☐	☐
get their attention early by having an interesting opening?	☐	☐	☐
signpost the body of the talk and work logically from point to point?	☐	☐	☐
finish the presentation strongly by requesting specific action and thanking the audience for their interest and support?	☐	☐	☐
manage all their support materials efficiently?	☐	☐	☐
field questions confidently, honestly and accurately?	☐	☐	☐

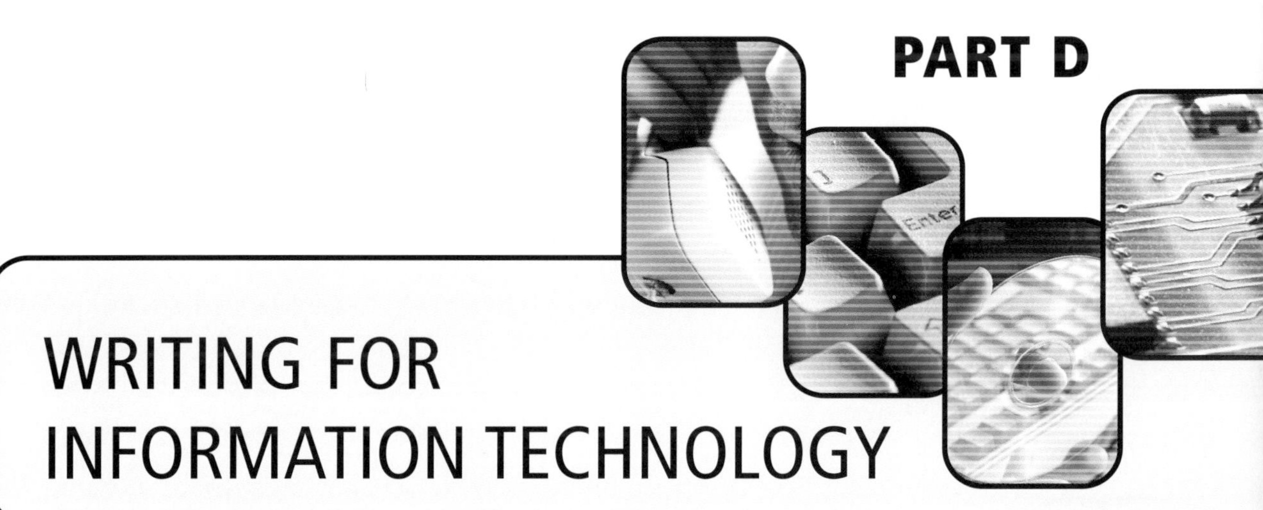

WRITING FOR INFORMATION TECHNOLOGY

CHAPTER 7

PRINCIPLES OF EFFECTIVE WRITING

COMPETENCIES

This chapter is linked to elements contained in the following competencies which are in the Information Technology Training Package.

- Receive and Process Oral and Written Communication ICAITD003B
- Create User and Technical Documentation ICAITD128A
- Interact With Clients ICAITS009B
- Relate to Clients on a Business Level ICAITTW027B
- Confirm Client Business Needs ICAITAD042A
- Develop and Present a Feasibility Report ICAITAD043A
- Establish and Maintain Client User Liaison ICAITS102A
- Record Client Support Requirements ICAITS016B
- Determine Client Computing Problems and Action ICAITS022B
- Record Client Support Requirements ICAITS016B
- Provide One on One Instruction ICAITS023B
- Assist with Policy Development for Client Support Procedures ICAITS033B
- Apply Skills in Communications BSX154L407
- Guide Application of Communications Management BSX154L507
- Manage Communications BSX154L608
- Apply Occupational Health and Safety Procedures ICAITU00B

The aim of this chapter is to provide you with techniques for effective business and technical writing. It deals with using language and format to convey your message accurately to your readers.

Working in the IT industry requires excellent written communication skills. With the growing dependence on intranet within organisations, and email and internet use both internally and externally, the ability to present information clearly and unambiguously is essential. Providing clear instruction manuals for quite complex software and hardware is another challenging written communication task.

Writing clear, courteous and informative documents involves finding answers to the following questions:

- How is business and technical writing different from the writing I did at school?
- Is business and technical writing different from everyday writing?
- How do I get my point across concisely?
- How do I refer to my reader/s in a document?
- How do I avoid sounding stuffy or distant in my writing?
- What do I look for when checking drafts of my documents?

TOPICS DISCUSSED

- Writing in five stages
- Thinking and planning
- Thinking about the reader/s
- Capturing ideas
- Organising the shape and structure
- Editing, revising and proofreading
- Using plain English
- Effective layout
- Inclusive language

INTRODUCTION

Writing at work means communicating for and with people. It is an excellent way to exchange information, but equally important is its ability to create bonds of understanding. Writing skills rely on knowing your purpose and using the tools of language to create meaning. People write to communicate ideas in a way that elicits the desired response from the receiver.

You have probably seen a great range of business writing, such as promotional material that enters your home and office daily, letters, and reports. There are many forms of business writing and you must decide what is the best way to get your message across.

The words you choose set the tone of the message and influence the response of the receiver. The way you structure your writing gives power to the ideas you express.

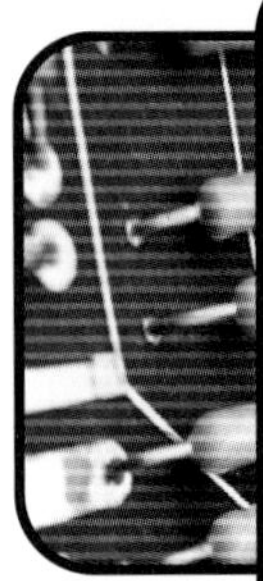

Activity 7.1

Types of written communication

Think about the different types of written communication relevant to the IT industry. Collect examples related to the type of documents listed and complete the remaining sections of the table.

Document examples	Intended readership
Letters	
Reports e.g. project management, feasibility	
Email	
Web-based documents	
Instructions	
Questionnaires/surveys	
Other documents	

WRITING IN FIVE STAGES

Many people consider writing to be hard work. It does not have to be: if you go about it the right way, business writing can be productive and enjoyable. One approach is to write according to the five stages listed in Table 7.1.

THINKING AND PLANNING

Think of yourself as the engineer, architect or designer of your written message. How can you build a worthwhile letter or report if you do not have a plan? When you start to write, you will work far more effectively if you understand:

- the situation (context) in which you are writing
- the topic you are writing about

- what you really want to tell your reader/s
- why you want to tell them this.

It is vital that your workplace writing does more than simply represent your interests. When readers receive your documents they need to understand the situation that led you to write and why your information is important and interesting to them.

Table 7.1
General guidelines for business writers

	Stage	Task	Result
1	Thinking and planning	Deciding why you are writing and what you want to achieve	A list of ideas, topics
2	Thinking about the reader/s	Who are they and what do they need to know?	An edited version of your list above due to the elimination of unnecessary items
3	Capturing ideas	Jotting down ideas as they occur to you	A rough draft
4	Organising the shape and structure	Developing a layout and a logical sequence of ideas in sentences and paragraphs	A second draft with headings and outline
5	Editing, revising and proofreading	Rewriting, improving language, style and tone; proofing for errors	A final draft, then the finished version

Activity 7.2

Written communication in the workplace

1. Make a list of the different people you need to communicate with in writing, e.g. external clients, internal clients or your supervisor.
2. List the types of written documents you would be expected to prepare for each person.

THINKING ABOUT THE READER/S

The real or actual written communication is not the words you use but what your reader understands when they receive the written document. You need to analyse your reader and understand:

- the person or reader group to whom you are writing
- what they know about the topic or issue you are writing about
- how much technical knowledge they understand
- any opinions they may have about the topic
- how many people will be reading this document.

Effective written communication takes into account the needs of the reader.

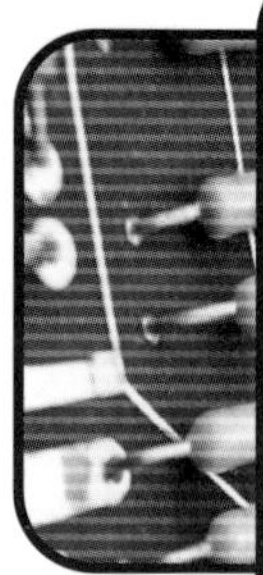

Activity 7.3

Identifying the purpose and reader

Find examples of the following documents and identify the purpose and reader.

Document	Purpose	Reader
An advertisement in a daily newspaper about selling second-hand laptops		
An article in a computer magazine about the development of new software		
An invoice to a company for repair and servicing of computers		
A webpage providing tutorials on Microsoft applications for the office		
A document that you are currently writing OR have recently completed		

CAPTURING IDEAS

Refine your documents by drafting and redrafting. Never expect to perfect any workplace documents in one go. Trying to organise whole paragraphs in your head can be quite difficult; so many ideas get lost while you try to think of the right words and put them in the right order. The technique called 'random writing' is among the best of all methods for avoiding writer's block.

Rules for random writing

1. To begin with, write down your thoughts as they come to you. Do not worry about:
   (a) choice of words
   (b) grammar, spelling, or the way sentences are put together
   (c) sequence
   (d) appearance—draft writing does not have to be neat and tidy.
2. Do not try to work out specific details. Unless they come readily to mind, leave them until later.
3. Use diagrams, shapes or symbols. They're often faster to use than words when you want to capture an overall idea.
4. Do not let anyone see your first draft.
5. Allow yourself the freedom to make as many alterations and corrections as you like. Once your thoughts are on paper it is easier to judge their value.

ORGANISING THE SHAPE AND STRUCTURE

People need to see not only each idea clearly, but also the connection between one topic and the next. The rules for organising ideas and grouping topics according to their content can be summed up in two lines:

- keep similar topics together
- keep different topics apart.

Deciding on the format or type of document you need

Look at the purpose of your document and the context in which you are going to use it. Use this to decide what form your document needs.

It is common in the IT industry to use different forms of electronic documents. An electronic document is defined by its content and format. Content is the information contained in the document and format is the method by which the information is stored and displayed. Electronic documents may include text files, spreadsheets, presentations, scanned images, faxes, and video and audio information.

Think back to Activity 7.1 and the list of the different kinds of documents used in a typical IT environment (both paper and electronic). You need to apply the principles of effective writing to all of these documents.

Written format

The basic structure of any written format is an introduction, a body and a conclusion.
The introduction:

- presents the topic for discussion
- indicates the direction your writing will take
- encourages the reader's interest.

In other words, it lets the reader know what you plan to tell them.

The body is made up of one or more paragraphs dealing with your topic or issue. These paragraphs:

- set out the facts
- detail arguments
- support the facts with references or more detailed information.
  The conclusion:
- summarises the issue and draws together the main points
- states exactly what needs to be done in response to the issue.

Organising sentences and paragraphs

Sentences are separate ideas that form a complete statement. They combine to form a paragraph. In business writing, sentences are shorter and to the point, as opposed to a piece of creative writing.

Check that the ideas in each sentence link up to present a logical and sequential flow of information which is easy for the reader to understand.

Activity 7.4

Communicating information clearly

1. Express the ideas in the wordy and rambling sentences below in five or six simple sentences. Reorganise the information so that the client/reader's most important information needs are met first.

   New Era Communications has moved to new premises as this will give us more room to improve our customer service by expanding our existing product range and services to include after-sales telephone support and an

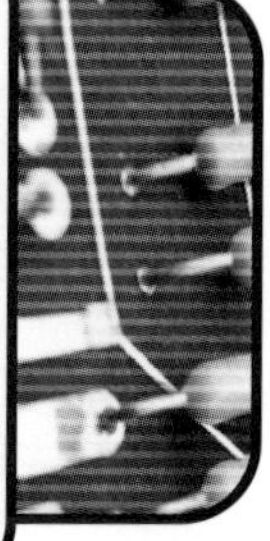

> *extended recreational software range. Our new offices and showroom at 47 King St will open from 9 am until 6 pm six days a week including Saturdays from Monday 1 June, to give customers a chance to experience the new software which we will run in interactive workshops and demonstrations on 6 and 7 June.*
> 2. What would be the best way to communicate this information (spoken, written, letter, email, etc.)? Why?

A **paragraph** is a set of 3 or 4 related sentences. The **topic sentence**, usually the first sentence in a paragraph, indicates what the paragraph is about and is a general statement giving an overview of the paragraph. **Supporting sentences** follow the topic sentence and develop it by giving specific details about aspects of the topic.

In deciding when to end a paragraph, ask yourself: 'Does the next sentence relate to this topic or to a new one?'. If it is a new topic, start a new paragraph.

Finding the 'right' tone

Everything you write has a mixture of verbal and non-verbal meaning. While it is relatively easy to convey objective fact and instructions clearly, it is harder to create a positive, efficient and reader-friendly tone in your writing.

'Tone' describes sound; in writing, tone affects the way a message 'sounds' to the reader, helping to signal the kind of writer–reader relationship you want to establish. Letters can have a friendly or a formal tone. They can sound angry, sad, happy, gloating, respectful, loving or bored.

The tone of a letter may project trust and personal respect for the reader, yet the words 'respect' and 'trust' may be nowhere in the text. Tone may depend on the choice of words (and the way they are put together), but may just as easily be conveyed by words that are left out; this is why tone is classed as a non-verbal characteristic. Typical words and phrases that signal tone are shown in Table 7.2. Perhaps you will need words like these to project the precise non-verbal tone you want to convey. But be careful! If you write this way, your feelings are showing.

Adjust your tone to the situation, the topic and the reader

If you are writing to someone who is in a position of authority and appreciates formality, use an appropriately formal tone. If you are organising a follow-up service meeting with a long-term client to discuss a new system installation, you may use a more informal tone.

Personalise tone whenever possible

Keeping the above point in mind, use a tone which communicates your own individual message, reflecting the way you feel about people. Present a true picture of your personality. For example, 'We have mailed you a brochure' becomes 'You will soon receive a brochure outlining all the features of the system'.

Be wary of using a critical tone

A critical or parental tone is more likely to produce a negative response than an adult tone. Check to see that you have not created this tone unwittingly. For example, 'I expect to receive a response from you by next week' becomes 'I look forward to reading your response to our proposal next week'.

Be cautious about using other people's words

Copying words and phrases used by others means copying non-verbal content as well. If you must use someone else's words, check that the between-the-lines meanings are appropriate to your message.

Table 7.2
Typical words and phrases that signal tone

Tone	Signals	Examples
Urgent	imperative statements	'it is essential that'
	timing adverbs	
Informal	abbreviations	'let's', 'you'll'
	colloquial phrases	'I'll get in touch'
Distrustful	extra-polite phrases	'I must ask you for confirmation of'
	qualifying phrases	'If, in fact'
	mitigating adjectives	'your alleged malfunction'
Negative	bad news to follow	'unfortunately'
	criticism of reader	'you neglected to'
Pompous	outdated, pseudo-legal jargon	'the above-mentioned persons'
		'moreover'
		'quintessential'

Activity 7.5

Selecting an appropriate tone

Rewrite the following sentences using a more appropriate tone.
1. We must have a 10% deposit to secure the order.
2. Our service department will be closed next week for systems maintenance so you will have to ring the number below.

EDITING, REVISING AND PROOFREADING

Editing your writing can be enjoyable. Once you take responsibility for this extra step, you will discover your full potential as a writer. Professional writers often spend as much time on editing and polishing as they do on any of the other stages. Polishing can also include adapting your own or others' writing to fit the needs of special readers.

- Experiment. You still have your previous version if the trial does not work out.
- Be self-critical. Every writer has weak points of which they are not aware. If you can discover yours, you can learn to overcome them.
- Let others read your draft, and welcome their reactions. The faults you miss are the ones others detect and tell you about.
- Work with one aspect in mind at a time (for instance, continuity). If you try to cover everything from grammar to discrimination at one sitting, you will lose concentration. If you have the time, put the work aside for a day, a week, or longer.

Using the RIPPA formula

The RIPPA formula lists five essential topics that you need to cover in most business communication. Use it as a further check in polishing your message. The initial letters of the key words give the formula name, RIPPA.

1. Establish the RELATIONSHIP	**R**
2. Give the reader INFORMATION	**I**
3. Persuade POINT by POINT	**P**
4. Strengthen the argument with a PICTURE	**P**
5. Close by asking for ACTION	**A**

The relationship

Will this document have a positive effect on your business relationship? If you are writing about an overdue account but you really want to maintain a sound business relationship with a valued client, have you emphasised the relationship? Or have you ignored the relationship and mentioned only the outstanding debt?

Exchanging information

Have you included the right kinds of information? Have you given too much or too little?

Point-by-point persuasion

If you are writing in order to gain agreement, have you highlighted points that will appeal to the specific reader?

Painting a clear picture

Will the reader be able to see clearly what you want? Have you used white space, graphics and illustrations to ensure visual appeal?

Getting action

Have you described the action you want in clear, straightforward terms? Have you asked for feedback in the form of a reply or confirmation? Have you told the reader how to let you know that the action has been carried through?

Rewriting

Rewriting may involve experimenting, trying different arrangements of ideas and different styles. You could try moving around paragraphs. The more you write about a subject, the more knowledgeable you become about it. Often you find your most powerful ideas at the end of a section. If you think a later statement would have more impact at the start, move it.

Rewriting may simply involve rephrasing—changing the word order here and there or substituting a better, more descriptive word for a less effective one.

Revising your edit

Your final message needs to be clear, concise, correct and easy to understand. Read it through and change anything that does not meet the standards you have set.

- **Check your language.** Concentrate on the quality of the words. Change vague, abstract phrases into short, straightforward and direct ones.
- **Proofread every line.** Check grammar, spelling and punctuation. Double-check numerical data.
- **Review the tone and style.** Check for minor points of style such as passive sentences, repetition and redundancy.

The principles of good writing that apply to written documents also apply to digital documents. Clarity of purpose, attractive layout, highlighting, cohesion and a focus on the reader are still just as important. Sometimes the ease and immediacy of digital communication discourages attention to detail: good planning is still needed if you want to get your message across in the most effective and economical way possible.

Knowing that your pages have a stronger appeal and that your message makes good sense adds to your confidence in your writing ability. Because the format makes reading easier and topics are displayed more clearly, you and your readers find the message easier to remember.

USING PLAIN ENGLISH

Plain English is basically good writing and involves:

- knowing what the reader wants and being aware of good writing habits
- recognising the limitations of the language we use when writing
- developing the habit of thinking about what we want to say and then planning how to say it.

Writing in plain English means that you use clear, straightforward English and 'current' language, with a logical organisation of words, sentences and paragraphs. Plain English is flexible and is composed of a set of broad principles and suggestions for usage designed to help both writer and reader. Some of these principles are as follows:

1. The writing should have a clear purpose.
2. The intended reader should be comfortable with the style and form of writing.
3. It should be clearly written so that the reader can find the information required.
4. The document should clearly tell the reader what he or she wants to know.
5. Technical terms, acronyms and abbreviations should be clearly explained and used sparingly.
6. Use short sentences wherever possible.
7. Use active voice.
8. Consider the layout and format to improve the readability of the document.

Reader–centred writing

Try to maintain the approach known as the 'you' attitude where relevant. This conveys a sense of partnership: it reflects a special interest in the person you are writing to and recognises that person as an individual.

- Describe the situation as the reader would see it, e.g., ' repair of your scanner' rather than 'Customer complaint no: 765432'.
- Tell readers all they need to know. Leaving out essential details suggests a lack of 'you' attitude. When writing a repeat order, for instance, restate the details of item type and quantities required rather than writing, 'Send a further shipment as previously'.
- Use an adult-to-adult style rather than a critical or patronising tone.
- Avoid talking too much about yourself.
- Avoid using out-of-date or pompous expressions.

Notice that strengthening the 'you' attitude requires more than simply using the word 'you' a few extra times, or sounding polite and courteous.

Table 7.3
Alternatives to overused, out-of-date or unnecessary expressions

Do not use	Use
terminate	end
commence	begin
assistance	help
endeavour	try
require	need
in the event that	if
at this point in time	now
owing to the fact that	because
attached herewith	attached
in the near future	soon
with reference to	about

Tips for plain English

- Use more full stops. Shorter sentences can cut wordiness and confusion. If a sentence contains two ideas, divide it.
- Follow a long sentence (thirty or more words) with a short one.
- Use shorter words.
- Use direct, specific (concrete) words, the kind that readers find easy to picture.
- Put long words (three or more syllables) in short sentences or surround them with short words.
- Add a short example or explanation to clarify the meaning of an abstract (hard-to-picture) word (as this paragraph does to explain 'abstract').
- Use direct, positive statements in place of abstract and/or negative ones.
- Use shorter paragraphs.

Active voice

When you speak, you use active sentences such as: 'I am very interested in your submission'. It makes sense to write this way, too.

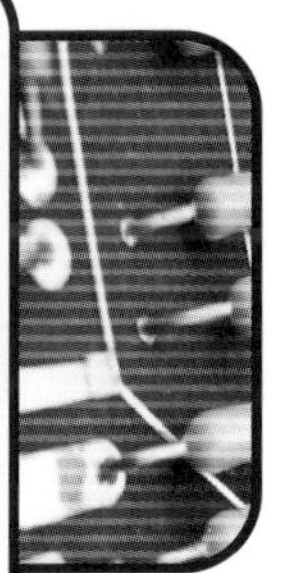

Activity 7.6

Writing in plain English

Rewrite the following passage in plain English:

Asset deployment management systems

Deployment management products (also called 'asset tracking' or 'inventory' products) are the most recognisable types of asset management applications. These include real-time inventory, software distribution and electronic licensing tools. Typically, deployment management applications are used by the same technical staffers who install, upgrade, repair and otherwise maintain the organisation's hardware and software. The most tactical reasons for implementing deployment management tools are to help automate the installation of assets and to measure the tangible indicators of asset usage. A broader reason is to gather data necessary for making strategic technology decisions. If you have accurate counts and configuration details of assets you have actually deployed, you can perform better evaluations of your technology alternatives and arrive at money-saving decisions.

When someone writes: 'Your submission has attracted considerable interest', the effect is passive because emphasis is shifted from the action and from the person involved. The action is focused on the submission, and just who exactly is interested remains a mystery.

The telltale sign of a passive sentence is the complex verb consisting of two or (usually) three words. You will always find a form of the verb 'to be' ('is', 'was', 'were', 'am', 'are' and so on) in this arrangement. When verbs such as 'will be kept', 'are being made' and 'was not received' appear in your writing, consider reducing your word count and acknowledging who is responsible for the action by changing from passive to active.

Passive sentence: 'The contract is being signed on Monday by the client'. This sentence, though short, is impersonal. The contract (an inanimate object) is being signed (action) by the client (the person taking the action). What happens if, instead, the sentence starts by naming the person taking the action?

Active sentence: 'The client will sign the contract on Monday'. Notice the improvement in style and tone, as well as the shorter sentence. Passive sentences, however, can be useful at times to:

- distance yourself from a decision: 'Your application has been unsuccessful' rather than 'We have rejected your application'
- put an intentional emphasis on the object: 'Payments can be approved only by an authorised officer'
- provide variety in a long text—too many active sentences together can be overpowering.

EFFECTIVE LAYOUT

First impressions are as important in writing as they are in face-to-face communication. In some ways they are more important because you do not have access to the receiver's

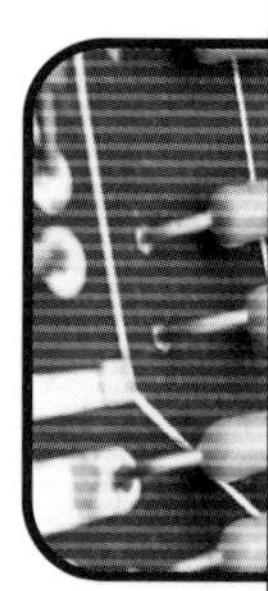

Activity 7.7

Using the active voice

Change the following sentences from passive to active voice.

1. The faults in the program have been analysed and will be rectified as soon as possible.
2. Documents can be edited by selecting the options located in the edit menu.
3. Upon completion of the spreadsheet tutorials, participants are asked to email their answers to the trainer.
4. In order to minimise problems with your computer, you are asked to define the nature of your problems accurately before contacting the help desk.
5. Your letter has been received by us. Hearing from a regular client such as yourself is a pleasure to us, and we must thank you for same.
6. Until authorisation has been confirmed by our head office, this network account is not to be operated by persons other than yourself.

signals to help you adjust your style of presentation. A high-class layout will not fix bad writing, but it will put the reader into a positive frame of mind. Remember the importance of attractive layout.

Give your pages 'eye appeal'

In today's busy world, words alone cannot create clear communication. What you write must also look attractive. From the very first glance, your readers should be convinced that what is in front of them will be:

- easy to read
- easy to understand
- easy to remember.

Use business format

To get your message through to busy readers:

- use one topic per sentence or paragraph
- leave blank lines between paragraphs to show where each topic starts and ends
- use numbered headings to help people follow your topics in a step-by-step sequence.

Use appropriate graphics

This involves striking a balance between words and pictures. Use graphics to summarise complex issues, give information, and break the tedium of large blocks of print. Avoid using graphics for the sake of it. Always ask yourself: 'What is the purpose of this graphic? What will it do for the reader?'.

Organise information

As a rule, put the most important thing first. Give the reader the key information they want, then organise all the supporting material so it follows in a logical way. There may be

Activity 7.8

Evaluating layout

Look at a collection of documents and evaluate their layouts using the following table.

Features	Comments
What makes my job easy as a reader? Consider simplicity, clarity, style, tone and jargon.	
What makes it difficult? Consider overlong sentences, grammar, awkward construction, confusing information and poor spelling.	
Is the layout appropriate for the type of document? Consider fonts, headings, diagrams, graphics and amount of text.	
Would the inclusion of additional graphics be useful?	
How is white space used?	
Is the intended audience clear?	
Does the document achieve its purpose?	
What changes would you make if any?	

---

instances when you want to hide the key points or move from the general to the particular, but this should be the exception and done for a clear purpose.

INCLUSIVE LANGUAGE

It is very important for good business relationships that you do not offend, embarrass or alienate your audience. There are also ramifications if you breach anti-discrimination laws. Any message that highlights characteristics such as sex, race, religion, marital status or nationality suggests that these details are significant and that the receivers need to know about them to judge the subject's worth. The following guidelines will help you to use inclusive language.

- Use the plural form to avoid use of he or she. For example, 'The applicant should complete the quiz using his or her own computer' should be changed to 'The applicants should complete the quiz using their own computers'.
- Eliminate the use of personal pronouns altogether by rewording the sentence. For example, 'Use a computer to complete the quiz'.
- Use an alternative word that does not contain 'man' at the end of the word. For example, 'A layman could configure this software' should be changed to 'A computer novice could configure this software'.
- Use the 'person' alternative. For example, 'spokesman' should be changed to 'spokesperson'.

- Do not use terms that stereotype any group. For example, 'Disabled people can use a mouse adaptor' should be changed to 'A person with limited use of their hands can use the mouse adaptor'.
- Do not use terms that are racist, sexist or give an impression of being helpless.

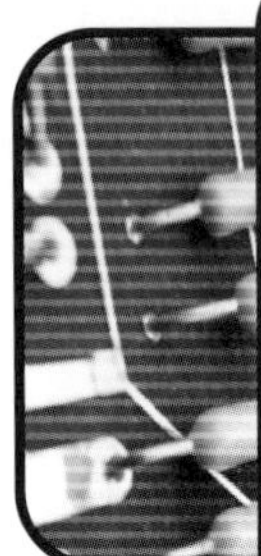

Activity 7.9

Writing clearly and accurately

Reword the following sentences to improve style and clarity, and to remove errors. You can change any or all of the original words as long as your answer conveys the same meaning. Your versions should be active, free of discrimination and shorter than the originals.

1. It is imperative that each manager arranges for his staff to receive full training before any of the men commence actual usage of the new equipment.
2. A spokesman for the Computer Engineers Training Association said he expected more money to be made available to train Aboriginal students next year.
3. The new chairman of the Manpower Resources Team is Ms Jill Lee, a recently arrived migrant from New Zealand. Her husband is a well-known newsman on TV.
4. When a new logistics manager takes up his duties, he should always tell his secretary how he wants her to handle his calls.
5. We are pleased to advise that we have just opened a new branch of our firm, ACME Communications, in this town, and invite any local businessman who would like his computing system upgraded to kindly contact us.
6. Our new sales representative is Ms Laurena Lamb, a shapely 22-year-old female graduate from Queensland. With her looks, she's already managed to raise our sales figures by 10 per cent.
7. Ask your secretary what she thinks of the new PCR70 word processor, and she'll tell you it makes her job twice as easy.

ACTION POINTS

You will write well for business purposes if you:

- think of workplace writing as a way of building your relationships with clients and customers
- plan before you write so that you understand clearly why you are writing and what your reader most needs to know
- draft your documents using the method that works best for you
- edit your work carefully to ensure that the language, tone and information match your purpose and your reader's needs
- use a direct, well set-out business format
- avoid offending readers with discriminatory language.

Write in five stages. Think and plan. Once you have captured your ideas, organising them will be easy. After that—check, correct, clarify. Some writers begin with a written outline—a detailed list of every topic they intend to write about. Others find more open methods, such as 'random writing', are more effective.

Sit in the reader's chair. The average reader prefers to do business with someone whose correspondence has a personal approach, is friendly, and appears to be written with the receiver in mind. Readers need to see each idea clearly, so write about only one topic in each paragraph, use blank lines to separate paragraphs, use headings as signposts and number important headings and subheadings.

The only correct words are those which carry your meaning clearly and accurately. Use plain English and avoid discriminatory language. Concentrate on the quality of the words as well as on grammar, spelling and punctuation. Avoid passive sentences that signal a distant and formal attitude, which usually has a negative effect on the business relationship. Ask yourself whether the langauge is concise, descriptive, accurate and up-to-date.

Tone and style affect responses to the content and meaning of written messages. They also help to signal the state of the writer–reader relationship. Tone is judged by the way written messages 'sound' to the reader.

Many word processing software packages now include templates and wizards to save you time when creating many common types of documents. In most cases, all you need to do is select the appropriate template or wizard when opening a new document. Remember that the principles of good writing that apply to written documents also apply to digital documents.

Evaluate your workplace writing

Collect three pieces of workplace writing you have completed in the past month. Ask a co-worker, supervisor or friend to evaluate your writing using the checklist below.

I can:	Yes	No	Not sure
plan and draft my work to meet my own and my reader's needs	☐	☐	☐
write short, complete, cohesive sentences	☐	☐	☐
organise my ideas in well-structured, logically connected paragraphs	☐	☐	☐
edit my work to remove all unnecessary words	☐	☐	☐
identify passive writing and replace it with active expression	☐	☐	☐
produce writing which creates a positive impression by being friendly and informative	☐	☐	☐

Action plan

1. What principles of effective writing do you wish to develop in your own writing?
2. How do you plan to achieve this? Make a list of specific strategies you will apply to your own writing.

CHAPTER 8

WORKPLACE DOCUMENTS

COMPETENCIES

This chapter is linked to elements contained in the following competencies which are in the Information Technology Training Package.

- Receive and Process Oral and Written Communication ICAITD003B
- Create User and Technical Documentation ICAITD128A
- Interact with Clients ICAITS009B
- Relate to Clients on a Business Level ICAITTW027B
- Confirm Client Business Needs ICAITAD042A
- Develop and Present a Feasibility Report ICAITAD043A
- Establish and Maintain Client User Liaison ICAITS102A
- Record Client Support Requirements ICAITS016B
- Determine Client Computing Problems and Action ICAITS022B
- Record Client Support Requirements ICAITS016B
- Provide One on One Instruction ICAITS023B
- Assist with Policy Development for Client Support Procedures ICAITS033B
- Apply Skills in Communications BSX154L407
- Guide Application of Communications Management BSX154L507
- Manage Communications BSX154L608
- Apply Occupational Health and Safety Procedures ICAITU00B

The aim of this chapter is to help you plan and write effective work-related documents. Successful workplace documents are well received by readers and achieve your aims. Contemporary business writing is strongly influenced by technology, time pressure and the impact of plain English. Templates for a range of workplace documents are readily available on the internet and in software packages. Word processing packages assist with formatting as well as grammar and spelling. Email, with its speed and informality, competes with memos and letters as a preferred method of business and personal communication. Plain English, with its emphasis on direct 'reader-centred' language and spacious layout, has changed the way we write at work. Today most readers are busy and will not give priority to, or persist with, long, overly formal, or wordy documents.

We will deal with many of the frequently asked questions about everyday workplace documents including:

- How do I choose the right type of document?
- How do I start?
- How do I organise my thoughts on paper?
- How can I show readers that I understand their perspective?
- How much information should I include in a business document?
- How can I persuade my reader to act on what I am proposing?
- How can I sound like myself in print?

TOPICS DISCUSSED

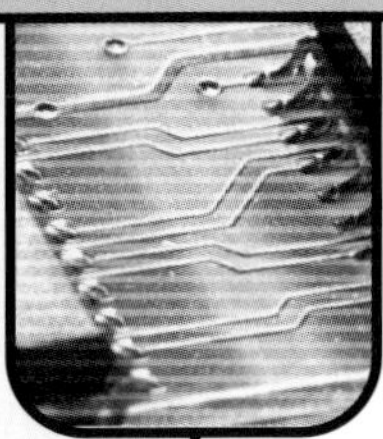

- Planning your documents
- Letters
- Emails and memos
- Web documents
- Short reports
- Instructions
- Newsletters
- Leaflets

INTRODUCTION

Your workplace documents will often have to compete with other people's communication for a share of your reader's attention. How can you ensure that your documents are read, understood and acted upon by your reader? Chapter 7 looks at organising your thoughts and choosing the best words, and introduces the RIPPA formula for structuring your workplace writing. It also covers the principles of plain English. In this chapter we will look at the uses of a range of routine workplace documents and suggest strategies for planning and writing them well.

Figure 8.1
An urgent message

PLANNING YOUR DOCUMENTS

Workplace documents are not written in isolation. We need to plan and write them in the context of our wider involvement with clients and colleagues. They represent steps in the sequence of actions and consequences that make up our working lives.

Imagine you want to send an email to all the staff in your office asking them to restrict their use of the photocopier. Currently, your staff have unrestricted access to the copier and your department has used two-thirds of its annual copying budget in three months. Unless forced to do so, you are reluctant to introduce restrictions, which can be expensive to install and cumbersome to administer.

Your aims (purposes) for this memo, in priority order, are to do the following.

1. Motivate the staff to cooperate by reducing the number of copies.
2. Outline the current serious budget overrun.
3. Set reasonable limits for copying.
4. List your options if voluntary reductions do not occur.

Your reader/audience includes *all* your staff, some of whom are minimal copiers and conscientious recyclers. Others may be abusing the free access, copying more than they

Figure 8.2
Workplace documents are not written in isolation

need for work and making personal copies on the machine. Some of your staff have a genuine need to make frequent copies while others hardly ever need to use it.

The context for this message is tricky, as your readers are likely to react negatively to its message. You want to send a clear disciplinary message to the overusers without alienating people who do the right thing. You also need to acknowledge the differing copy requirements in your department. This is your first formal communication on this issue and you do not want to be too heavy-handed. You *do* want to describe the problem, the action you require and the consequences of inaction in clear and specific terms.

Once you have an outline of the purpose and context of your document, list the information you will include. You need to have a clear idea of how each piece of information relates to your aims.

This email could include the following information:

- the extent of the budget overrun, and the amount of money and time remaining in the current budget (*establishes the extent of the problem*)
- a reminder that personal copying is an abuse of the free-access system and contrary to the widely endorsed staff Code of Conduct—note that you found a sports club newsletter left in the machine (*restates accepted ground rules on behaviour and provides evidence of abuse*)
- a list of suitable allocations for individuals or sections stating numbers of copies per week (*sets fair and appropriate targets which can be monitored*)
- a list of options to control copy access and volume, such as key-cards or paper allocation (*warns staff that failing to act voluntarily will bring enforced restrictions*)
- a date for reviewing usage and introducing restrictions if necessary (*gives everyone a timeframe to work to and signals that you are absolutely serious about this issue*)
- a request that everyone does the right thing and an offer to discuss copier allocations with anyone who is interested (*appeals to a sense of fair play and shows that you are open to suggestions on handling the problem*).

This example shows how careful planning can establish strategies to meet all the aims of your document. Complex problem-solving documents work well when you provide evidence to substantiate the problem, outline potential solutions and give people a chance to influence the outcome.

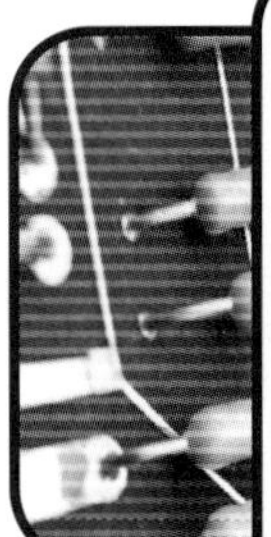

Activity 8.1

Writing emails

Write the above email and show it to a colleague for comment.

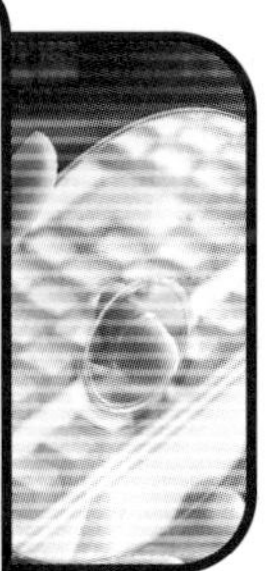

> ## Case study 8.1
>
> ### The Connectnow revival
>
> You recently bought a suburban computer company, Connectnow. Don Line, the previous owner, had let the business run down and now he has left the country. You need to deal with the following problems:
>
> - dissatisfied clients who are waiting for equipment and software that they ordered some time ago
> - angry creditors whose accounts need urgent attention
> - dedicated, capable staff who are suffering from low morale and uncertainty about job security.
>
> You bought the business cheaply as Don Line was desperate for cash. You feel confident you can rebuild and expand it into a thriving and profitable operation. Your immediate aims are to:
>
> - contact former clients to clarify outstanding orders and arrange delivery
> - notify suppliers about your new management and arrange new credit facilities
> - promote your business locally and offer 'opening' specials
> - reassure staff that you support them and their jobs are safe
> - book a working lunch at a nearby restaurant to build team spirit and give staff a chance to air their concerns.
>
> ### Case study activities
>
> 1. Discuss the different types of communication you could use to meet these aims. Consider when email, fax, brochure, letter, face-to-face or phone call would be most appropriate. Select an appropriate document type for each aim.
> 2. Plan the documents you would write for each situation. Make sure that each includes your purposes (practical and persuasive), identifies your audience (reader) and their concerns, establishes the context (how is the reader likely to react to your message?), and lists the information you will include in the document to achieve your aims.

LETTERS

Letters are common workplace documents used to communicate with clients and other organisations. They are used to convey the relevant facts and they propose action. They also provide an opportunity to maximise building relationships with clients and promote your organisation. However, as letters are being increasingly replaced by other forms of communication, such as fax and email, it is important to consider the guidelines for effective letters when writing all forms of correspondence.

Business letters are broadly categorised by their purpose as follows:

- **neutral or good-news letters** conveying positive messages such as:
  —agreeing to a request
  —introducing your organisation
  —requesting information
  —ordering goods
- **bad-news letters** conveying disappointing or upsetting messages such as:
  —refusing adjustment or supply
  —declining an offer, request or application

- **persuasive letters** conveying messages aimed to convince the reader to:
  —pay an account
  —buy a product
  —support a project
  —accept a proposal.

Defining the purpose

Firstly you need to decide what the letter is about. What do you want the letter to achieve? What are the most important issues and key facts? Similar aims apply to virtually all letters:

- **strengthening** the relationship between you and your reader
- **sharing information** that will make it easier to reach agreement
- **getting agreement** from the reader so that they will be more inclined to respond in the way you want
- **creating** action or movement.

Second, decide on the specific action you are seeking. What *exactly* do you want the reader to do? What kind of response do you expect? When and how do you want it done? As you answer these questions, start making rough notes. When choosing the key issues and information, remember that it is a mistake to communicate about two totally different topics in one letter. Write two letters, even if you put them in the same envelope.

Deciding on the length

Set a limit and stick to it, wherever possible aiming for one page. For most readers, under two pages is the absolute limit.

Only key facts need to go in the letter. Information is far easier to read in business format than in letter form, so if you need to include detailed facts such as an itinerary, a résumé or a list of expenses, make sure that the bulk of the material is attached to the letter, not part of the letter.

Organising shape and structure

Once you have your rough ideas written down, you can rearrange them using the RIPPA sequence as a checklist. Organise the various points so that they form a logical and coherent plan that fits the three different sections of the letter. This method is explained in Chapter 7 under the heading 'Using the RIPPA formula', as are techniques for writing in easy stages in the section 'Writing in five stages'.

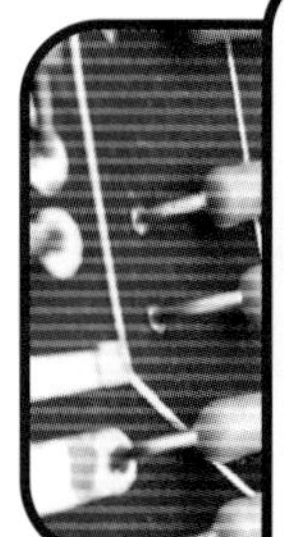

Activity 8.2

Planning a document

Choose a letter you would need to write for the Connectnow revival in Case study 8.1 and use the RIPPA sequence to plan the document. Use the information in Figure 8.3 to help you.

Figure 8.3
Planning two letters using the RIPPA sequence

Example A	Account overdue	
Opening	Remind reader about our agreement	R
Body	List outstanding amounts	I
	Explain why payment is needed now	P
	Note advantage of keeping account open	P
Ending	Ask for a cheque before 27th	A

Example B	Job application	
Opening	Note my special interest for *this* job	R
Body	List my qualifications for job	I
	Support my case by pointing to résumé	P
	Suggest a meeting to clarify picture	P
Ending	Suggest phone call regarding interview time	A

Letter layout

Word-processing software provides templates for a variety of styles in letter layout. All government departments and many businesses have conventions for document layout and presentation. When you start a new job, ask for a copy of any guidelines or manuals instructing you on particular conventions in written communication.

Various styles are available for the layout of letters. Fully blocked style is the most acceptable in business letters.

Writing effective subject lines

Subject lines help your letters (and other documents) draw the reader's attention. They act like newspaper headlines enticing the reader to pursue useful and interesting information. They should also:

- identify the topic and the type of letter
- identify the message to which you are replying
- list reference codes from the previous message.
  There is no need for 'Re:' or 'Ref:' at the start.
  Examples of subject lines might be:
- Request for information—National Sales Report
- Confirmation of fax—Approval for contract, 21 Pan Rd Norgate TxCode 4021/K Recd: 12 May 4:26 pm
- Your advertisement—Computer Programmer, Grade 3
- The *Australian*, Sat 22 July, page 34 Ref: 34M/87
  Subject lines can be 'you' oriented or 'action' oriented. You-oriented lines refer to the reader's communication: 'Your request for', 'Your inquiry on' or 'Your advertisement for'. Action-oriented lines refer directly to action that has been or will be taken as a result of this correspondence. The first words might be 'Approval of', 'Information on', 'Request for' or 'Delivery arrangements'.

Figure 8.4
Layout styles of letters

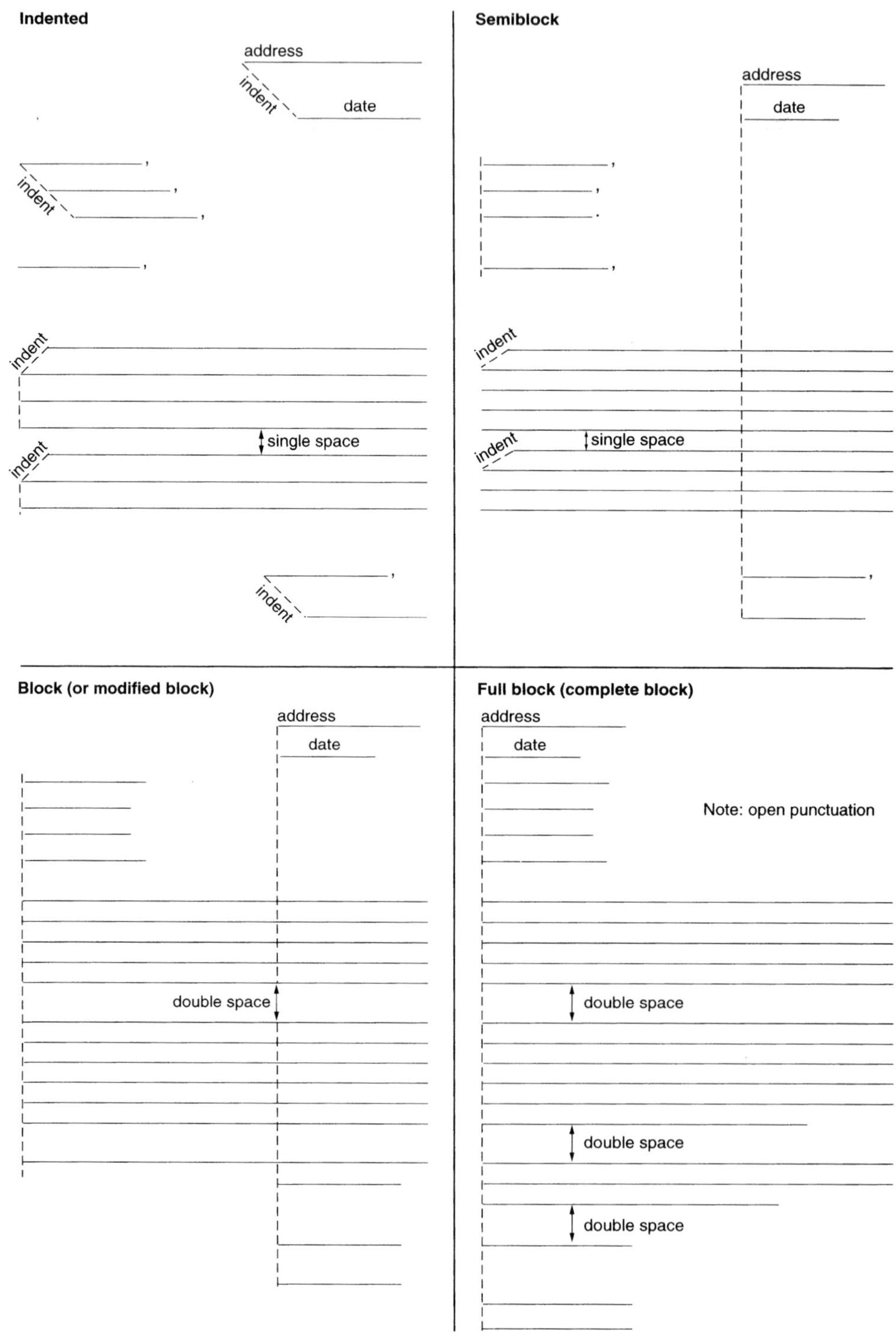

Make your subject lines work by:

- using positive terms: 'Your request for action' instead of 'Your complaint about a delay', or 'Final request for payment' instead of 'Delinquent account (legal action pending)'
- outlining the topic or topics in as few words as possible, ending with relevant file codes or numbers and the date of the original message. If acknowledging a phone call, fax or computer message, include both the identification number and the time received.

Figure 8.5
Accurate, descriptive subject lines will give your documents an edge

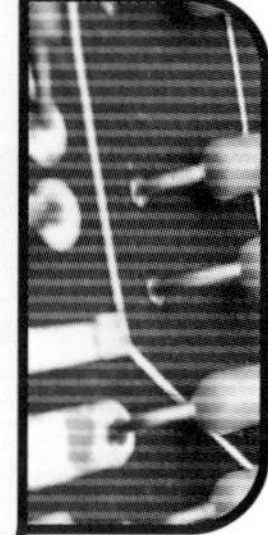

Activity 8.3

Writing subject lines

Return to your list of documents in question one of Case study 8.1. Write a subject line for each document. Make sure the subject lines reflect the reader's interests and convey the essence of your message.

Organising and drafting the letter

The first paragraph

Once you have captured your reader's attention with an engaging and informative subject line, give your letter a good start by:

- showing readers where they stand with you
- referring to the main topic or purpose of the letter
- switching the reader on and building interest
- expressing appreciation and giving acknowledgment.

Use an appreciative tone. Bridge-building works best if you pay a compliment. Integrate this with the factual information you wish to convey:

> *Your firm has been recommended to me by Peter Green of Brighton. He says your software has given better results than any previous products he has used. Could you produce something similar to meet our needs? I am interested in costs, design options and timeframes for delivery.*

The body of the letter

Thanks to your opening paragraph and subject lines, readers now know what your letter is about and where they stand with you. This makes it easier to concentrate on exchanging information and developing agreement. You will now need sound facts and logical reasoning (based on those facts), plus other supporting material, to persuade your reader to act in accordance with your aims.

The body of our sample letter could include information on numbers of software products, target audiences, potential content and suggested timeframes for production.

The final paragraph

End the letter by stating exactly what you will do next and outlining the action you want the reader to take. Be specific and avoid vague and open-ended finishes such as 'Looking forward to hearing from you soon' or 'Please reply at your earliest convenience'. A suitable end to our sample letter could be: 'Please email me an initial costing based on the information provided. I will call you on Friday to discuss my software requirements'.

If the letter is about a straightforward business matter such as an order, explain what you want, then make a direct request for action: 'I need the disk before Monday 2 May. Please send it by express mail'.

If you know the reader well you can be more personal, yet still direct: 'It's a good idea, Gil. Send me full details'.

If you do not want to sound too demanding (when asking a favour), add 'can', 'could' or 'would' at the start: 'Could you phone and advise what date suits you for next month's meeting?'.

If a series of actions is needed, list all steps, explaining how they are to be carried out and in what order: 'Please send the disk express mail. Charge the cost to our account, no. QV32618. Send a copy of the disk to our regional office in Adelaide'.

If you are fairly confident of acceptance, state the action you are ready to take, ending with a description of what you will do (unless the reader disagrees): 'Would you please phone and confirm the plan? I will then arrange for one of our software specialists to discuss your needs in more detail on June 20'.

Even if you covered all the important points in the body of the letter, you can close with a quick recap: 'It would help if you could arrange a meeting with the engineer to discuss the changes, as outlined above'.

Figure 8.6
Organising your letters

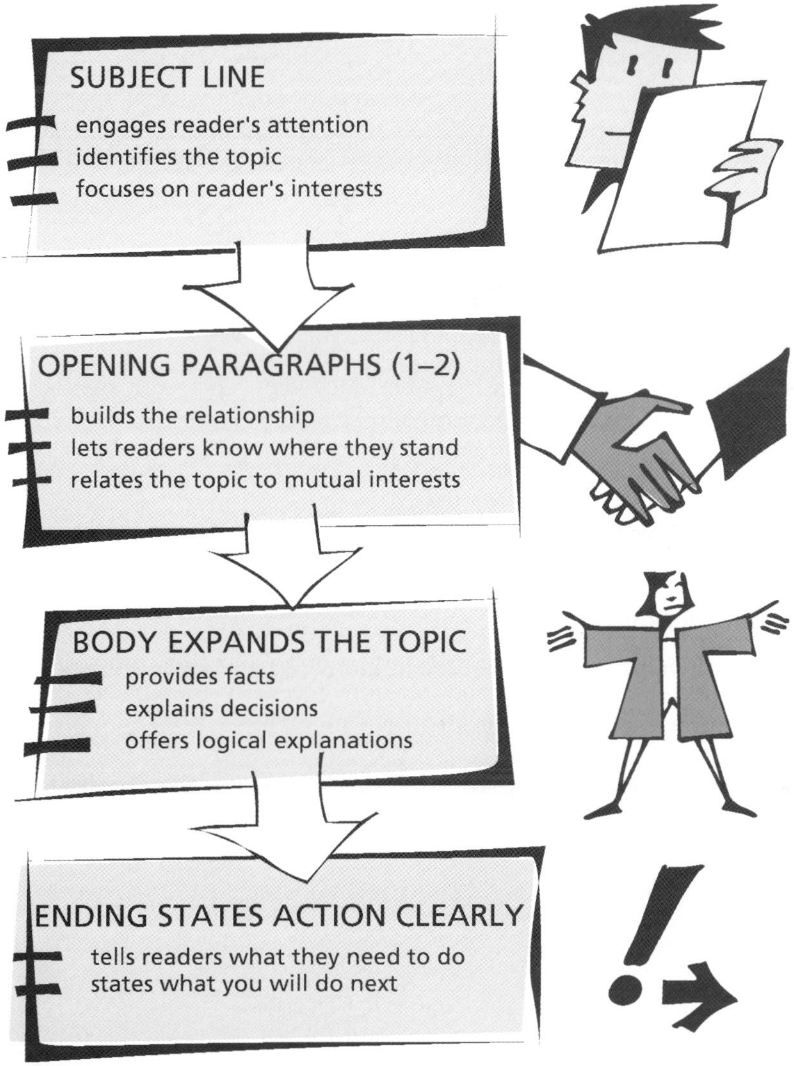

Activity 8.4

Writing letters

Write the Connectnow letter you have planned in Activity 8.2. Use the guidelines in the text and the letter in Figure 8.7 to help you.

The seven Cs

Use the seven Cs to add clarity and credibility to all your documents.

1. **Count and measure.** State facts in precise (countable) units: dollars, metres, grams or other standard measures. Non-measurable words such as 'cheap', 'expensive', 'heavy', 'light', 'far' or 'close' are emotive, unclear and less persuasive.

2. **Calendar.** State the precise dates. Do not say 'rather lengthy delays'—be specific. Instead of 'as soon as possible', say 'by 30 March'. Avoid 'next week', 'recently', or jargon such as 'inst' (instant) or 'ult' (ultimate).

3. **Clock.** State exact times rather than 'after lunch' or 'later on'.

4. **Country.** State locations precisely, give the exact position or address; do not rely on terms like 'nearby' or 'centrally located'.

5. **Character.** Name people responsible for the facts. Include the names of experts or authorities and, if necessary, list their professional qualifications.

6. **Copies.** Instead of describing a problem document, enclose a photocopy so that the reader can see exactly what is causing the trouble.

7. **Camera.** Enclose a photograph with a letter if it helps to increase clarity or reinforce the truth.

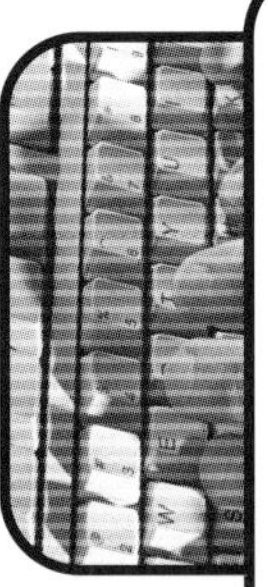

Checklist 8.1

Writing business letters

Write a letter to a company that has sent you an invoice for computing components but has not included all of the information necessary for you to pay the invoice correctly. Then complete this checklist.

I have:	Yes	No	Not sure
planned the letter to explain my purpose clearly and acknowledge my reader's interests	☐	☐	☐
written an engaging, informative subject line, using the first paragraph to build the relationship with the reader	☐	☐	☐
provided all relevant facts and supporting detail in the body of the letter	☐	☐	☐
ended the letter describing specific action required by both parties	☐	☐	☐
attached copies of relevant documents	☐	☐	☐
used complete letter format which conforms to my organisation's standards	☐	☐	☐
written in plain English, using direct language and spacious layout	☐	☐	☐
used a personal, friendly tone which highlights my concern for the reader's needs	☐	☐	☐
proofread the letter carefully to correct any errors in expression or fact	☐	☐	☐

Presenting bad news

Letters containing messages the reader does not want to hear are difficult to write. How can you convey an unwelcome message and retain the reader's goodwill? Enhance your chances of doing this successfully by explaining your position clearly and objectively. Where possible, focus on what the reader can do to remedy the situation.

Figure 8.7
Format of a well-written letter. Notice the positive tone used throughout the letter. It would have been easy to make a negative comment about Glenn Wilde's initial failure to provide the information, but the writer's idea is to get the account opened rather than worry about what is past.

McPherson's Computing Pty Ltd
Credit Department

21 March 2002

Glenn Wilde
Manager
Ultra Office Industries
PO Box 8576
Sydney NSW 2001

Dear Glenn,

**Details Needed to Finalise Account Opening
Your Enquiry Ref: GW/pn 23897 Dated: 17 September**

We are always happy to welcome new clients. Thank you for your application for a business account.

Although Ultra Office Industries is well known to us as a successful business, we need some additional information to help finalise the opening of your account:

- Three references from firms with whom you already have similar types of accounts.
- The name and address of your bank.

Once we have this information we can finalise the account arrangements. Our Autumn sale begins on Tuesday 2 April, but provided you reply by Friday 29 March we can open your account before then. This will help you take full advantage of our special sale discount.

As soon as we receive your reply we can advise all branches that you are a business client.

Yours sincerely

Andrew McPherson

Andrew McPherson
GENERAL MANAGER

Make the actual refusal as brief as you can. **Build your letter on positive issues, perhaps on maintaining a good working relationship despite the present trouble.** Make this appear to be your main reason for writing, and be sure that the closing paragraph stresses this positively, as part of the action ending.

The KKK formula

This old formula is still one of the best: Kiss first (positive opening), then Kick (the bad news in the body) and finally Kiss again (positive action ending). If you feel that a negative message is the best way to gain agreement, then be careful where you place it in the letter. Keep the first and last paragraphs of the letter free of any reference to the bad news. Where the action ending cannot be entirely positive, use a conditional ending to present the reader's options and outline the consequences of inaction. Collection letters, for example, need this type of ending.

Organising and drafting bad-news letters

The opening paragraph

Your bad-news letter will already have a subject line that immediately identifies the problem and may also state the action you require.

Use the opening paragraph to establish 'neutral ground' and express empathy for the reader's position. How you do this depends on your subject. You could thank the reader for their application, order or request, and acknowledge their interest in submitting it to you. If you are asking for payment, outline your organisation's credit terms and explain the mutual benefits of maintaining these conditions. Similarly, if you are refusing credit, you can state your organisation's criteria for granting credit. You are then 'set up' to use the following paragraphs to explain how the client might arrange payment or meet credit requirements.

Letters carrying bad news are more acceptable if you talk with the readers and show that you understand their concerns. Empathy links you to the reader who may then be less likely to see you as the enemy and more amenable to working with you on solutions to the problem. 'I can appreciate your feelings about the delay', 'We recognise your position and the effect this change will have on your plans', or 'I can understand your concern about the present arrangement' are ways to express empathy for your reader.

The body of the letter

Your reader deserves a direct answer so give your refusal clearly and do not labour the apologies. An extended apology in a business letter will seldom sound really sincere and phrases such as 'I'm terribly sorry' or 'We sincerely regret' only emphasise bad news and add to the reader's sense of loss.

Dwelling on the bad news and expressing doubt, criticism or anger, greatly reduces your chances of a positive response. **Once you have stated the refusal, talk about alternatives, help your reader feel empowered to respond positively to the refusal and express confidence in their abilities.** Describe the solution rather than the problem and avoid victimising the reader and questioning their credibility.

The following example is negative, impersonal and disapproving and implies that the reader is an idiot.

> *We cannot supply the software at academic prices for you at this point in time. Although you seem genuine, clients who are charged academic prices need to show proof that they are employed at or are currently enrolled as students of a Registered Training Organisation. Unfortunately you have neglected to do this, so I regret that I have no alternative but to reject your application until same are supplied on the attached form.*

The real message is positive: the price will almost certainly be approved, with only a short delay.

Activity 8.5

Writing positive letters

Rewrite the negative letter quoted on page 192 so that it:
- has an effective subject line
- has an empathetic and neutral opening
- explains the requirements clearly for purchasing products at academic prices
- tells the reader what exactly to do
- outlines the likely consequences of his or her actions
- has a positive, professional and reader-friendly tone.

Compare the following extracts from letters refusing a request for a donation for ex-lease office computers.

Our firm recognises the excellent work that you are doing in helping unemployed youth, and I have been asked by the board to convey their congratulations to you. We make annual donations to community groups in May each year and we would be very happy to receive an application from you next year when we are making this distribution. As long as your submission reaches us before 1 May, you can be confident that it will receive full consideration.

In this letter, the writer explains clearly why a request was not granted and suggests a positive alternative. It was not necessary in this case to give an actual refusal in the letter; the absence of a cheque in the envelope made it clear enough. The reader can also see that part of the problem was the lateness of the application although the word 'late' is never mentioned.

We are sorry to advise you that we cannot make a donation to your group as you failed to apply for same before the closing date, namely 1 May. Unfortunately, we do not consider late applications. Please ensure that any future applications are not submitted after 30 April each year.

In this extract so much emphasis is placed on the negative aspects that the apology is wasted. The writer gives a direct refusal, then proceeds to stress the applicant's shortcomings and dwell on the 'unfortunate' results for the reader. Its abrupt and unfriendly tone suggests that the reader is disorganised and stupid.

Ending the letter

Use the last two or three sentences in the letter to help readers see exactly what you are asking of them. **The best endings use direct, active language, and suggest that you have confidence in the reader's capacity to act.** Vary your endings according to how strongly you wish to stress the desired outcome.

A conditional ending based on the 'If you do X, we will do Y' formula stresses the benefits of action by stating the results. This ending retains a positive tone while reminding the reader firmly but tactfully of the risk in failing to act: 'Your network is due to be connected next Monday, and if you finalise your account by 4 pm on Friday we will be able to arrange training on new procedures within one week of installation'.

Threats like 'Unless you pay by Friday …' create resentment and ill feeling. People pay, but they appear to 'lose face' acting under duress. Describing the benefits of immediate action encourages readers to act promptly: 'We will phone you as soon as we receive the documents and your name has been registered'.

If legal action is likely, do not say so in your letters. Once matters reach that point, hand them over to legal or debt-collection experts because it is they, not you, who will be responsible for carrying the action through.

Checklist 8.2

Writing bad-news letters

Write a letter asking for payment from a business that owes you money. Then complete this checklist.

I have:	Yes	No	Not sure
expressed empathy for the reader's situation	☐	☐	☐
explained my organisation's position	☐	☐	☐
provided all the facts	☐	☐	☐
concentrated on maintaining our relationship	☐	☐	☐
not overdone the apology	☐	☐	☐
stated the necessary action clearly	☐	☐	☐
explained the consequences of inaction	☐	☐	☐
used a positive tone which helps the reader feel able to act	☐	☐	☐

Outlines for persuasive letters

Apply the planning and writing principles described in this chapter to all of the following reasons for correspondence. These outlines will help you select and order your information effectively.

Making a written complaint

People sometimes complain that they write letters to express some grievance and receive an inadequate response or no reply at all. Frequently, the fault lies in the wording of the complaint. Avoid using this opportunity to vent your frustrations (however justified) in aggressive terms. Written complaints, like all business correspondence, should state your intentions clearly, allowing the receiver to trace the source of your problem and act on it promptly.

Tips for writing complaints are:

- identify the product or service and state the history of the complaint
- list all the information the reader requires to follow it up
- tell the reader exactly what you want done
- avoid sounding rude or condescending
- convey your faith in the integrity of the business and their willingness to deal with your problem
- do not include irrelevant information in the letter.

Answering complaints

Dealing fairly and efficiently with complaints is an essential skill in customer service. Empathise with the client—see the problem from their perspective. Letters responding to complaints should aim to retain goodwill by offering the client reasonable compensation.

When writing responses to complaints:

- acknowledge the complaint so that the recipient feels understood and taken seriously
- give clear and appropriate explanations or reasons for the recipient's problem
- request clarification of unclear details
- clearly indicate any further action required by the recipient
- offer recompense where appropriate, or show regret if you are unable to rectify the problem (refer to the standard practice or policy of your organisation so that the client knows it is not a personal refusal)
- assure the person of their value to your organisation in a goodwill final paragraph
- use a polite and assertive tone showing the person that you are in control of the situation
- never blame your organisation—merely apologise for the specific inconvenience to the client.

Activity 8.6

Written complaints

1. Compare the following written complaints and assess them against what you know about effective writing.
2. Plan and write a reply to each of the complaints.

Computer warranty

I am writing about the appalling way your staff have treated me. When I phoned up to find out what had happened to my computer I was told that everything was all right. I was naive enough to think that Australia was a fair place and I'd be looked after. Well, I came in to pick it up and paid with a cheque. I asked for a receipt but the lady said that everything was recorded on my file and that she could not print a receipt at this time. She would post one to me. It seems incredible that a big organisation like yours cannot afford a stamp! Anyway, the computer still has the same problem and I have lots of error messages. I checked with the bank and the cheque had never been cashed. Whose fault is that? I've lost my valuable time because you were too inefficient to fix my computer properly.

Scanner warranty

When I bought my scanner from your firm in July last year I was looking forward to a year's trouble-free use and the protection of a one-year warranty. I decided to buy from you as I had heard good reports from other customers about your after-sales service.

I have received friendly and courteous assistance on my numerous visits but it has not been effective, although I have brought the scanner in twice in the past eight months for repair.

> *On Monday 19 June I will be leaving scanner Model HJ 260 at your service centre for its final check before the warranty expires. Please ensure that it is given the same skilful care and attention your other satisfied customers enjoy.*
>
> *I have enclosed photocopies of samples of work produced using this scanner. This will allow you to see the problems I am experiencing. I will give a copy of this letter to the head of your service division when I leave the scanner there on Monday.*
>
> *Please send me a brief acknowledgment of this letter. I hope that I will not have to take up any more of your time, as I much would prefer to add my name to your list of satisfied customers.*

Please-pay letters

Most organisations have a sequence of collection letters designed to prompt clients to pay their accounts. These rely on the persuasive power of appeals to conscience, pride and (ultimately) self-interest. Correspondence at all stages of the process should follow these guidelines aimed to extract payment and retain the business relationship:

- specify outstanding amounts, account numbers and when the account was due
- invite the reader to contact you to discuss the account
- stress the positive aspects of payment, such as keeping a sound credit rating and ensuring uninterrupted service
- inform the reader of the consequences of not paying the account.

Table 8.1
Letter types

Letter type	Opening	Body	Ending
Neutral, good news, bad news, persuasive	Builds the relationship States your position	Provides facts, logical explanations and supporting details	States action clearly
'Please-pay' (overdue credit card account)		'Credit will be maintained if the account is paid within ten days' 'Our customer service officers are available to discuss payment options'	
Request for quotation (supply and installation of an administration network)			'Please fax me your quote by 28 July. I will contact the successful suppliers on 14 August'
Refusal to speak at a seminar (too busy)	'Thank you for considering me a suitable speaker at your seminar. I wish I could accept your offer'		

EMAILS AND MEMOS

Emails and memos are used for many routine purposes at work and are a vital part of the formal communication systems in most organisations. Some are like letters, others more like reports, but the essential requirement is that they should be kept short.

Internal emails or memos are forms of written communication used *within* an organisation, with emails replacing memos in many organisations. The use of emails as a replacement for letters or telephone calls to external clients is also widespread. However, the principles are similar whether you are writing a memo, or an internal or external email.

Writing a memo or email gives you the chance to draft and redraft your message to make sure that it will not be taken the wrong way. You cannot do this when speaking face-to-face or on the phone. A personal message also gives both parties a record of the message to serve as a reminder.

If a phone call will produce the same result, choose it in preference to an email or memo. You can sound petty, even ridiculous, if you use an email or memo to deal with issues such as the purchase of a new teapot!

Use emails or memos to:

- request information
- respond to requests
- give notification (instructions or explanations of procedures)
- report on events.

Emails and memos work best for conveying good news or simple requests for action that require no special persuasion and will be easy to agree to. If an issue is complicated or controversial, face-to-face communication may be called for.

When not to use emails or memos

Giving bad news

Give the message face-to-face or write a letter. This applies in particular to any kind of reprimand or withdrawal of privileges: a memo or email is not a good channel if you have to assert your authority. Never use one to say things you are not prepared to say to a person's face.

'Pep-up' messages

Morale-boosting requires personal leadership and face-to-face contact. You cannot lead people or change attitudes by writing memos; in fact, the opposite effect is more likely. If you try to lead in this way you will be seen as weak and ineffectual.

Conveying personal news

Use a letter to advise people of promotion or to welcome someone to a new job. Similarly, use a letter to offer congratulations on personal success.

If the matter is urgent

Senior managers tend to forget that if a memo arrives after 11 am the reader may have already made plans for the day or be busy with another urgent task. If an issue needs action in under three or four days, other communication methods are safer.

Distributing material not related to your workplace

This includes unsolicited junk mail or forwarding/replying to emails not related to work.

Emails

The following are some of the advantages of emails.

- **Immediacy.** The recipient can often see the document within minutes of it being sent.
- **Retrieval.** Email documents can be easily stored, sorted, searched for and retrieved.
- **Records.** You have a record of what you send as well as what you receive.
- **Distribution.** Documents can be shared with others, sent to multiple recipients and replied to at the touch of a button.
- **Ability to attach other material.** You can send other material such as a draft report, URL or spreadsheet as part of the message.

Figure 8.8
Plan the content of your message

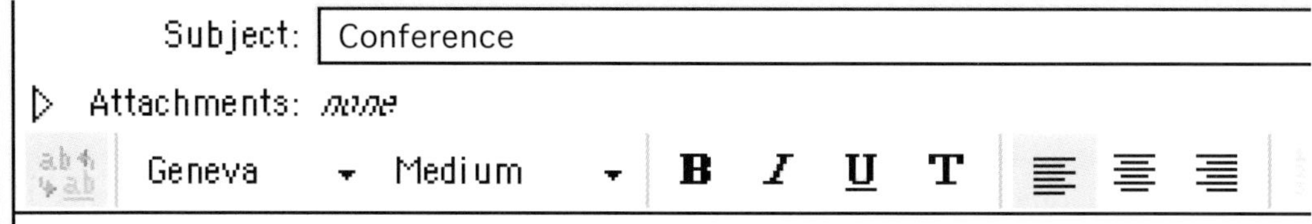

The message in Figure 8.8 is contradictory and confusing, consisting of a series of 'unprocessed' thoughts. The writer looks indecisive and disorganised while the recipients of the email are left not knowing what to do. Plan the content and timing of your email message as carefully as you would for any other workplace document.

While an informal conversational tone is often appropriate for an email message there are also protocols and company policies to consider. Most organisations have strict codes of conduct regarding the use of email and inappropriate or frivolous use can lead to serious consequences for the employees involved.

Memos

A complex format wastes the time memos are intended to save: avoid all unnecessary detail. Many organisations provide employees with pre-printed forms. Memos should contain headings (To, From, Date, Subject). Figure 8.9 shows how to format a memo.

Tips for writing emails or memos

Keep emails and memos short

Use short words and short sentences. Deal with only one idea in any one paragraph. Complete sentences are not essential; if you list points you use fewer words. Long memos do not work.

Figure 8.9
Sample memo

Date: 1/5/02
To: Jane Lee
From: Terry Wang
Subject: Software Development Team Meeting

The Software Development Team Meeting will be on Tuesday 7/5/02 in meeting Room 3, Level 5, 2–4 pm.

The agenda is:

1. Training budget for 20 staff—Rob to present the final proposal. Copies of this will be sent to you next Friday before the meeting.
2. Common problems with network compatibility—Jane Lee to present.
3. Questions and review of progress—Kevin to facilitate.

See you there.

Terry

Check spelling and grammar

People often use abbreviations or other shortcuts when using email, for example, 'u' instead of 'you'. This may be appropriate for very informal messages but if the email concerns confirmation of important organisational issues, use correct forms of spelling and grammar.

State your purpose clearly

Write an informative subject line and present your material in order of importance. Divide your content into sections and number each point if this clarifies a sequence or ranks the information. Use subheadings to achieve this result in longer memos.

Use face-to-face language

Use the active tense. Be direct and personal. Let your document be more like an extension of conversation.

Avoid bureaucratic jargon

Some emails and memos are filled with worn-out phrases like 'in reference to the above matter'. Some (misguided) writers believe that long words are necessary to make them professional.

Monitor background signals and tone

Emails and memos contain non-verbal messages whether you want them to or not! Before you send the message, read it aloud to yourself or to a colleague. If it sounds artificial, or like a parent chastising a child, rewrite it.

Remember that messages can be recorded

Remember, email messages and memos are part of the record system for organisations. They can be read and used by management. There have been instances where emails have been used in a legal context for issues such as harassment and contractual disputes.

Allow sufficient time for replies

Everyone replies to messages at different rates and an email may not be read until much later than you think. Consider this delay when asking for a reply by a certain date.

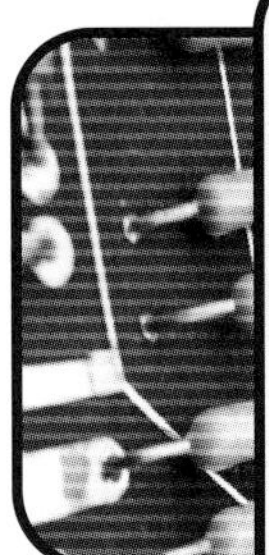

Activity 8.7

Writing emails and memos

1. List three situations at work which might call for writing emails or memos.
2. Why are emails or memos unsuitable for giving bad news or pep talks?
3. Choose an email or memo from Case study 8.1 and write it following the guidelines given in the text.

WEB DOCUMENTS

Most software applications allow you to save documents as HTML files (these are files used in webpages that can be viewed on the internet). The more adventurous user can then try creating documents using webpage editors which allow for much more creativity in terms of features that can be incorporated into the document. Most internet service providers (ISPs) can offer advice about access to these programs.

SHORT REPORTS

All reports, regardless of length, investigate a specific subject and provide documentary evidence of findings. They provide objective information as a basis for assessing progress and making decisions.

The principles for writing either a short or long report are the same. Chapter 9 covers the planning and writing of long reports in depth. Here we look at the uses of short reports and at routine or progress reporting.

Attaching short reports to letters

Business letters lose impact if you 'overload' them with more than one or two detailed body paragraphs. Often you need to share much more information than this with the reader.

Figure 8.10
Short reports or internal documents are often presented in memo format

National Training Council

To: Chairman, National Conference Committee
From: Deputy Director, National Training Council
Date: 21 October 2001
Subject: Venue for national conference—Booking problems

1. INTRODUCTION

This report presents the results of the recent investigation into booking problems experienced at the National Conference.

2. BACKGROUND

The conference was held at _____ on _____ ...

If the information is very detailed, particularly if it contains figures and statistics (for instance, a quotation for supply of goods or services), attach it as a separate document.

If you present it in report format using numbered headings and white space, it will be more accessible to your reader. Information received in this way is more easily understood and more likely to gain agreement than if it 'clogs up' the middle of your letter.

Examples of attached reports include:

- **a résumé**, which should never be included within a letter
- facts and figures on a firm's financial position
- a statement presenting a series of problems, and complex technical data.

Each is, in effect, a report in that it contains collected and collated information arranged according to type. It makes sense to present it in a way that will make it clear and easy to follow.

Writing routine reports

Most organisations require regular reports to update information on sales levels, staffing changes and other activities which measure an organisation's wellbeing. This type of reporting is also used to describe and monitor progress on projects. The frequency varies according to an organisation's needs and expectations but routine monthly reporting is fairly common practice.

In many cases these reports follow a standard format, with only figures, times and places changed to reflect the operations for the period covered. This is purely 'informational' reporting with no analysis of the data or recommendations for change. These reports, however, can become the basis for decision making and must record the facts accurately and completely. Alternatively, if you have the authority to interpret data and suggest action, do so, basing your analysis solidly on the facts you have presented.

Avoid the following 'pitfalls' in analytical reporting.

- **Contamination.** Do not combine your research and analysis in the same sections. Present all the facts before you draw conclusions. Similarly, separate your conclusions (analysis) from your recommendations—the action you are proposing. The clarity, logic and overall integrity of a report depends heavily on presenting these three different yet interconnected types of information separately and in sequence.
- **Black holes.** Ensure that your analysis and recommendations are fully supported by the facts. Report writers are often 'hit' by a radical and inspired solution to their problem towards the end of the reporting process. This may not be linked to the recorded research and analysis in the report. If you are suddenly struck by a viable solution and want to include it in your recommendations, you need to add the relevant facts and analysis to support it.
- **Blithering.** Write the report in plain English using language your readers understand. **Whether the same word is jargon or good technical language depends on who is reading it.** Match your language to your reader's needs and vocabulary. Report the facts objectively and accurately and save your opinions for the section on findings or conclusions.

The characteristics of sound routine reporting include:

- highlighting any change or variation from normal procedures—*if sales in the region have fallen sharply, the report format must be such that the drop cannot be hidden among other data*
- discussing a problem and suggesting reasons for the change—*help others understand what is happening*
- knowing the procedure for recording anything that has not changed—*is it left out altogether or recorded for statistical purposes?*
- expressing expert opinions on local matters—*this is not confined to problem solving; try to predict future trends and suggest improvements.*

Pre-printed forms may not be sufficiently flexible and comprehensive for routine reporting. Even if they are designed to cover every possible situation, by having the writer tick boxes or cross out items that do not apply, they can serve to hide most of the items listed above while highlighting routine data.

A well-designed form with the initial section devoted to variations and problems and the last page used for routine items, such as stock on hand, will serve both purposes and still save time. A recent variation supplies the 'blank form' on a computer disk. The writer types in the figures and the report is submitted by email or a copy on disk by post. This allows collation of facts and figures from various sources without retyping.

Activity 8.8

Writing reports

1. List the kinds of information best included in a report attached to a business letter.
2. Why is routine reporting useful to organisations?
3. What are the limitations of pro forma reporting?
4. Separate the facts, conclusions and recommendations in this badly contaminated extract from a report on internet security. Identify any 'black holes' and reorganise and rewrite it using suitable headings and plain English.

From wide area networks to the World Wide Web, from the committees of Parliament House to the cubicles of corporate Australia, systems security is all the rage. Witness the plethora of products goaded by the promise of digitised dollars, corporate concern over information assets easily shared over local area networks, intranets and extranets, and the Federal Government's ongoing struggle to come to grips with issues like encryption. Then there are the workshops, seminars and conferences.

Taking the topic to the other extreme by proclaiming the coming 'death of the intranet' as a stand-alone network and the advent of a 'universal infraware', Moon Microsystems Inc. is pushing its own network security solution, which includes its Moonbeam products line. CEO Chris Wood claims this will serve as the means for companies to use the internet with full assurance of safety, 'making the internet secure enough to be the backbone of business communications', according to its corporate materials.

Overall, the critical importance of security technology was reinforced last month with the announcement of a new partnership by the Australian Security Intelligence Organisation and the National Institute of Standards and Technology. The agencies plan to set up the so-called National Information Assurance Partnership (NIAP). Ultimately, NIAP should provide 'independent evaluators and product producers with objective measures for evaluating the quality and security of these products', according to the agencies' news release.

The partnership will provide evaluators and product producers with 'a common language to define the security features and assurance of products as well as a defined common test methodology to evaluate products'. The common language as well as the test methodology 'will be based upon the International Common Criteria for Information Technology Security Evaluation'. With security stretching its tentacles to the other end of the geopolitical spectrum, making the internet secure is a top priority.

For those seeking to create an operational framework for systems security, Wood profiles what she considers the five essential policy positions. The first is risk assessment, in which the organisation looks at its own unique circumstances and the value, criticality and sensitivity of its information. The second is contingency planning, where you have an ongoing effort to look at how you will, for example,

> *back up and restore your system, recognising your need to be able to roll back to a prior version and abandon unliveable circumstances. The third essential policy is documenting applications developed in-house as well as testing them. Wood admits she is often amazed at the state of an organisation's documentation; in many cases there is none. Fourth is change control, that is, a formal proposal for initiating change. For instance, an organisation cannot reconfigure its system in the middle of the day. The final step is establishing a level of need and defining access to the systems based on this need to know.*

INSTRUCTIONS

Often you will give instructions face-to-face at work but you may also have to write a clear set of instructions or procedures for staff (how to operate a new piece of equipment or how to find client information). Too often people find written instructions frustrating because they are confusing and not properly sequenced. Careful planning, clear writing and thorough testing can prevent much of this confusion.

Whenever you can, support written instructions by demonstrating the procedure. Be patient and empathetic with your audience and ask for feedback on their understanding of the task. Provide written instructions as a back-up to reinforce your demonstration and verbal explanations.

Guidelines for writing instructions

Analyse your audience

How much information is needed to complete the task? Is background information required to put the task in context? Do you need to motivate your audience by clearly stating the purpose of the task so that they are then willing to learn the procedure?

Analyse the procedure

Perform the task yourself and break it down into its parts. Consider the timeframe and how long it takes to perform each part of the task. Then consider whether each step is really necessary.

Include necessary steps in the task

So often instructions do not discriminate between essential steps and what is merely recommended. Ask yourself: 'What is crucial for the reader to know?'.

Highlight vital safety information

Write 'Warning' or 'Caution' and use bold type to identify and describe risks and their consequences.

Test your instructions

Ask someone unfamiliar with the task to try to follow your instructions. Then ask for feedback, checking on steps they were uncertain about or found difficult. Do they need further explanation? If necessary, revise and test your instructions again.

Be clear and accurate
Operating instructions often affect personal safety or the protection of costly equipment, so write clear instructions.

Avoid negative words in instructions
Instead of saying 'Do not disassemble the printer when changing paper', it is better to write 'Leave the printer assembled when you change the paper'.

Use the 'you' approach
Direct the instructions at the reader: 'Turn the printer off' rather than 'The printer should be turned off'.

Use active voice
Active voice focuses responsibility on the person performing the task and is more effective than passive voice: 'You must disconnect the power at the controller's desk' works better than 'Power must be disconnected at the controller's desk'.

Use action words
A verb indicates the action the reader needs to take, so start each instruction with a verb as shown in the following examples.
1. Read the manual.
2. Turn the printer on.
3. Set the program to the desired font.

Leave out unnecessary words
Instead of 'In order to accomplish the effective changing of the printer paper', simply write 'To change the printer paper'.

Write the instruction before the explanation
Your readers are most interested in what they have to do. 'Turn on your computer. This will start Windows, and launch the Microsoft Word for Windows program' is better than 'Launch your Microsoft Word for Windows program by starting up Windows after you have turned on your computer'.

Sequence information
Arrange the instructions in chronological order and number the steps. This allows the reader to follow easily the proper sequence of actions. Use headings to organise procedures into clusters of related steps.

Separate instructions from explanations
Use different fonts, or put instructions in bold and explanations in italics. This distinguishes actions from consequences and clarifies the process for the reader.

Use illustrations and white space
Well-labelled diagrams can illustrate some concepts better than words. Plenty of white space and wide margins make instructions easier to read and allow the reader to write additional notes.

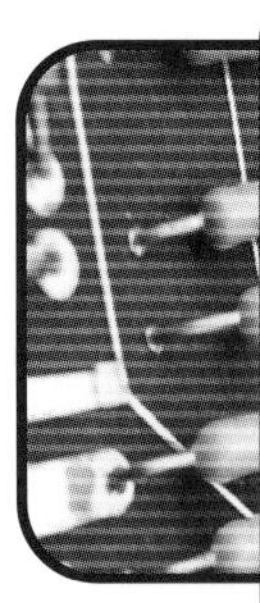

Activity 8.9

Writing instructions

1. What information can you include before the actual instruction to entice your reader to learn a procedure?
2. Why is it useful to separate instructions from explanations and to put the instruction first?
3. When is a diagram or an illustration better than a written instruction?
4. How can subheadings improve the clarity and flow in written instructions?
5. Plan and write a set of clear, complete instructions for one of the following tasks:
   (a) creating a new folder in Windows Explorer
   (b) attaching a URL to an email
   (c) editing bookmarks/favourites
   (d) saving a file to a floppy disk.
6. Test your instructions and rewrite the steps that do not work well.

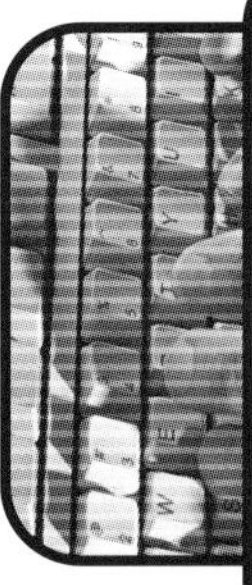

Checklist 8.3

Writing instructions

Imagine you are going on holiday and someone is filling in for you. Write a set of instructions telling them what to do on the first day, then complete this checklist.

I have:	Yes	No	Not sure
motivated the reader to learn the procedure by describing its uses and advantages	☐	☐	☐
included all crucial steps	☐	☐	☐
sequenced and numbered the steps, writing one instruction per number	☐	☐	☐
used subheadings to identify stages of the procedure	☐	☐	☐
separated instructions from explanations	☐	☐	☐
begun each step with an action word (verb)	☐	☐	☐
written in active language directed at the reader	☐	☐	☐
highlighted risks and described the potential consequences	☐	☐	☐
used diagrams (if appropriate) and ample white space	☐	☐	☐
removed all unnecessary descriptions and wording	☐	☐	☐
tested the instructions and adjusted them if necessary	☐	☐	☐

NEWSLETTERS

Newsletters and in-house publications provide an excellent communication channel for all levels of an organisation. In business you often become involved in producing newsletters. Provided they are read, in-house publications can:

- raise morale
- build team spirit and unify staff
- inform and educate on policy and practice
- provide a forum for discussing issues and ideas.

Guidelines for producing readable, effective newsletters

Focus on special interests

Divide a newsletter into sections, each clearly identified, so that it attracts its regular readership. In reality, most people skim through newsletters searching for items of interest to them and ignoring the rest, so the best way to plan and write a newsletter is to forget about cover-to-cover readers.

Balance text and visual content

Remember that some of your readers are visually oriented while others—the aurally oriented—are more concerned with words. Editors with too strong an aural background can produce a publication with too many words and little visual appeal. They tend to use small type and few pictures (to fit in as many words as possible), whereas visually oriented editors produce pages with strong eye appeal but less material content. This draws criticism from aural readers. Balance visuals and text in your publication.

Choose the content carefully

The content of any internal publication must have some special, original appeal, something that readers cannot get watching television or reading commercial magazines. Reproducing items already used in a hundred other newsletters destroys this element. Include a mixture of:

- useful facts that readers cannot get elsewhere
- items giving recognition to organisation members who have succeeded at work or in sport or community activities
- news of successes attained by the organisation as a whole—victories that everyone can share
- reminders of coming events, particularly of deadlines and closing dates
- information on new technology for use at work or at home
- ideas on management and company policies—make your newsletter a forum where individuals can put these forward
- high-quality, original humour—this is always popular, but also rare (it is better to have none than to lower your standards).

Know your reading public

Print what people want to read, not what you or anyone else thinks they ought to read. Experiment with new features, but test them for audience appeal. If a regular feature is no longer popular, drop it.

Do not rely on casual reader judgment

People who have no experience in publishing or editing will offer critical advice on your performance as editor. Do not take this too seriously. If there are ten sections in your newsletter, you will find a group of readers who support one or two, tolerate a couple more and want you to cut out all the rest. As soon as you address this you will find that the deleted items were at the top of another group's list of favourites. If you want to measure popularity ratings, conduct a full survey.

What not to include

An editor is legally responsible for what appears in any publication. This responsibility also carries considerable power and authority to decide what will be printed and what will not. Sometimes people mistakenly assume that an editor must print anything submitted, and cannot alter it in any way. This is not correct. You have the right to reject, condense and, if necessary, alter the content of any item before it goes to print. In such cases it is wise, however, to advise the contributor of the changes and seek approval. If you make major changes, the article should carry a note: 'Condensed from a report supplied by', or 'This article is an edited or condensed version of text supplied by'.

Committee reports or technical papers

Technical writers and committee leaders may contribute regularly. They often have a strong desire to see their work in print but the material seldom has mass audience appeal. Short extracts, heavily edited, may be worth including, but leave it at that.

Management 'pep talks'

Sincere and well-deserved praise from management deserves a place. However, if a paper contains what appears to be corporate propaganda, its credibility is reduced. A boss who feels that a newsletter is a personal mouthpiece should be discouraged.

Extreme or biased points of view

If the newsletter appears to be a platform for a few individuals wanting to air extreme views, it will lose the support of the majority of middle-ground readers. For the same reason, it is best to avoid political content.

Gossip

Rumours and gossip may guarantee readership, but will lower the standard of the publication beyond the point where it will be taken seriously.

Page design and layout

A two- or three-column layout improves readability, because the short lines are easier to read. A three-column format is also easier to work with when you are fitting in artwork or photos alongside text.

- Use plenty of headings and subheadings to break up the text. Bold lettering and capital letters emphasise important points and look more professional than underlining.
- Use a right-hand page for important items or to start an article that runs over several pages. It attracts more attention than a left-hand page.
- Use the page centre and the top and bottom right-hand corners for pictures or graphics.

- Use photographs, provided your printing system can reproduce them clearly. Put one or two on each page. This is better than making some pages all pictorial and some all text.
- Stick to a few standard typefaces, even if your printer can produce more. A mix of too many type styles marks you as an amateur.

Desktop publishing

If you wish to produce a professional-looking newsletter, leaflet or brochure you should use a desktop publishing software package. You can use word-processing packages but you are limited in the use of graphics and they cannot be manipulated on most applications. Laser printing can produce artwork good enough for publications.

Activity 8.10

Writing newsletters

1. List some practical ways a newsletter can help to motivate and unify staff.
2. Why might readers lose interest in their in-house newsletter?
3. Collect some workplace newsletters and assess them against the guidelines in this section.
4. You are producing a newsletter for staff of an ISP.
   (a) What are your aims for this newsletter?
   (b) Who will read it?
   (c) How might your readers react to the content of the newsletter?
   (d) List the likely sections.
   (e) Plan and write the content for one of your sections.

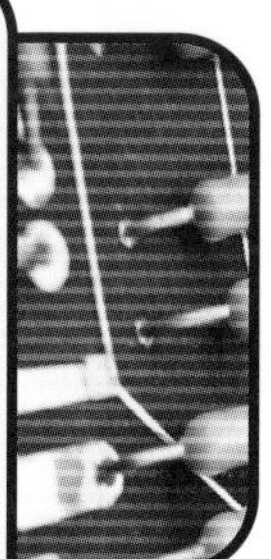

LEAFLETS

Advertising a coming event can be costly if done by professionals. A well-planned leaflet is easy to produce yourself and can provide just as good a result. A leaflet should give all the information an interested reader needs to participate in the event.

- Use language that sounds enthusiastic, but do not exaggerate.
- Choose a catchy title.
- Run off hundreds of leaflets rather than ten or twenty. Mass coverage is the secret of successful do-it-yourself publicity.
- Display them everywhere.
- Establish the wording and format and use similar versions for local newspaper advertisements, signs in windows, and brochures.
- Include a short, tear-off section at the bottom which can be detached and posted with payment or as a form of enrolment. This saves people having to write a note to send with their money.
- The leaflet in Figure 8.11 highlights all the important points without cluttering the layout. A contact telephone number enables anyone with additional questions to get an immediate answer.

Figure 8.11
Example of a well-produced leaflet

Greenlands Community College

49 Universal Drive Nirvana QLD 4269 ABN 78 426 438 195

One-day computer expo for the small-business operator

WEDNESDAY 25 JUNE   9 AM TO 10 PM

See demonstrations of the latest hardware and software designed for self-employed business owners and small-business managers.

Latest version of Austro Spreadsheet
New laser printers
Scanners and digitisers

Get expert advice on your business's computing needs from our special guest Professor Rita Robbins from Stanfield University of Technology.

Design your own accounting system
Experiment with desktop editing and printing

Admission: $10.00 adults (cash or credit card)
$3.00 Student card holders
$2.00 under 14 years
Includes morning tea. Lunch available on site.
Contact: Ricky Cousins, Computer Dept, Greenlands College
Phone: (07) 9783 2814 Email: rcousins@greenlands.com.au
Sponsored by Greenlands Community College Council

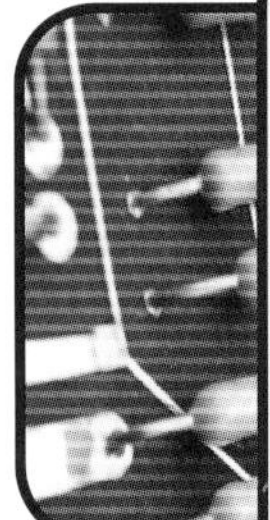

Activity 8.11

Creating leaflets

1. Discuss the pros and cons of designing a leaflet yourself compared with having it done professionally.
2. List the possible outlets for distributing the Greenlands Community College leaflet.
3. Plan and produce a leaflet for a series of special prices on home computing systems.

ACTION POINTS

You will write well at work if you:

- identify all the aims for your document
- plan around your reader's information needs
- select the type of document most appropriate for your message
- empathise with your reader's situation and feelings
- keep your documents brief while including all essential information
- support your position with fact and logical reasoning
- state all the necessary actions clearly and specifically
- use simple, direct language to convey information clearly
- set your documents out clearly with plenty of white space
- use your documents to improve cooperative working relationships
- edit and proofread your documents carefully.

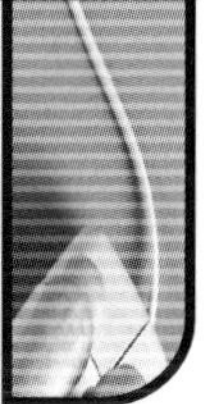

Planning workplace documents

Careful planning will overcome many of the obstacles to successful business writing. Workplace writing needs to fit the context of your broader dealings with clients and colleagues. Plan your documents to convey your message clearly in terms that represent the reader's interests. Documents that are clear and complete will be well received by readers and save everyone's time.

Write all your documents to express empathy for the reader's position however straightforward or complex their circumstances. Trust your instinct. If you feel uncertain about the draft of a document it probably needs rewriting. A word processor will help you draft and edit your documents quickly and efficiently.

Letters

Letters convey information *and* reflect your organisation's image. Contemporary business letters are shorter than they used to be, so use subject lines to define your topic and engage the reader's attention.

Letters have three parts: the opening, the body and the action ending. The opening tells the reader where they stand and expands on the topic. The body supplies the reader with facts, logical explanations and an appropriately persuasive appeal. The action ending tells the reader exactly what they need to do next as well as what you will be doing about the matter.

Bad-news letters focus on maintaining the working relationship with the reader. The KKK formula helps you convey unwelcome messages in a tactful way.

Emails and memos

Emails and memos are key forms of communication within an organisation. Immediacy and informality are the key benefits of email, however, think before you type your message. Clogging the system with copious messages sent to indifferent readers reduces the efficiency of email. Training is essential for all users of an email system.

A simple four-section heading is all the heading you need for memos. Effective memos are short and action oriented, using face-to-face language.

Short reports

'Bulk' information likely to 'overload' the body of a letter is more accessible in an attached report. Memo format is common for short reports, followed by conventional reporting structure based on headed sections and decimal numbering.

Present facts before interpretations and recommendations. Routine reporting records the status quo. It should also identify changes and problems.

Instructions

Your instructions begin where the readers' knowledge ends, so find out what they already know about the procedure. A brief explanation of the benefits of the procedure will motivate your reader to follow an instruction. Logical, numbered sequencing is essential for written instructions to be effective.

Newsletters

Topical, well-presented newsletters can build staff unity, celebrate an organisation's achievements and provide a forum for discussion. Originality is a key ingredient in successful newsletters. Provide information and opportunities for comment that staff cannot get elsewhere. Appeal to both visual and aural readers by balancing text and visual content.

A newsletter editor is legally responsible for the publication's contents but is entitled to reject, condense or amend any item before it goes to print.

Leaflets

It is possible to create eye-catching, informative leaflets without expensive, professional production. Leaflets must include all the information the reader needs to participate in the advertised event or activity. A contact phone number allows readers to follow up this information. Distribute leaflets as widely as possible.

TRAINING LOG

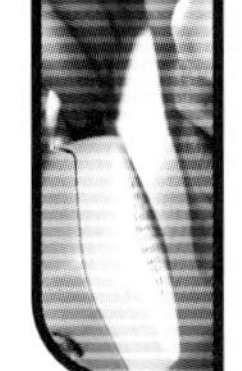

Workplace writing

1. Keep a record for five days of the documents you write.

Type of document	Audience	Length	First draft or edited?

2. Choose one of the letter-writing activities you have completed in this chapter. Revise and edit your draft and publish a professional version suitable for the IT industry. Ask a co-worker, supervisor or friend to evaluate your published version.

3. In most organisations there are a number of policies and protocols related to the use of email. Interview three people working in an IT environment and draw up a list of guidelines for email etiquette.

Action plan

1. Write, edit and send an email to someone in your organisation requesting a meeting about an IT-related matter. Use the meeting organiser facility on your PC, if available. Include the following:
   (a) background information
   (b) reason for the meeting
   (c) location and time
   (d) an attached file with the meeting agenda.
   Use the guidelines on pages 198–200 to help you.

2. Ask the recipient to evaluate your email by completing the following checklist.

I have:	Yes	No	Not sure
decided that an email is the appropriate form for this message	☐	☐	☐
expressed the essence of the message in the subject line	☐	☐	☐
presented the information clearly and concisely	☐	☐	☐
ended by stating the action required	☐	☐	☐
used subheadings, numbering and full stops appropriately	☐	☐	☐
written in active, direct language	☐	☐	☐
set an efficient and friendly tone	☐	☐	☐
allowed sufficient time for replies	☐	☐	☐

CHAPTER 9

WRITING REPORTS

COMPETENCIES

This chapter is linked to elements contained in the following competencies which are in the Information Technology Training Package.

- Create User and Technical Documentation ICAITD128A
- Interact with Clients ICAITS009B
- Develop and Present a Feasibility Report ICAITAD043A
- Record Client Support Requirements ICAITS016B
- Assist with Policy Development for Client Support Procedures ICAITS033B
- Apply Skills in Communications BSX154L407
- Guide Application of Communications Management BSX154L507
- Manage Communications BSX154L608
- Apply Occupational Health and Safety Procedures ICAITU00B

The aim of this chapter is to help you develop the skills to plan your report or submission, organise information from research into a form that can be easily incorporated into a document, analyse information to generate options and solutions, and draft and revise the document.

You will deal with some of the more common questions concerning reports and submissions:

- What is the best approach to gathering information for a report or submission?
- How do you set out the ideas in a report so that they are clear and logical?
- How do you make sure the reader gets the message?
- What techniques help the reader clearly see what has to be done, how and when?
- Is there anything particularly hard about writing technical documents?
- How can graphics be used effectively?
- What is involved in packaging a submission or report so that it looks professional?

TOPICS DISCUSSED

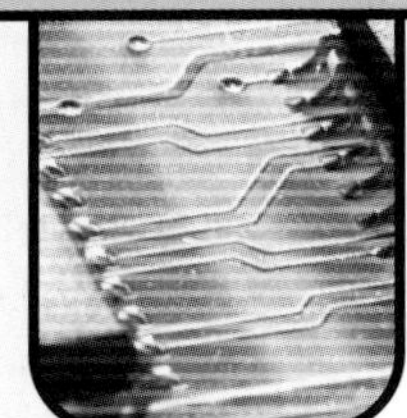

- What is a report?
- Planning the report
- Gathering the data
- Producing an outline
- Organising information
- Writing the report
- Quotations, references and acknowledgments
- Editing the report
- Appendixes
- Condensing a report
- Packaging the report
- Submissions, proposals and feasibility studies
- Technical writing
- Presenting the report to an audience
- Sample report

INTRODUCTION

We all write reports. The range includes:

- progress reports on new developments on both hardware and software
- feasibility reports on implementing new technology and procedures
- proposals or tender documents for provision of user support services
- accident/critical incident reports
- reports on the evaluation of training or implementation of technology
- project management reports
- occupational health and safety policies
- productivity report.

Learning to write effective reports is important because reports are used to share ideas at many levels of an organisation. As well as explaining how to prepare and present a report, this chapter provides formats that will attract positive attention and hold the audience's interest. Examples are given to show how an effective report and presentation should look and sound. Clear reports and presentations minimise misunderstanding and ambiguity, helping to avoid costly mistakes caused by poor communication.

WHAT IS A REPORT?

A report is a presentation containing logically organised information, usually based on an investigation. The information is the basis for analysis and recommendations which may be incorporated in the report. In some cases the report leaves the analysis and recommendations to the reader/s. In any case, the information contained in a report usually points to some action to be taken. The action could be as simple as the decision to do nothing about a situation, or it could be a complex set of recommendations outlining essential changes. Figure 9.1 shows some of the elements involved in producing a report.

Given that reports are often the basis for work-related decisions, it is important that they are presented in a logical and coherent way. This helps people who may have to act on the information in the report to understand the outcomes and the basis for the outcomes. **Even reports written on the most complex subjects must be accessible to people who, although they may understand the technical issues, may not have strong language or literacy skills.**

Reports can be presented in writing, orally, or as a combination of the two, however they are made up of more than words. Today's reports usually include graphs, pictures and other non-verbal material. Videotapes and on-screen computer graphics—anything that helps get meaning through—are often used as well, in the form of appendixes. Some of the skills you will need to develop in order to become effective at presenting reports include the following:

- problem solving
- planning
- researching
- writing in plain English
- speaking
- using audiovisual materials.

Figure 9.1
Producing a report

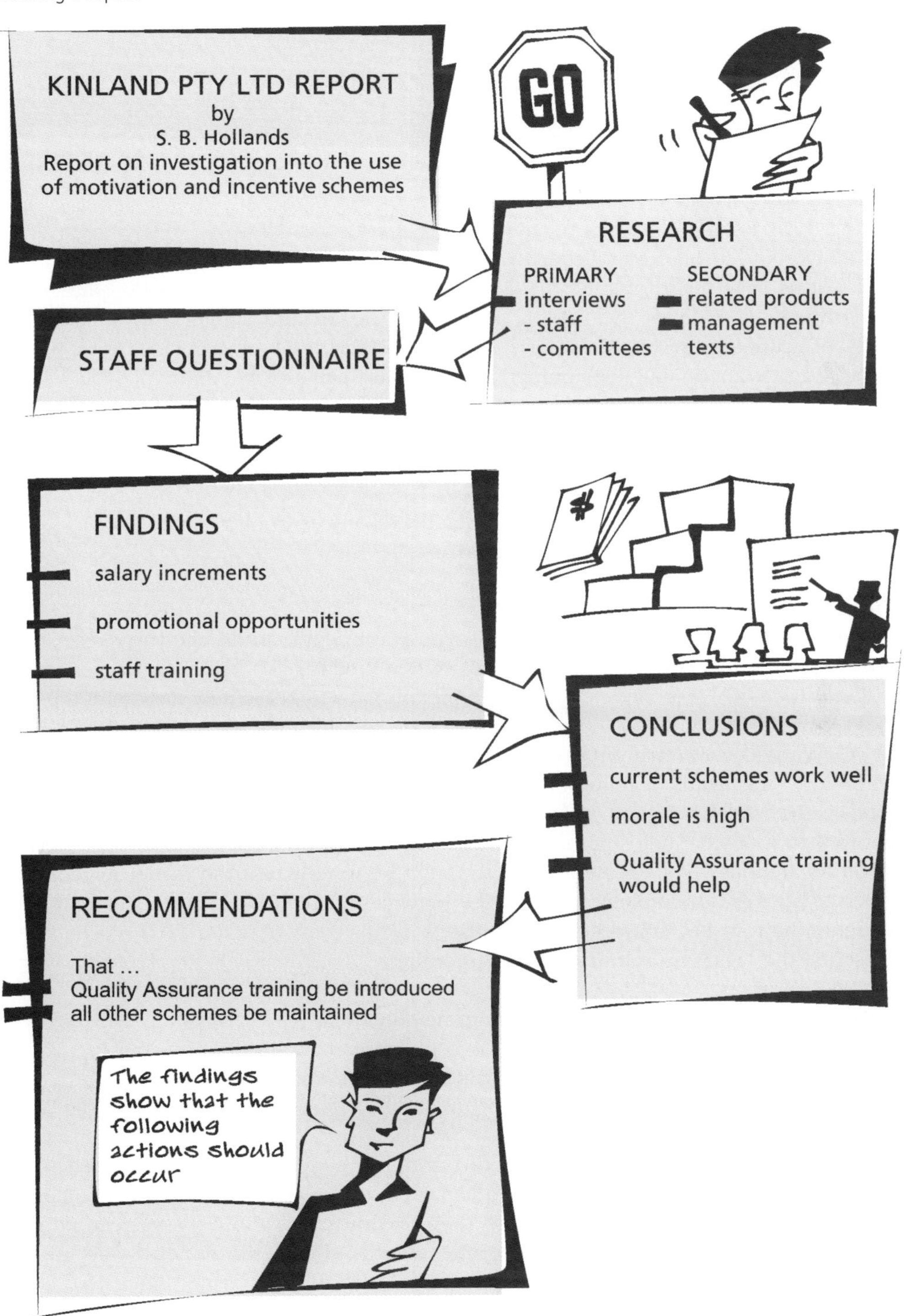

The five stages of writing a report

1. Plan the report.
2. Gather data.
3. Produce an outline.
4. Write the report.
5. Edit, proofread and rewrite the report.

PLANNING THE REPORT

'Planning is a hassle—a waste of time!'
'I don't have time to plan—it's better to just get on and do it!'

Most of us have heard or used these excuses. In reality, planning can be quite simple. Done properly, it reduces the time it takes to do a job and significantly increases the chances of getting the result you want. You can probably think of many examples where a job was done without much planning, but planning can be the difference between an acceptable outcome and exceeding expectations.

What is planning? At its simplest, planning is making sure you are clear about:

- why you are doing this (**the purpose**)
- who you are doing this for (**the audience**)
- how much you can achieve with the time and resources available (**the scope**)
- how you intend to go about it (**the actions**).

The purpose

Why are you writing the report and what do you want people to do after they read it? One way to approach this is to think to yourself: 'When (*the reader*) has read this report, they will (*specify action*)'. To complete this statement you have to know how important the issues addressed by the report are to the readers, and ways in which the report is likely to be used.

If you want to get action on a particular issue or problem, what specific outcomes must you aim for? This means deciding on a *general purpose* and a *specific purpose*. The general purpose is the overall outcome while the specific purpose is a short list of outcomes (usually no more than four) that help sharpen your focus. In a report aimed at improving safety in a computer warehouse, your general purpose might be to convince the reader to reduce the number of hazards and implement safe work practices. Your specific purpose might be to:

- identify the four key sources of accidents
- describe the legal implications of doing nothing
- list the solutions
- recommend a program for implementing the solutions.

You might not need to distinguish the two purposes in a short report, but it is a useful tool when writing long reports or where you are addressing complex issues.

The audience

Who is going to read your report? Is there only one reader? Apart from the person who commissioned the report, other likely readers include those who have to implement the recommendations. Ask yourself how much they already know about the subject, and what their attitude may be towards the report and towards you as the writer. Some might be supportive and interested while others are opposed to your ideas or not interested. Do you have to win the 'opposition' over or can you ignore them?

Approaches to working out what the audience expects include:

- asking them what they expect
- asking for an example of the sort of thing they have been happy with before
- asking others who have had dealings with the audience.

You also need to consider the language and style that will make it easy for the reader to understand your message and accept your conclusions and/or suggestions. Ask yourself the following questions.

- What are their reading skills like? Should I use simple language or can I use more complex language?
- Do the readers have prior knowledge of the situation? Can I leave out a lot of detailed explanation?
- How 'technical' is the audience? Will I need to avoid jargon and/or provide a detailed explanation of terms (e.g. a glossary)?

Knowing the kind of language that suits your readers is as important as getting the facts right. People are not going to take you seriously if they think that you have ignored their needs as readers.

The scope

Which factors will limit how much you can achieve? Apart from time and cost, factors such as the quality of primary and secondary sources of information, how much effort the reader is likely to put into reading the report (let alone implement its recommendations), and your degree of expertise, will have an impact on the outcome.

If there is not enough time to do primary research, how can you make sure the data you include will withstand critical scrutiny? A survey or questionnaire may be the best way to get accurate information, but it is not worth doing if you do not have the resources to do it properly.

You need to list the factors that are likely to limit the scope of the report and then decide how significant they are. Some you simply have to live with. Others, such as time frames, finances and human resources, may have such a marked impact that you will need to address them.

The actions

When should you stop collecting information and start analysing it? How much time can you then spend writing? For a straightforward report, it might be enough to set aside a day to write. For most reports, though, this is not an option, so you need to produce a timetable. Now most of us are not good at this sort of thing so we tend to avoid it, which is why many reports never fully achieve their aims. At least make a note of the milestones, as in Table 9.1.

Table 9.1
Make a note of the milestones

What	By when
Finish collecting information	23 June
Complete the outline	30 June
Feedback from Marie	4 July
Finish first draft	12 July
Feedback from Marie	14 July
Finish report	21 July

Do not fall into the trap of drawing up your plan and then forgetting about it as you go off and start gathering information. Use the plan to keep your work focused, to help make the best use of your time. Sit down with the plan and draw up a list of issues and ideas relevant to the purpose of your report. Next to each issue make a list of types and sources of information that will help achieve the report's purpose.

Table 9.2
Factors to consider when planning your report

Purpose of the report (Purpose)	Is the aim to inform or convince? A report that needs to *convince* its readers needs more supporting information than one aimed simply at presenting facts about a situation.
Nature of the problem being addressed (Scope)	Complex problems such as those involving significant financial risk or issues of public safety may require more data than, say, a report on car-parking facilities.
Amount of time available (Scope)	If time is limited, then you need to think about priorities (i.e. how much time to spend gathering new information already available).
Anticipated opposition to the report (Audience)	If you believe that the report will come under critical scrutiny, it may be necessary to support your case with more information/evidence than if you believe it will be well accepted.
How important the report is to you (Planning)	You need to decide whether or not you will use the report as an example of how well you do your job. A report that you use to show-case your skills will obviously need to be well planned and researched.

Table 9.3
Timetable for a well-planned report

Stage	Activity	Expected completion date
Investigation and research	Study history of problem	10/03/02
	Begin interviews	17/03/02
	Draw up questionnaire	04/04/02
	Distribute questionnaire	14/04/02
Analysing results	Collect answers	27/04/02
	Analyse results	10/05/02
Planning the report	Write ideas down first	
	Produce the outline	22/05/02
Writing	Complete all sections	01/06/02
Improving	Rewrite (final draft)	19/06/02
Editing	Edit, proofread	29/06/02
	Prepare index, contents page, etc.	04/07/02
	Safety margin (two weeks to go to annual meeting)	
	Printing, binding, etc.	11/07/02
Presenting report	Board's monthly meeting	19/07/02

Make a list to ensure you have addressed all the issues. Record the issue and the source of information for each issue. Take care at this stage—too much information can be as bad as too little, because too much information makes it hard to know where to start or what to leave in and what to leave out. Once you have decided how to go about this task, the next step is to start gathering information (i.e. researching, interviewing, observing, etc.).

GATHERING THE DATA

Sometimes you will have all the information needed to write your report, but in most cases you will have to gather it from a range of sources.

Researching

The purpose of research is to extend both your knowledge and your viewpoint. Most projects you work on will be related to issues you already know something about; however, what you know may represent only one view. Your final presentation needs to cover the whole picture.

Most investigations involve research of both primary and secondary sources, so part of the initial planning for any project is to decide on the proportion of your work that will be given to each.

Primary sources

If you have access to facts, figures and photographs, the report should be easier to write and have a better chance of gaining agreement. Data based on actual tests or measurements or on personal observations that you know are reliable will enable you to write more directly and concisely. You need to carefully record your sources of primary data. You may be asked 'Who said that?' or 'Where did you get that from?'. You have to be able to respond accurately and list the sources in the bibliography.

There are many advantages in using facts you uncover yourself. The data that you count, measure or observe yourself is relevant to the local situation. It may also be more up-to-date than published research. On the other hand, investigation of primary sources may take more time and may be costly in comparison with using information in secondary sources such as books, journals and computer databases. Sources of this information include the following.

Direct observation

For example, if you are researching a problem in meeting deadlines, go and look at conditions in the section involved. Weigh up what you see and compare it with data obtained from other sources.

Interviews

Face-to-face interviews can produce essential facts, but even if they fail to uncover the data you were looking for they play a vital part in adding to your understanding of the topic. Information obtained in this way is not always reliable, but it can provide clues. What is unsaid may be more significant than the words you hear. Interviews can be quite informal—just talking with colleagues and other employees—or can follow a structured format.

The effectiveness of interviews as a source of data can be improved if you follow these suggestions.

Talk to people who disagree with you

Their points of view will add balance and depth to your study. A short interview with people who have recently left a firm may reveal information that current employees may not be so ready to share.

Talk to experts

If your research involves front-line issues, particularly 'people problems', some of the most useful information can come from individuals who are familiar with the issue at the hands-on level. Talk to your own front-line operators—sales staff, trainers, delivery drivers, switch operators and repair technicians—all those who spend their time dealing directly with customers and clients. Also consult associates who have recently dealt with similar issues and have up-to-date information from their front lines.

Ask interviewees

Ask interviewees: 'Is there anyone else you can suggest who could help me?'. While the people you are speaking to may all hold similar views, someone else might have vital bits of information you could miss.

Follow up clues or leads

Plan your questions in advance to give you control of the discussion, but tune in to any new or unexpected topics that are mentioned during the interview.

Use the telephone

Telephone interviews allow you to talk to people who you cannot meet personally. As long as you are friendly and informal, and explain what you are looking for, people are usually willing to give information over the phone.

Surveys and questionnaires

These must be well planned. A lot of inaccurate information is worse than none at all. Decide whether you are seeking facts or opinions, and do not mix the two in the same survey. Make sure you have a balanced sample by distributing the survey among a range of people representing the target population. If a college has 1000 full-time students attending on weekdays, 400 part-time students attending at night and another 100 on Saturdays and Sundays, all these groups must be covered in roughly the same proportion in a survey about student access to the internet. When surveying for factual data you can find out, for instance, what proportion of people use the internet, what kind of information they are looking for, how many hours per week they use the internet, and what sites they visit.

Questionnaires need to be carefully prepared to avoid leading questions (i.e. not phrased so that the questions tend to suggest answers). Here are some general guidelines for designing surveys.

Use short, simple statements that cannot be misunderstood

Decide whether you will get more accurate answers by asking people to tick boxes ('Yes', 'No', 'Not sure') or to mark a position on a line with contrasting words at each end.

The computers in the library are fast enough to meet the demands of the internet.

agree	7	6	5	4	3	2	1	disagree

The linear scale discourages inaccurate mid-point responses suggested by words such as 'undecided' in a verbal scale. Few people want to say they are uncertain, nor is uncertainty necessarily located in the middle of the scale.

Keep the number of questions to a minimum

The easier it is for people to answer a questionnaire, the more likely they are to cooperate.

Avoid open-ended questions

Instead, provide a number of alternatives covering a range of possible answers. Questions requiring long, written answers can be hard to interpret.

Always have a trial run

Field-testing of your draft questionnaire is vital before you launch the main survey. Use a small sample group to make sure your questions are clear and that the words do not convey double meanings.

Surveys must be voluntary

Explain to respondents how cooperation may benefit them personally. For example, if you are seeking data on the work habits of employees, point out the use of such information for research into workplace accident patterns.

Use survey data carefully

You need to be careful that the design of the survey does not distort the information you gain. For example, someone may make the statement that 'sixty-six per cent of answers indicate agreement with our present policies. That means two out of every three members want the rules left the way they are'. The speaker is probably misinterpreting the results. What happened was that two of every three of the people who replied ticked a 'yes' box beside a particular question. Ticking a box does not tell you how strongly people agree or whether they might have made other suggestions if asked additional questions. It tells you nothing about the views of people who did not reply. Even if everybody who replies says 'yes', this does not prove the rules are sound.

At best, surveys can provide a useful guide to trends or general viewpoints. Never treat figures or percentages from such a survey as though they represent factual data. Surveys need to be supported by additional data or analysis before you can be confident of the conclusions that you draw. Possible survey sample groups include:

- **Commercial and industrial sources.** People who sell and service a product will naturally be biased in the advice they offer about it, but this does not mean that they cannot give valuable information. For a start, they can tell you about faults in opposition products. Service technicians can supply facts about the technology behind their products that sales staff often do not want to discuss, and they appreciate being asked.

- **Industry-based organisations.** Most industries have one or more associations or federations that collect data on the industry concerned. They are usually happy to share this with interested students. As long as you weigh advice from these sources more carefully than that from independent experts, the data can be extremely valuable.
- **Community groups.** If you, as a student, are looking for a topic for a thesis or project, community bodies offer a fruitful area because most organisations like to be involved in studies by educational institutions.

Secondary sources

Quoting expert data that reinforces your own case is an excellent aid to persuasion, and there are many possible sources.

Past reports and projects

There may be past records of surveys similar to yours, or a project or thesis on the same topic. There may also be reports or general files at work dealing with similar topics, so check with your records section as the incidence of the problem you are investigating may be traced back over some time.

Networks and organisations

Many other sources of information are worth looking into. If your study is concerned with political or social issues, such as access to computers, there will be a number of special-interest organisations who can put you in touch with up-to-date material, including research already completed.

Often there is an information network already in existence on the subject, with its own library or computer database, and because these groups rely on public support they are usually happy to share their data and publications.

Library resources

Libraries are naturally among the richest of all sources of secondary material, including the following:

- printed material—books, journals, articles, magazines, technical reports
- audiovisual and graphic media—videotapes, tape recordings, films, slides and photographs, drawings and sketches
- computerised databanks in which you use key words to call up the precise data you want
- general reference books—encyclopaedias, atlases, yearbooks, directories and back copies of newspapers
- citation lists, abstracts and bibliographies.

A major advantage of library research is that the information is already sorted and indexed. However, in using libraries look for more than just facts and figures. Discover opinions expressed and conclusions drawn by those who are authorities in their fields.

Other sources of secondary data you could consider include:

- **conferences or seminars**
- **government departments**
- **personal contacts**
- **competitors.**

Using statistics

Statistics can give powerful support to your case, but like any data, they need to be used properly. Statistical measurements must be valid and appropriate, and the results must be interpreted correctly. Use statistics from reputable sources such as the Australian Bureau of Statistics (ABS) or an organisation's specialised internal statistics unit. If you have to use a particular test regularly, find out all you can about it. Get a good book on the method involved and keep it handy.

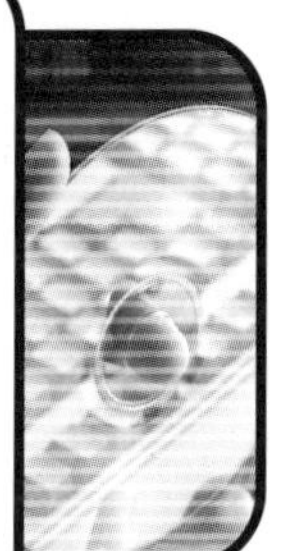

Case study 9.1

Communication technology at JoMat

Paul works for JoMat, a wholesaler of computer hardware. Sales representatives in each capital city generate eighty per cent of sales. The balance of sales come through responses to advertisements in trade magazines.

For some time now, Alicia, the managing director, has been concerned about the impact of ecommerce on the way the company does business. She is aware that many companies have spent a great deal of time and money setting up websites without seeing any real return on their investment.

Although Alicia believes that ecommerce is an important part of business, she also understands that it must be managed carefully.

Paul has been asked to prepare a report on the costs and benefits of selling computer hardware on the internet.

Case study activities

1. What will be the purpose of the report?
2. Who will be the main audience?
3. What will influence the scope of the report?
4. What are some of the issues that the report will have to address?
5. How should Paul research the report? What kinds of research would be relevant?
6. What kind of data should Paul collect?
7. What are some of the primary sources of data?
8. Where would Paul look for secondary sources of data?
9. What kind of reaction or resistance is Paul likely to encounter when he does his research? How can he overcome this?

PRODUCING AN OUTLINE

Once you have gathered your data, have another look at your purpose and audience, and decide on the report structure that will help you achieve your goal. One way that will help you organise your ideas into a logical sequence and help make sure all important points are covered is to use an *outline*. This section looks at how using an outline can help you organise your ideas, set out the information and prepare headings and numbering for a report.

Setting out the report

Although the number of divisions in any report and the names for them vary, there are some that are common to most reports. These include the following.

Introduction

The introduction establishes a credible relationship between writer and reader; it explains the purpose and scope of the report. Here you answer questions such as 'What is this about?' and 'Why should I read this?'. Use this section to map the path you plan to follow in the report.

Findings or results

This is objective information; it gives the facts, as a basis for later discussion. Tell the reader what you found. No discussion or interpretation is included here, just the results of your investigation.

Analysis or discussion

This section builds agreement through logical reasoning and rational argument. It points the reader towards the action proposed at the end of the report, explains what recommendations will be made and why they are necessary, and 'paints a picture' of the expected outcome. The reader wants to know what all the facts you have gathered mean. Discuss what the information means in terms of the problem the report is addressing. What are the implications of the data? What are the options?

Recommendations

This is the action ending. The recommendations set out exactly what has to be done, and the report ends with a request for approval or a proposed specific course of action. Each recommendation describes what has to be done, by whom and by when. There are no new ideas or discussions in this section.

Summary/executive summary

As its name suggests, this is a summary of the whole report. It comprises a brief introduction, the main findings or results, a summary of the analysis, and the key recommendations. The reader can, at a glance, see what is in each section of the report. Although written last, the summary/executive summary is not part of the report. It appears as a separate section at the front of the report after the contents pages.

There will, of course, be more sections than this in many reports. A twelve-page document might need eight or nine such divisions, each of which needs a heading; you will then have many different headings, as shown in the sample report on pages 252–7.

Wherever possible, give each section a clear, descriptive heading that tells the reader something about what they will find. Terms like 'Findings' or 'Analysis', although accurate, are not all that helpful. Headings such as 'Safety conditions in warehouse' give the reader a much clearer guide to the structure of the report and make referring to it easier.

For each section of the outline, summarise the main points or ideas. This helps you see whether there are any glaring gaps in your data or ideas. Decide on heading names and numbering (they can always be changed when you write up the report in full).

Subsections

The major sections are further divided as writing progresses. Each subsection should be identified with its own numbered subheading. Here is an example of an introduction divided into four subsections:

1   INTRODUCTION
1.1 Aim
1.2 Authorisation
1.3 Sources of information
1.4 Overview and historical background

The findings section could be divided into three subsections as follows:

2   PRESENT SITUATION IN THE MARKETING DEPARTMENT
2.1 Data from observations
2.2 Interviews with staff
2.3 Research data

Advantages of subdividing

Dividing a report into smaller units breaks the content into more easily understood packages. As long as they flow smoothly from one to the next, the overall effect is to create a sense of logic and clear thinking, which encourages agreement.

Some subsections may need to be split even further. This is no problem as long as you arrange them so that one part complements the next and together they give a balanced picture of the topic.

Create a logical sequence

Aim for a step-by-step sequence of ideas that will have meaning for the reader as well as for yourself. Group similar topics together. In reports it is also essential to separate material with differing levels of objectivity.

Keep facts and opinions apart

It makes sense to use the findings section for facts and the analysis section for opinions and proposals. Readers need to be able to clearly distinguish proposed future action from description of past events. Use plenty of headings and subheadings to indicate each change of direction.

Organise report topics

Table 9.4 will help you to organise topics into appropriate sections according to their type.
- Column 1 lists the different aims for each set of headings, using the RIPPA formula as a key (see Chapter 7).
- Column 2 lists 'sample' (not standard) headings suggested for a typical business report on a problem situation.
- The questions in column 3 help you decide where each topic or type of information can best be used.

Table 9.4
Organising report topics

Sequence	Report headings	Questions
R Helps to establish a good businesslike relationship	1 Introduction 1.1 Aim 1.2 Authorisation 1.3 Sources of information	What is this about? What is the aim of the report? Who asked you to write it? Where did you get the facts?
I Information, facts, data, what did you find?	2 Findings 2.1 Problem 2.2 Causes 2.3 Effects	Has your investigation clarified the problem? Is the information valid? If so, is this the kind of material that should go into the findings?
P Opinions, explanation, logical reasoning, point-by-point persuasion	3 Analysis 3.1 Reasons a change is needed	Is this material part of a reasoned argument that is intended to persuade the reader or support the aim of the report?
P Paint picture of solution	3.2 Options 3.3 Advantages and disadvantages of each option 3.4 Best option	Does it lead to a proposal for a specific course of action?
A Step-by-step set of proposals for action	4 Recommendations 4.1 That all new staff have … 4.2 That the changeover date … Writer's signature	Is each recommendation supported by the facts and analysis? Does it clearly identify the action that has to be taken? Do not include any reasons or discussion in this section. The name and signature of whoever is responsible for the recommendation should appear at the end of the report.

Source: © Downs Holdings Pty Ltd.

ORGANISING INFORMATION

To be persuasive, your information must be well organised. The sequence of your argument must be apparent to your readers. The main rules for organising ideas are the following.

1. Group similar topics together: 'Five similar problems have been observed with this type of software. They are …'.

2. Keep topics of different kinds apart: 'The advantages of leasing are listed here. Disadvantages are discussed on page 5'.

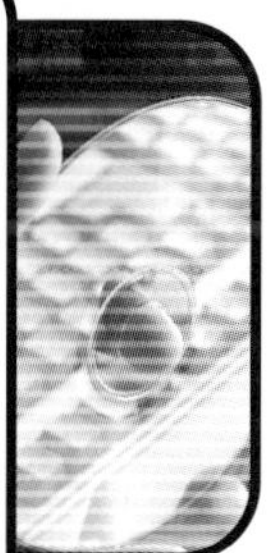

Case study 9.2

Dr Cureall

Dr Cureall, a representative of a large local medical practice, has spoken to you and asked your company to prepare a feasibility report on the use of voice recognition software. Dr Cureall would like to be able to dictate reports, letters and add to a patient's file notes using voice recognition software. He has asked you to research current programs and estimate the practicability and cost of using this system. Dr Cureall has a basic working knowledge of PCs, but little or no familiarity with the technology behind voice recognition software, its limitations, or the various products on the market.

Case study activities

Prepare an outline for the report requested by Dr Cureall including possible headings and sections.

3. Follow familiar sequences where possible: 'The problem will be discussed in two sections: Part A deals with actual issues both past and present; Part B deals with possible future effects'.

Sequences for headings and subheadings

Different sequences suit different topics. Some useful arrangements are shown here, although there are many others. The simplest are often the best.

Order of time

This is used in any discussion related to the clock, calendar or time sheet. For example:

    2.1   Installation of new machines
    2.2   Testing system in use
    2.3   Disposal of old machines

Order of location

A study of future markets for a product might look at the potential for sales in the city first, then in the country and then overseas.

Order of importance or rank

It is logical to list ideas in order of ascending or descending importance. For example:

    2.1   Discussions with manager
    2.2   Discussions with sales staff
    2.3   Discussions with drivers

Order of familiarity

Tell people first about familiar aspects of a situation before introducing new or unfamiliar topics.

Contrasting pairs

Understanding of a topic is increased when writers contrast opposite ideas. For example:

3.1   Features of old network system
3.2   Features of new network system

Other examples of pairing include question and answer, before and after, and cause and effect.

Parallel order

There is usually more than one way of dividing a set of ideas. For instance, if you are investigating which of two different models should be purchased, it might at first seem a good idea to set out your findings this way:

2   RESULTS OF COMPARISONS AND TESTING
2.1   Software A
2.1.1   Cost of purchase and running
2.1.2   Compatibility and limitations
2.1.3   Reliability
2.2   Software B
2.2.1   Cost of purchase and running
2.2.2   Compatibility and limitations
2.2.3   Reliability

Is this the most useful way of presenting the facts? Anyone who wants to compare costs has to move from 2.1 to 2.2 to find the difference in price for brands A and B. Depending on the purpose of the submission, the arrangement below may be more effective.

2   RESULTS OF COMPARISONS AND TESTING
2.1   Cost of purchase and running
      Brand A
      Brand B
2.2   Reliability and accuracy
      Brand A
      Brand B
2.3   Maintenance and repairs
      Brand A
      Brand B

Numbering the headings

The numbers to the left of the heading work in much the same way as the distance marks on a road map, telling readers where they are in the report or indicating the location of important items. **Numbering needs to follow a clear, straightforward system.**

The metric or decimal style uses numbers separated by decimal points. It is much clearer and easier to use than traditional letter–number systems, particularly if you want to renumber paragraphs. An example of decimal numbering and bullet points in a report is given in Figure 9.2.

The levels of numbering will be influenced by the length of the report. A short report will probably only need two levels of numbering. Too much numbering does not serve any useful purpose and tends to clutter the report.

Activity 9.1

Producing an outline

Look back at Case study 9.1, 'Communication technology at JoMat'.
1. List the main headings Paul might use.
2. What are the key points that should be addressed?
3. List four different items that should be included in the report title.
4. Produce a brief outline for the report Paul would write.

Working on this task with someone else or in a group will make it easier to come up with ideas for what will be in the report. Remember, the purpose of this activity is to practise producing an outline, not writing the definitive report.

Figure 9.2
Example report with decimal numbering and bullet points

1 Sources of information
1.1 Secondary sources

Libraries are naturally among the richest of all sources of secondary material, including:
* print media—books, journals, articles, magazines, technical reports and so on
* audiovisual and graphic media—videotapes, tape recordings, films, slides and photographs, drawings and sketches
* computerised databanks—in which you use keywords to call up the precise data you want
* general reference books—encyclopaedias, atlases, yearbooks, bibliographies, directories, and back copies of newspapers.

A major advantage of library research is that the information is already sorted and indexed. However, in using libraries, look for more than just facts and figures. Discover opinions expressed and conclusions drawn by those who are authorities in their fields.

1.2 Primary sources

* Community groups. If you are looking for a topic for a study thesis or project, community bodies offer a fruitful area because most organisations like to be involved in studies by education institutions. Some even offer financial support.
* Conferences or seminars. Meetings of any kind conducted by any special interest group or organisation are a source of alternative viewpoints and the latest research findings in your area of investigation.
* Government departments. If there is a government department that deals with the topic you are researching, contact the departmental public relations office responsible for study material.

WRITING THE REPORT

Now it is time for you to take the ideas, data and structure developed in your outline, and tell your reader what they need to know. The basic elements of the report structure were developed in the outline section; this section looks at the components of a report in more detail. **If you have trouble getting started, concentrate on ideas rather than on words.** Do not try to write the whole report at one time. Write a rough draft, look over it, consider the main ideas, and then decide how they need to be organised.

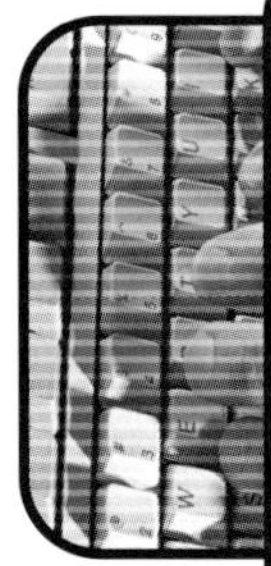

Checklist 9.1

The written report

Use this checklist as a guide when writing the report and as a final check when you have completed the report. It is useful to give your report to someone else when you have finished and ask them to check the document using the checklist.

	Yes	No	Not sure
Prescribed sections of the report are included.	☐	☐	☐
Presentation of the report:			
• is neatly and clearly set out	☐	☐	☐
• is free of error and suitably bound	☐	☐	☐
• uses appropriate conventions.	☐	☐	☐
Information from an investigation relevant to the report is included.	☐	☐	☐
General and specific purposes of the report are clear from the content.	☐	☐	☐
Introduction identifies the reader, purpose and scope of the report.	☐	☐	☐
The summary/executive summary is a complete précis of the report.	☐	☐	☐
Recommendations:			
• are logical and follow from the facts presented	☐	☐	☐
and the conclusions:			
• are brief and specify action to be taken	☐	☐	☐
• specify who is to implement them	☐	☐	☐
• specify timeframe.	☐	☐	☐
Words and style used are appropriate to the readership.	☐	☐	☐
Body contains factual information and the facts support the statements that are made.	☐	☐	☐
Facts explain the recommendations to be made and the reasons for recommendations.	☐	☐	☐
Conclusion (discussion) summarises the facts and points to the future.	☐	☐	☐
Charts, diagrams or photographs are included.	☐	☐	☐
Information from additional sources has been included.	☐	☐	☐
Appendixes are directly referred to and supplement the report.	☐	☐	☐
Bibliography is relevant.	☐	☐	☐

The introduction

The introduction also helps to establish a positive, professional reader–writer relationship, which encourages trust and confidence in the writer. Readers need to know why it is important for them to read the report and take its findings seriously.

Guidelines for writing the introduction

- Help the reader; anticipate questions like, 'On whose instructions did you write the report?' and 'What were those instructions?', and answer them as part of your introduction.
- Explain the purpose of the report in one short sentence (aim).
- State who asked you to write the report, the date you were asked, and any conditions or terms of reference. If the request is on record as a memo or a letter, mention this (authorisation).
- Identify your main sources of information—meetings, interviews, personal observations, and particularly the methods used to obtain figures or accounting data. Reassure readers that the report is genuine, and the result of thorough investigation. Readers like to know:
  —what kind of facts will be presented and how reliable they are
  —how they were obtained (careful research, detailed interviews or guesswork)
  —whether the views expressed are expert opinions or just the writer's ideas.

This may require a fourth heading in the introduction: 'Method of investigation'. If so, just give a brief summary. The details belong with the facts in the body of the report.

The introduction also provides a map or guide to how the report is set out. In the case of the report for Dr Cureall (Case study 9.2) on costs and benefits of introducing voice recognition the introduction may be:

This report investigates four of the leading voice recognition applications to determine whether this technology has become a practical option for use in a medical practice and to determine which application is the best choice.

Findings—results of investigation

Clear, specific information helps readers to engage with what you say. Use examples to illustrate important points.

- Important data should be stated in kilometres, kilograms or similar measures rather than words that mean different things to different people.
- If you cannot produce figures, use precise descriptive words.
- If lengthy statistical data, complex specifications and so on threaten to overfill the findings (or if any numerical tables run to more than half a page), summarise the data in that section and include the full item as an appendix.
- Give sources of important findings. If experts supplied factual information, do not just say 'experts suggest ...'—identify them: give names, technical qualifications, and where they can be contacted. If quoting from audited accounts, name the auditor and the audit date.
- If your information was obtained by personal observation, say so. If test equipment was used, describe it. List statistical tests used to verify data.
- If you can, it is better to show than to tell. Use photographs. Illustrations make a page more interesting and facts more credible. Use graphs, tables and diagrams. If important evidence is contained in specific documents, certified photocopies are more reassuring than quoted contents.

- Set the information out in a clear and logical sequence. For instance, your main findings could be either in chronological order or grouped by function or features, according to the topic.

  Do not comment on or make judgments about any *findings* in this section.

  Figure 9.3 is an example of findings that could be used in the Dr Cureall scenario.

Figure 9.3
Example of findings to be used in a report

Requirements for the purchase of voice recognition software

After discussion with the staff, the following conditions were established:

- Continuous speech recognition software is preferred, rather than the slower, more unnatural discrete speech recognition software.
- The application must run on a Pentium-powered PC with Windows NT and be able integrate with Office 2000.
- The software program must be compatible with all the current computers.
- The program must be one that can be learned and customised reasonably quickly by nearly anyone in the office.
- The cost limit is $2500.

Points of comparison

The different voice recognition software programs compared are Dragon Systems' NaturallySpeaking 5.0 Preferred Edition, L&H Voice Xpress Plus, IBM ViaVoice 98 Executive and Philips FreeSpeech 98.

Eight categories of comparison will be made in order to effectively evaluate these competing programs.

1. Accuracy.
2. Minimum system requirements.
3. Capacity to manage a specialised medical vocabulary and medical records.
4. Integration with Microsoft Word.
5. Ease and speed of installation, customisation and use.
6. Industry ratings and awards.
7. Inclusion of microphones.
8. Cost.

Accuracy. Accuracy is the single most significant consideration. Without it, the program is useless.

Table 1
Comparison of accuracy

Software	Average accuracy expressed as a percentage
Dragon	91
L&H	87
IBM	85
Philips	80

At first glance, these percentages, particularly the top two, may not seem significantly different. Consider, however, that for every 1000 words, an accuracy rate of 87 per cent means that 130 words must be corrected. An accuracy rate of 91 per cent represents an average of 90 errors per 1000 words, while an 80 per cent rate means that 200 out of every 1000 words must be corrected.

Minimum system requirements. All four programs run on Pentium-powered PCs utilising Microsoft Windows NT 4.0, and require 16-bit SoundBlaster-compatible sound cards. Random access memory (RAM) requirements for software run under Windows NT are higher for all of these programs.

Table 2

Comparison of minimum system requirements

Software	CPU	RAM	Hard disk space	L2 cache
Dragon	Pentium 300 MHz	32 MB	180 MB	none
L&H	Pentium 500 MHz	40 MB	130 MB	none
IBM	Pentium 500 MHz	32 MB	180 MB	256 KB
Philips	Pentium 500 MHz	32 MB	150 MB	none

It is important to recall that significantly greater system resources are recommended to optimise performance. Given the sufficient system resources, none of these software programs should present a problem for the existing system.

Capacity to manage a customisable, specialised medical vocabulary. Medicine in general, and each medical specialty in particular, have their own complex, specialised vocabularies.

- Dragon Systems NaturallySpeaking offers a so-called Medical Suite targeted to medical professionals and specified as an alternative to transcription. Marketing materials state that an extensive vocabulary of thousands of words, including medical procedures, terms, drugs, diagnoses and symptoms, are included. The software allows creation of multiple vocabularies for specialty customisation if desired.
- IBM offers add-on VoiceType Vocabularies for use with ViaVoice. The medical vocabularies available are for Emergency Medicine Dictation and Radiology Dictation. No other specialty customisation is available.
- L&H Voice Xpress and Philips FreeSpeech 98 do not offer medical vocabularies, either as add-ons or bundled with the software.

Integration with Microsoft Word. All four programs integrate with Microsoft Word and can, therefore, be used with existing word processing software.

Ease and speed of installation, customisation and use. Each of the four programs use 'wizards' to install and configure hardware, and all programs support macros for frequently used phrases.

- Dragon Systems' NaturallySpeaking uses its wizard to train the system to recognise the user's voice within 4 minutes. Material is provided so that about 30 minutes of reading aloud will improve accuracy. Electronic medical documents can be analysed automatically to 'learn' new specialised terms and proper names. Its CommandWizard feature enables any user to create medical-specialty macros. Commonly used and required medical forms, electronically stored, can be readily called up and the user is prompted to fill out each section of a form.

- IBM's ViaVoice also trains the system by means of reading from selected texts for about 30 minutes, and its wizard adjusts microphone and speaker volume levels.
- L&H Voice Xpress Plus directs the user to read chapters of a book, and in *PC Magazine*'s tests, about 75 minutes was required for the process.
- Philips FreeSpeech 98 directs the user to read selected text for about 15 minutes; ten training topics are available for the user's review.

Industry ratings and awards. Only one of these products refers to and lists awards on its web site, and that is Dragon Systems' NaturallySpeaking. None of the other three products has any such mention anywhere on its site, nor do any awards or industry recognition show up on multiple web searches for the products.

Inclusion of microphones. As previously noted, a microphone is necessary for capture of spoken words.
- Dragon Systems ships with a VXI Parrott 10-3 microphone.
- IBM's ViaVoice and L&H Voice Xpress Plus both provide an Andrea NC-80 microphone.
- Philips FreeSpeech 98 does not include a microphone; it recommends its own SpeechMike at an extra cost of $69.95.

Cost. Highly significant price differences exist among these programs.
- The Dragon Systems' NaturallySpeaking $379 when purchased directly from Dragon or through resellers. NaturallySpeaking Medical Suite is available for $1595. An Add-On Medical Specialty Vocabulary is $49. One year of 1800-number telephone support for all products is an additional $199, for a total cost of $2,043, exclusive of tax and shipping costs, for the Medical Suite.
- IBM's ViaVoice Executive software program costs $450, and the medical specialty add-ons are $540. However, these add-ons are for emergency medicine and radiology only.
- L&H Voice Xpress Plus is $270.
- Philips Free Speech 98 costs $139 and includes no microphone. A Philips SpeechMike can be ordered for $69.95, for a total cost of $208.95, exclusive of tax and shipping costs.

Analysis or discussion

This section explains why action should be taken, what the options are, what decisions are proposed and why readers should support specific actions (recommendations). In formal or academic reports this section is often titled 'Conclusions'; in business reports 'Analysis' or 'Discussion' is a more appropriate heading.

Begin with a 'where we are now' statement

Summarise important points from the findings and highlight the present position.

Make a logical analysis of the facts

Discuss how facts, findings and expert opinions should be interpreted. This requires a mixture of both logical and persuasive writing.

Identify options where appropriate

Show the reader you have considered more than one credible path. Explain why you are excluding options.

Discuss options

Use sound, logical argument to steer readers towards a specific action. Explain the reasons behind each option.

Give predicted results

Include details such as the estimated cost of implementing the options.

Have confidence in your position as an 'expert'

Your own opinions are important. The more time you spend investigating, collecting evidence and talking to people, the more qualified you are to offer specialist views.

Argue your case

Although a report should be written objectively, it is reasonable to put a powerful argument that 'steers' the reader towards agreement, as the following example illustrates:

Need for immediate approval

If the new system can be installed and fully operative before the end of the financial year, it is predicted that savings in administration time alone should pay for the cost of installation.

The summary

The summary is one of the most important sections of a report. It is used to:

- decide whether the report is relevant to the reader and therefore needs to be read (save time)
- help managers decide who should deal with the report (manage resources)
- provide an overview of the content, making the report easier to read (improve comprehension)
- highlight the most important features of the report (maximise impact)
- help people looking through a large number of reports for a specific piece of information (improve efficiency/save time).

More people read a summary because it takes less time to read than the report. As well as highlighting important ideas, it helps to create interest. **An effective summary should arouse sufficient interest for a reader to want to find out more about the topic.** They may even want to read the full-length report from which your summary was condensed.

For these reasons, a summary should be complete. This means it should contain the key facts, analysis and recommendations. Each major section should be summarised, including the introduction. Figure 9.4 is an example of a summary from Dr Cureall (Case study 9.2).

Where should you put the summary—at the front or back of a report? Given that the summary is usually the first (if not only, for some) part read, it is best to place it at the front of the report, immediately after the contents page.

Figure 9.4
Example of a summary from a report

Summary
Accurate and complete records are crucial to staff and patients of a medical practice. This report examines the use of voice recognition software as a means of recording important medical information.

To date, the weakest link in voice recognition technology has been accuracy. This is fast changing, and current software programs have improved. The conclusions were:
1. Four products were evaluated with Dragon Systems' NaturallySpeaking Medical Suite outperforming the three alternative programs.
2. All programs specify system requirements that are well within the specifications of the existing computing systems of the practice.
3. All programs integrate with the existing word processing software, Microsoft Office 2000.
4. Dragon Systems' NaturallySpeaking Medical Suite is by far the most expensive voice recognition program at $2043, including one year of technical support.
5. Dragon Systems' NaturallySpeaking Medical Suite with Add-On Vocabularies can be customised to specific needs of different practices for specialised medical vocabulary and medical forms.
6. Dragon Systems' NaturallySpeaking technology is the most accurate of the four programs tested.
7. Although Dragon Systems' NaturallySpeaking is the most expensive, it offers the best function while the other options considered are barely adequate.
8. The best choice of the four applications considered is Dragon Systems' NaturallySpeaking.

Using graphics

Any visual item or any non-verbal material that helps understanding can be termed 'graphic'. Graphs and drawings add appeal to any written or printed page: people will understand more, and will be motivated to keep on reading. Chapter 10 has detailed guidelines on how to produce graphics for your documents.

The following guidelines will help you make effective use of graphics in reports:
- Keep the graphics as simple as possible.
- Provide clear, descriptive headings and a brief explanation with each graphic.
- Include a brief interpretation of data with each graph or chart.
- Keep the graphic as close as possible to the text to which it relates.

Recommendations

Recommendations are a recipe for action. The analysis/discussion identifies what should happen in general terms. Recommendations tell readers exactly what, when and how action needs to be taken. The less room there is for doubt, the more confident busy readers will feel about accepting your recommendations.

You are the one who has researched and prepared the report, so you should be in a position to offer the reader complete details of what has to be done to implement the recommendations. This does not mean they have to be longwinded, just complete. Each recommendation should, where practicable, answer four questions.

1. What has to be done? Describe the action that follows from your analysis and conclusions. Use active language, starting each recommendation wherever possible with clear direction as to what has to be done.
2. Who should do it? In many cases we take it for granted that the reader is going to implement the recommendations. What you should do, wherever possible, is to give an indication of the person most likely to be able to take responsibility for achieving the suggested outcome. For example, it might be the design engineer in the case of software development, or a consultant who you know has the skills to deal with what is recommended.
3. When should it be done by? In some instances this is implied, such as when one recommendation is dependent on another being implemented. In other cases, you may list the recommendations in priority order, as may be the case with something that affects safety or market share.
4. What is it likely to cost? If possible, give some indication of what it will cost to act on what you are recommending. Money is not limitless in many organisations and readers need to have some basis for deciding on priorities and allocating available resources.

There are two ways of starting a recommendation. The example shown in Figure 9.5 illustrates the usual concise style. To save repetition, start with a single line: 'It is recommended that ...'. Sentences often leave out all but the most essential words.

Figure 9.5
Example of a recommendations section in a report

Recommendations

It is recommended that:
1. Dragon Systems' NaturallySpeaking Medical Suite is selected for voice recognition.
2. An evaluation copy is purchased for $500 and evaluated for three months by Dr Cureall.
3. Six thousand dollars be allocated for purchase, installation and training staff in the use of the program if the evaluation is positive.

For formal reports just add the phrase 'That approval be given for ...' at the start of every recommendation. This style is preferable if approval is being recorded in minutes or formal documents. Use full sentences (no missing words).

Guidelines for writing recommendations

List recommendations in a logical sequence

Notice that in Figure 9.5 that the second recommendation is for a trial evaluation. Until this is approved, other proposals cannot be considered. End with low-priority items needed just to tie up loose ends.

Give only one item per recommendation

Each one needs to be discussed and approved individually. Combining items increases the chance of rejection.

Number recommendations individually

In meetings, people can then refer to them easily: 'Recommendation 4.5 cannot be considered until we discuss 4.4'.

Be specific

If equipment is needed, give the technical name, the model number and the supplier's name and address. State exact dates and amounts. Ask that 'the current travel fund ($2000) for the financial year commencing 1 July be increased to $2250', not that 'the travel allowance for next year be increased'. Provided each proposal appears as a numbered item, there is no need for headings. However, if recommendations can be grouped according to topics, list them under appropriate subheadings.

Use direct, active language

Do not be apologetic, or beat about the bush. Do not make a recommendation that is not supported by the analysis. If you think of an extra proposal, be sure to add the topic concerned to the analysis.

Keep explanations and reasons out

Keep recommendations free from any discussion for or against the ideas. Some writers feel the need to support each idea by including reasons for acceptance. Arguments in favour of the proposals should be included in the analysis.

When you are in doubt

Sometimes you just cannot get the facts you need to help you make clear recommendations. It is better in such cases to suggest further investigation than to make recommendations based on insufficient data.

Safeguarding recommendations

Some decision makers may reject a recommendation unless they are sure the request does not 'exceed the guidelines'. For this kind of reader, recommendations 4.2 and 4.3 in the following example add assurance that it is safe for them to say 'yes'.

    4. RECOMMENDATIONS

    It is recommended that:

    4.1 The equipment allowance for the Perth and Hobart branches be increased by $60 000.

    4.2 State managers in each branch be responsible for authorising use of this additional allowance.

4.3 All officers be advised that the restrictions applying to equipment allowances as listed on pp. 34 and 35 of the Administrative Handbook, and in Par 2.4 of this report, are to be adhered to.

'Either/or' recommendations

These leave decision makers free to choose a number of different 'cut-off' points. Notice in the following case how recommendation 4.2 suggests two alternatives, allowing the reader to select the one that best fits the current situation.

It is recommended that:

4.1 The equipment allowance for the Perth and Hobart branches be increased.

4.2 This increase be either $5000 for the present half-year or $2500 for the present and $2500 for the following half-year.

QUOTATIONS, REFERENCES AND ACKNOWLEDGMENTS

Referencing information

If you want people to support your reasoning, it is important to tell them where you obtained your information. In particular, numeric data such as statistics or accounting figures need a source reference. Even if you do not have a well-known 'name' to quote as your source—for instance, if the data were obtained through personal observation by your own team—identify the people involved and state their qualifications. Helping readers who doubt your data (or your quotes) to locate the primary source increases their confidence in what you are saying. If they need reassurance that your facts or figures are correct, they can check for themselves.

Quotes and acknowledgments

Whenever you quote from any source, include a clear and obvious acknowledgment. Give readers all the information they need to locate the original. You can do this in one of three ways.

1. Footnote references.
2. Reference to title and year of publication only.
3. Full reference in body text.

Giving the full reference as a footnote is the simplest and fastest form of acknowledgment. Use this method for ordinary business reports and submissions in which you are using few quotes or want to maintain an informal tone.

> *Peters and Waterman[1] say that in the USA participative management schemes offer the best means of encouraging employees to strive towards higher standards in client service.*

1. Peters, T. J. & Waterman, R. H., 1984 *In Search of Excellence*, Harper & Row, (Aust edn.), Sydney.

The quotation or information referred to is numbered in the body of the report, and the full reference is listed under a matching number at the foot of the same page. Remember to include full details of the reference in your bibliography. Note that as well as the author and title, the reference includes the year and the country in which the book was published. Chapter number and page references are optional, but helpful.

If you know a particular reader needs only a basic reference, just give the author and title, without publication details, as in the following example.

Ron and Dianne Baldwin, in The Export Credits Plan, *take a more positive view. They say that once Australia's trade ratio comes into balance, the nation will have one of the most open economies in the world.*

Including the reference in the body of the text is an option, but this tends to disrupt the flow for the reader. Using footnotes gives the reader the choice of whether to look at it or keep reading.

In academic writing people tend to use far more references per page. Direct referencing as used above would break the flow of ideas, and would waste space if you quoted from the same source several times on each page. So only the author's surname and year of publication are given in the text body and the reader is expected to refer to the bibliography or book list at the end of the document for full details of the source. In the text, all the reader sees is this:

Peters and Waterman (1984) say that in the USA positive rewards motivate employees more than threats or punishments. Nutting (1985) agrees that the best way of encouraging Australians to take part in the 'pursuit of excellence' is by praise rather than criticism.

A quote from a well-known authority adds a professional touch to any business writing, particularly where you need to persuade or build agreement. You also strengthen both the quality of your findings and the power of your argument if you quote other books or journals that support your view. A lesser but still important reason for acknowledgment is to show that you are not trying to claim the ideas as your own.

The bibliography

A bibliography is a separate unit, placed at the end of the document. Regardless of the acknowledgment method used, it adds strength to the overall message. All references (including texts from which direct quotes were *not* used) are listed together with authors' surnames in alphabetical order. One system of referencing is the Harvard system. The author's surname is followed by the date, title and details about the publisher, and the place of publication, as shown in the sample bibliography in Figure 9.6. However, systems vary and you will need to check the conventions of your organisation or educational institution. Style guides explaining different systems are readily available in libraries, textbooks and on the internet.

Figure 9.6
Example of a bibliography listing a book, online journal, print journal and a video.

Abbot, H. 2000, *URLs for Everyone*. (4th Ed). Powerline Publishers, Sydney.

Alwang, G. 1998, Editors Choice. *PC Magazine Online* (online) 20 October 1998. http://www.zdnet.com/pcmag/features/specch98/edchoice.html [accessed 23 October 1998]

Forbes, B. & Smith, N. 1999, IT and communicating to the world. *Australian Journal of IT Speak*, **20**, pp. 26–30.

The Highwayman: Bill Gates and the super highway (video recording) 6 March 1995. ABC Television.

There are special rules that apply to setting out bibliography material in academic or high-level reports, but for ordinary business purposes clarity and ease of understanding are the main criteria.

Other acknowledgments

It is appropriate to make a formal acknowledgment of special assistance given to you in writing a report or submission, particularly help in obtaining information or data. The acknowledgment, however, should be low-key and formal. It usually goes at the end of the document unless the people named are important public figures, in which case acknowledgment might be better at the beginning (usually after the contents page).

Make sure that you spell the names of people correctly. In business writing it is usually not appropriate to acknowledge the help of your own family, but do thank teammates, fellow workers and supervisors if they gave valuable assistance. If family members gave professional help, acknowledge them by name, but not as 'my husband' or 'my children'.

Activity 9.3

Writing reports

1. List some reasons for having a separate introduction section in a business report.
2. What items should be included in the introduction? What items should not?
3. Why is it important to keep the material in the findings separate from other sections?
4. Give two guidelines a writer should follow in choosing and classifying material for use in an analysis section.
5. What kind of material or wording should not be included in the recommendations? Why?

EDITING THE REPORT

Editing, rewriting and polishing takes time, but it is rewarding to watch the report improving and know that its chances of success are increasing with each day's work. Some of the things you should look for include:

- cohesion and unity
- readability
- credibility
- errors (proofreading).

How long should the report be?

A report needs to be as long as is necessary to provide the reader with enough information to make them feel comfortable about implementing your recommendations. In many instances, reports are too long because the writer has not been sufficiently critical about what information is needed to support the arguments.

The simplest way of checking the length is to tell someone what the purpose of the report is and then ask them to read the draft. They should be able to tell you whether the content addresses the purpose in a succinct way, and the extent to which the recommendations are supported.

APPENDIXES

There may be several appendixes to one report, identified as A, B, C and so on. Some may even be larger than the report itself. Typical items in an appendix include:

- items that are too long or too bulky (maps, blueprints, computer printouts) or objects other than paper (videotapes, models, samples)
- items that are only supplementary to the main findings but cannot be left out altogether e.g. a copy of a staff survey assessing knowledge of software features
- raw unedited data or original material from which the figures in the report have been condensed
- supporting evidence—material that only a few readers need, but which (because those people are experts) could be vital for the report to get their backing
- other items to back up your results—photographs or calculations that prove your figures to be correct or add credibility to the findings
- background information—a course syllabus, another report, a technical manual—items that help readers put the report into perspective.

Appendixes used to support the report should be referred to in the body of the report. **Do not use appendixes to add 'bulk', making the report bigger than it needs to be.** Adding appendixes to a report that is too short to achieve its purpose will not impress any readers.

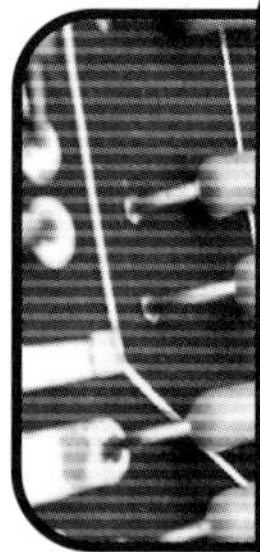

Activity 9.4

Appendixes

1. What kinds of appendixes would Paul attach to his report on ecommerce from Case study 9.1?
2. What type of material could go in an appendix to the Dr Cureall report on voice recognition software from Case study 9.2?

CONDENSING A REPORT

Sometimes you will be asked to produce a shortened version of a report. It may be to provide someone with a briefing paper for a press conference, or for a manager to gain an overview of reports prepared on issues affecting the organisation.

Select the key points from the main sections (Introduction, Findings, Analysis); recommendations are usually listed in full. The short version looks just like a full report, with a cover, contents page and summary, together with the condensed sections of the body of the full report.

PACKAGING THE REPORT

Cover page and title

Any report is worth presenting in the most professional way possible. As well as a separate contents page and synopsis, it should also have an outer cover, which should show:

- the full title in large lettering
- the name of the person or group for whom the report was prepared
- the name of the writer or writers and the group they represent, if any (in smaller lettering).

Writing the title

An effective title may have to be two or three lines long if it is to include the following items (each of which performs an important function):

- an opening phrase: 'Report on', 'Investigation into', 'Study of', or similar words
- a 'time word' relevant to the subject of the report—for example, a recent event, one that is current, or a proposed activity
- the main topic, and any sub-topics
- the name of the group, firm or organisation who will use the report (in a formal document this should appear as part of the title even if it is intended only for readers in the firm)
- the location (address, district or region) of the group referred to or of the activity dealt with in the text
- the period covered by the report (usually just the year, or year and month—this avoids confusion with other reports having similar titles but referring to different periods).

Investigation into recent changes in EDP System and resulting variation in policy—Northern Branch, Clearview Holdings Ltd—Manly, December 2001

A clear and concise title also helps people file a document more effectively, making it easier to retrieve later.

Table of contents

Even a short report benefits from having a table of contents listing headings (with page numbers). This provides a quick summary of the whole text as well as a means of finding a specific topic.

A contents list will show that the material has been organised clearly and logically. This increases reader confidence in the report and in you. If you used an outline (your collection of draft headings) as part of the early writing stage, you will have your table of contents almost completed. Many word-processor programs have an 'outline' function from which a contents table can be generated without your having to retype any headings.

Signature and position

A signature emphasises the writer's confidence in the reliability of the report. An unsigned document suggests (non-verbally) some doubt or uncertainty. If several people worked together to produce it, all can sign or one can sign as team leader.

- Signatures can be hard to read; print the names below them. If appropriate, add technical or academic qualifications.
- Under the name, give the position held. For example, Leader—Investigating team; Manager—Software Development Branch.

- If the report was prepared by a group, it is useful to include the name of the branch, committee or group responsible for producing it.
- Beneath the signature, add the date of signing to indicate exactly when the report was completed—an important piece of information.

Lyn McKay, B. Information Technology, UTS
Senior Software Development Manager
Alpha Communications Pty Ltd
15 August 2001

Other ways of improving a report

Each of the following, added to a report, can lift the overall standard of presentation.
- Glossary—this is an alphabetical list of special terms or phrases used in the report. A brief explanation is given for each item.
- Start each major section on a new page.
- Alphabetical index—this lists important subjects and other keywords used in the document (and relevant page numbers).
- Letter of transmittal—this is a short but formal letter accompanying a report or submission, which can be used to express views that could not be included in the report.
- Professional binding—first impressions always count, and the outside appearance of a report is important. Professional binding adds a strong visual appeal.

SUBMISSIONS, PROPOSALS AND FEASIBILITY STUDIES

A submission, like a report, is a way of communicating where it might otherwise be hard to make direct contact. You usually make a submission or present a feasibility study before you start a major project.

An important difference between these documents and reports is that there is usually only one report written on a given issue, whereas several (even hundreds) of submissions or proposals may be vying for one amount of money, resources or attention. Your job as the writer is to get the reader/s to accept your conclusions and think that your proposal is the best. It can involve a lot more selling than most writing.

Features

- There is usually a clearly defined target reader (or readers)—perhaps an accreditation committee, a government department, a purchasing board or a college council.
- The overall approach, the language and the tone need to be persuasive. Messages of this kind often face considerable resistance before they gain acceptance.
- **A submission should be built around a strong central argument and must close with a specific proposal or statement that follows logically from that argument.** It is not enough to give a list of facts and then leave it to your readers to work out a conclusion for themselves.

Organisation of submission topics

There is no standard format. A submission follows many of the conventions of a business report, as shown below, but the headings should be more specific.

Figure 9.7
Organisation of submission topics

PRELIMINARY PAGES
Cover
Title page
Official or formal project title
Name of organisation, branch, unit or individual responsible for project
Time (month, year)
Contents page
Summary

INTRODUCTION
1.   Outline.
2.   Briefly explain the project or activity for which approval is requested. Summarise major points to be made in the pages that follow.
3.   State the aim of the project or proposed activity.
4.   Set out the main goals or purpose of the proposed activity, program, project or purchase.
5.   Benefits—state value of proposed project or research program.
6.   Detail the value of the proposed program, especially from the reader's point of view. Explain exactly what benefits will result if the proposal or project goes ahead.
7.   Give sources of information.
8.   Say how and where objective data was obtained, to maintain validity.
9.   Outline historical background.
10.   Outline theoretical background—a theory or 'model' to show that your proposal or plan should work successfully.
11.   Describe the research method.
12.   If research is involved, explain how results will be measured to ensure accuracy. Describe the test design or equipment, using appropriate headings, for example:

Technique A, Technique B, Technique C, Location.

BODY OF DOCUMENT
The current situation
Give specific facts—presentation and content should be objective, similar to the findings section of a report. Readers may not agree with claims you make, so include evidence that proves the point.

The proposal
Describe in detail what is proposed. What will the project or research involve? Use diagrams to help make your case clear. If there are technical or statistical specifications involved, or if descriptions run to more than half a page, summarise only here and put the rest in an appendix. Whatever the topic, make your language as specific as possible. In your proposal section you could include:
•   *Timetable for stages in the program*
   Show clearly how long the project is expected to take. Be specific. Show the time set aside for each step (the plan in Table 9.1 is a good example).

- *People involved*
  Explain who will be involved and why they are well-suited for any special research.
- *Funding requirements/budget*
  Set this out logically, and in full detail. Be specific.

Central argument
Like the analysis section in a report, this section uses subjective material but, because it will meet stronger reader resistance, your argument will need to be logical, more detailed and more actively promoted.

Recommendation or formal statement of proposal
Word this in such a way that there is no doubt about what the reader will be saying 'Yes' or 'No' to. If it refers to several items (for instance, money, staffing, equipment or accommodation), list each separately.

APPENDIXES

Appendixes include any bulky items that would clutter the main document. For example:
Appendix A—Specifications of power supply and network configurations
Appendix B—Copies of original statements by experts, as quoted in submission

TECHNICAL WRITING

In the Information Technology industry, all written communication has a significant component of technical writing. Technical documents use the same principles of good writing that apply to all documents. The main difference is that they usually contain more technical information, graphics and numerical data.

This section is about keeping things simple in an area noted for complexity and confusion; it explains how to make technical writing clear, concise and helpful so that people who may not have a technical background can enjoy reading it. If there is no gain in understanding or accuracy, why do writers use complex terms in place of simple ones? Probably because they are following the style used by the writers who taught them. However, breaking this copy-the-leader cycle is important if technical writing is to help people rather than just impress them with complex vocabulary.

Will a short, non-technical explanation do?

Give enough detail to allow full understanding, but do not include unnecessary technical data. If a short, non-technical word will do, use it. Instead of writing 'AEU' (air-exchanger unit), call it a 'fan'. Ask yourself whether readers need to know the name, purpose and function of each internal part. If you feel some people might need extra details, attach a technical appendix. If you have to use a technical name, follow it with a non-technical description of what the object looks like and where it is.

Stick to one term for each part

If you do use a technical term, make sure you use the same word next time you talk about the object concerned.

Use visual explanations as well as words

Many of your readers will be visual or tactile thinkers. Add a diagram or a sketch showing the whole unit, with an arrow pointing, for instance, to the red control knob. Label other parts clearly, using the terms you use in the text. Appropriate **drawings, photographs and diagrams will make your writing a success where words alone cannot**.

Keep visual items and their verbal descriptions together

When readers need to refer from words to pictures, keep both on the same page or on facing pages. If you have to separate them, give page numbers as cross references both in the text and under the picture.

Put yourself in the position of the inexperienced reader

Recognise that some features will be so familiar to you that you may forget to include them in your instructions.

PRESENTING THE REPORT TO AN AUDIENCE

In many cases, when you have produced your report or submission, you will have to present it. This may be to the person who commissioned the report, a committee considering your proposal, or a group of specialists interested in the work you have done. Types of presentation could include:

- a formal speech to a large audience
- a one-to-one presentation
- an informal, discussion-group situation.
  Chapter 6 has more information on presentation skills.

SAMPLE REPORT

This model shows how a typical business report should look and sound, and how the topics should be organised. Notice the following points.

- The structure is developed from the original rough draft with objective items in the findings and subjective opinions and proposals in the analysis.
- The pages are set out to look attractive and are easy to follow. Notice the amount of 'white space', an essential requirement in a high-quality business report.
- The numbered headings support the structure. See how easily you can follow the hierarchy of ideas and locate major sections, subsections and minor units by following the system of numbering, indentation and underlining.
- The language is concise, direct and businesslike. Some information appears as listed facts instead of complete sentences. There is no use of 'I', 'me', 'we' or 'you', and no personal comment.
  Advice on how to write and edit particular sections of a report, including title page, synopsis, findings, analysis, recommendations and appendixes, follows the model.

KINLAND BUSINESS SOLUTIONS

Kinland Business Solutions is a medium-sized metropolitan business software company. The writer of this report is Kinland's personnel manager, Sandy Hollins, who has just completed a study of the methods currently in use by the company to motivate staff, and has been asked by Terry Cavill, the managing director, to write a report on the study. The report will be presented at a meeting of the Kinland board of directors on 25 November.

Sandy will have planned the investigation process to include information from a range of primary and secondary sources, including a series of interviews with various staff members and committees, reference to similar reports, and other reading. The questionnaire will have been trialled on several people who work with Sandy to ensure there are no ambiguities and the information from the questions can be easily analysed.

Sandy now has some draft notes (see Figure 9.8). They will give you a general idea of the topic and the context in which the report is being written. You will notice that the language and style in the draft are not appropriate for a report, but that they can be easily converted into report format.

In the final report, note the way the summary is centred in the page with wide margins top and bottom, and much wider margins on both left and right sides.

In a long report, you would normally start each main section on a new page. This has not been done in this report because it is an abbreviated version of a longer report.

Figure 9.8
Draft notes for Kinland Business Solutions report

Rough notes for report

1. Kinland Business Solutions uses the following methods to motivate employees. First we use a salary increment scheme. After the first twelve months' service, an employee receives yearly increases in salary. But payment of the increase is subject to the employee showing skills development in a number of areas. These include communication skills, technical skills and problem solving.
2. Secondly, we offer promotion opportunities to all employees. But promotion is not automatic. It depends on factors including proven ability to handle responsibility, high standard performance of duties and ability to work with others on a team basis. It also depends on what efforts the employee is making to improve work skills, as shown by additional study and training.
3. We have a staff training program too. For all staff, courses are run regularly on report writing, letter writing and public speaking. Supervisory staff are offered regular courses on basic supervision skills such as problem solving, decision making, negotiating skills and principles of management.
4. All the present schemes are operating well, and in my opinion should continue. The most obvious indicator is the extremely low turnover of younger staff (less than 2.5 per cent last year), which compares well with the industry average of over 10 per cent.
5. Morale is high, and when I interviewed them most employees expressed general satisfaction with the present program. (I wonder how reliable that sort of response really is. Would they tell me if they were not satisfied?)
6. Options include changing the incentive scheme and introducing additional training programs.
7. Changes to the financial incentives scheme have not worked elsewhere, whereas training programs in Quality Assurance have.
8. We should now start introducing some additional training programs.

9. Staff are enthusiastic about possible schemes, such as Total Quality Management. This should be tried next year. Efficiency and production levels could rise as a result if it works for us as it has in a couple of other local firms like ours. (I've got some data on this, too bulky for the report but could go in the Appendix along with my detailed plan for the new scheme.)

10. Planning should begin immediately so that we can start a trial Quality Assurance program in January. If this happens, there should be a visible indication of increase in both efficiency and production levels by mid-April.

11. My one worry is that if we do not move quickly, the present level of staff support for the idea may slacken off. There is a risk that opposition companies may introduce a similar plan in an effort to attract key customers away from Kinland, which may lead to our losing some of the best staff. I don't feel we should try any other schemes until the Total Quality Management program is working.

Figure 9.9
Sample report

Report on Investigation into the use of Motivation and Incentive Schemes

KINLAND Business Solutions

Prepared for the Board of Directors Meeting
25 January 2002
by S. B. Hollins Personnel Manager
and the staff of the Personnel Section
Kinland Business Solutions

Summary

Kinland's motivational schemes are an important feature of the firm's overall corporate strategy. Kinland uses several methods to motivate employees, starting with a salary increment scheme, subject to the employee showing an improvement in a number of areas. As the firm expands, promotion opportunities are opening constantly, but promotion depends on a number of factors such as technical and communication skills development. A staff training program covers areas such as management and negotiation. The present schemes are operating well. This report considers which ones should continue and whether new ones should be added. One option for improving productivity would be to train staff in Quality Assurance procedures. Unless the new scheme is approved for an early start next year, the firm may begin to lose key customers and staff. Recommendations for improving the quality of the workforce include the training of staff in Quality Assurance principles in July (2002) and the implementation of a Quality Assurance program in key departments on a trial basis in October 2002.

1

1. INTRODUCTION

1.1 Aim

To investigate the present systems of employee motivation and to suggest possible changes, where necessary.

1.2 Authorisation

As requested by T. G. Cavill, the Managing Director, on 5 September 2001, for presentation to the Board of Directors meeting on 25 January *2002*.

1.3 Sources of Information

- Questionnaire
- Discussions with supervisors
- Discussions with staff committees
- Reports on incentive schemes in other states
- Personnel section records
- Other sources: *Management of People at Work*, Donald S. Bauth, Penpress 1999

2. CURRENT MOTIVATION AND INCENTIVE PROGRAMS

The company currently uses three different types of motivation and incentive programs:

- An annual salary increment scheme, commencing after the first twelve months.
- Promotional opportunities, based on the undertaking of further part-time studies, plus development of other abilities (teamwork and responsibility).
- A staff development program intended to provide training in specific skills required by staff who are seeking promotion.

These are explained more fully below.

2.1 Annual Salary Increment Scheme

This commences at the end of the first twelve months with the firm. The employee is eligible for further increases in salary at the end of each twelve months from then on.

However, rises are not paid automatically. Each employee is required to maintain a satisfactory level of performance during the year. This is assessed according to the following criteria:

- communication skills
- job-specific technical competencies
- problem-solving skills

Assessment is carried out by the employee's immediate supervisor, at least twice during the year.

2.2 Promotional Opportunities

As Kinland is continuing to expand its operations, there are numerous opportunities for staff to apply for promotion. Employees are regularly advised that the factors that will increase their chance of gaining promotion include:

2.2.1 Demonstration of sound performance and working ability, including:

- proven ability to handle responsibility

2

- satisfactory performance in present position
- ability to work with others on a team basis

2.2.2 Additional Study Undertaken in Approved Programs

2.3 Staff Development Program

The staff development program for supervisors includes training courses on each of the following:
- team building
- client interaction
- problem solving
- negotiation skills
- principles of management

Other staff development programs, available to all employees, include courses on:
- report writing
- letter writing
- public speaking

2.4 Other Training and Motivation Schemes

The following schemes have been used by similar firms in this area and could be introduced in the future:
- Total Quality Management
- participative decision making
- delegation of responsibility

3. ANALYSIS

3.1 The Present Situation

Overall the firm's motivation and incentive schemes appear to be working soundly. The most obvious indicator of this is the extremely low loss of younger (16–22 years old) staff, which was less than 2.5 per cent over the last year. This compares favourably with the industry average loss for younger staff, which at present is over 10 per cent.

Morale is high, and most employees expressed general satisfaction with the program. (Although expressions of satisfaction are not always reliable indicators of true feelings.)

3.2 Options

The two main options are:
- a financial incentive scheme based on performance bonuses
- training in Quality Assurance based on a teamwork model and using staff to assist with its design

Financial incentives are not an option because they have been shown to diminish in effectiveness very quickly and then set a new base rate pay benchmark regardless of productivity.

3

3.2.1 Proposal to Introduce New Schemes

Staff are enthusiastic about the possibility of additional motivation schemes, including those mentioned in 2.4, and in particular the proposal to introduce a Quality Assurance program on a trial basis next year. To take advantage of this attitude, moves should begin immediately to introduce a trial program starting in January next year. (Recommendations 4.1 and 4.2)

3.2.2 Expected Results

If a Quality Assurance program is introduced next January, both efficiency and production levels should show a noticeable rise by mid-April. This prediction is consistent with similar experiences in other states where programs have resulted in increased output and efficiency. (See Appendix B.)

3.2.3 The Need for Immediate Action

If the firm does not move quickly, the present support for the idea may lessen. There is also a risk that opposition companies may introduce a similar plan in an effort to attract key customers and top staff away from Kinland. A detailed plan for the introduction of the scheme is attached in Appendix A.

3.2.4 Introduction of Other Schemes

Evidence from other states (see Appendix B) suggests that introduction of other schemes would also be beneficial. It is preferable, however, for changes of this kind to be introduced one by one. No consideration should therefore be given (at present) to any other schemes. (Recommendation 4.4)

4. RECOMMENDATIONS

4.1 That a Quality Assurance training program, as proposed in Appendix A, be approved and implemented by the Training Manager in consultation with the Operations Manager.

4.2 That the scheme commence on 4 June 2002.

4.3 That all other schemes operating at present continue in 2002.

4.4 That no other new schemes be introduced until the Quality Assurance program has been evaluated and shown to be contributing to improved productivity.

Sandy Hollins PERSONNEL MANAGER, KINLAND Business Solutions, 22 January 2002

APPENDIX A: Detailed proposal for introduction of a Quality Assurance program in January 2002.
APPENDIX B: Research findings on job rotation schemes and increased employee morale in NSW (1999–2000).

4

ACTION POINTS

- Ensure all important sections of the report are included.
- Aim for a document that is neat and clearly set out, is free of error and suitably bound, and uses appropriate conventions.
- Incorporate only relevant information from your investigation.
- Check that the general and specific purposes are clear from the content.
- Provide an introduction that identifies the reader, purpose and scope of the report.
- Include a summary that is a complete précis of the document.
- Ensure that the recommendations
  - are logical and follow from the facts presented and the conclusions
  - are brief and specify action to be taken
  - specify who is to implement them
  - specify a timeframe.
- Use words and style appropriate to the readership.
- Check that the body contains factual information and the facts support the statements that are made.
- Incorporate all facts needed to explain the recommendations and reasons for recommendations.
- Summarise the facts and point to the future in the conclusion/discussion.
- Include appropriate charts, diagrams or photographs.
- Ensure the appendixes are directly referred to and supplement the report.

SUMMARY

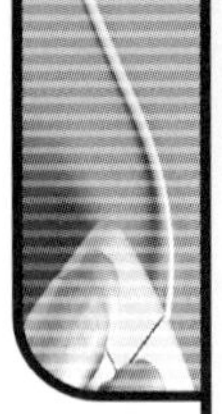

Easy-to-read reports are the ones most often read. The first barrier facing the report writer is reader resistance. Keep your report short and make each page attractive to the eye. Writing and setting out a report is a straightforward task and surprisingly easy to master. Reports are made up of more than words. They can include graphs, pictures and symbols.

Good planning is the basis for a report or submission that gets its message across to the audience. An effective plan addresses the purpose, audience, scope and actions needed to produce the document.

Remember that your document has to convince the reader—use a persuasive approach. Prepare an outline for your document to make sure all key issues are addressed and the ideas are set out logically. Have someone give you feedback on your outline.

There are four main divisions in a report. Names vary, but the most common are the following.

1. Introduction, which establishes the reader–writer relationship, outlines the purpose and scope of the report and states the aim.
2. Findings, which presents objective information—gives the facts as a basis for discussion.
3. Analysis, which tells readers what action is proposed and why, and builds support for the recommendations.
4. Recommendations, which make up the action ending, listing steps needed to get results.

In addition to these four sections, other items, even in a short report, include a summary or synopsis and (often) an appendix. A contents table shows that the report has been organised logically, with a clear division of ideas into sections. This increases reader confidence. When setting out the report, number all major headings. Metric- or decimal-style numbering has many advantages over letter–number systems.

Use a range of sources when researching a report. These should include both primary and secondary sources. Libraries and the Internet are excellent sources of information and assistance. Give a source reference for important findings. If experts supplied factual information for the report, identify them by name.

Always test surveys and questionnaires before distributing them. State important data in measures that have the same meaning for every reader (e.g. kilometres, kilograms).

Recommendations should provide the reader with details of what has to be done, by whom, and by when. However, remember that a summary takes less time to read than the original, so more people read it.

Always allow time for editing. Get someone else's advice on your work. If you cannot condense a long report to the required number of pages, an alternative is to write a special version known as an executive summary.

Keep personal views out of the report. Words such as 'I' or 'me' reduce the impersonal quality that conveys a sense of objectivity. However, it is still important to sign every report personally. An unsigned report suggests that the writer is lacking in confidence and commitment to the report.

A submission usually involves more 'selling' rather than 'telling' because several (even hundreds) of submissions or proposals may be vying for one amount of money, resources or attention. Your job as the writer is to get the reader/s to accept your conclusions and think that your proposal is the best. Your submission should be built around a strong central argument and must close with a specific proposal or statement that follows logically from that argument.

Technical documents use the same principles of good writing that apply to all documents. The main difference is that they usually contain more technical information, graphics and numerical data.

TRAINING LOG

Workplace reports

1. Collect three different types of reports from an IT workplace, by using the internet or researching in the library. You could include samples such as:
   (a) product evaluations
   (b) project proposals
   (c) occupational health and safety policy reviews
   (d) training needs analysis
   (e) productivity/section report.
2. Choose one of these reports and evaluate its effectiveness as a report according to the following criteria:

	Yes	No	Not sure
Prescribed sections of the report are included.	☐	☐	☐
Presentation of the report:			
• is neatly and clearly set out	☐	☐	☐
• is free of error and suitably bound	☐	☐	☐
• uses appropriate conventions.	☐	☐	☐
Information from an investigation relevant to the report is included.	☐	☐	☐
General and specific purposes of the report are clear from the content.	☐	☐	☐
Introduction identifies the reader, purpose and scope of the report.	☐	☐	☐
The summary/executive summary is a complete précis of the report.	☐	☐	☐
Recommendations:			
• are logical and follow from the facts presented	☐	☐	☐
and the conclusions:			
• are brief and specify action to be taken	☐	☐	☐
• specify who is to implement them	☐	☐	☐
• specify timeframe.	☐	☐	☐
Words and style used are appropriate to the readership.	☐	☐	☐
Body contains factual information and the facts support the statements that are made.	☐	☐	☐
Facts explain the recommendations to be made and the reasons for recommendations.	☐	☐	☐
Conclusion (discussion) summarises the facts and points to the future.	☐	☐	☐
Charts, diagrams or photographs are included.	☐	☐	☐
Information from additional sources has been included.	☐	☐	☐
Appendixes are directly referred to and supplement the report.	☐	☐	☐
Bibliography is relevant.	☐	☐	☐

Action plan

Write a report on a topic relevant to the IT industry. Use the information in this chapter as a guide. Possible topics include:

- evaluation of appropriate hardware requirements for a client
- evaluation of suitable software requirements for a client
- comparison of similar software products for a target group of users
- feasibility report on the use of web based trading for a client
- tender for provision of information technology support services
- occupational health and safety report
- an issue relevant to your workplace.

   Before you begin consider the following.

1. What is the aim or purpose of the report?
2. What sources of information will you access for the factual sections of the report? Identify likely sources under the headings 'Primary sources' and 'Secondary sources'.
3. List possible graphics that could be included in the report.
4. Prepare a report outline using the five-stage structure and descriptive headings.
5. Draft some possible recommendations.
6. Make a list of possible benefits that will result from the recommendations of your report. These will be incorporated into both the analysis and your presentation so they need to be ideas that will 'sell' the report.
7. Identify a range of techniques that could be incorporated into your presentation of the report at the next management meeting.
8. Look up the following Internet site for examples of how to include references, footnotes and how to write a bibliography: http://www.csu.edu.au/division/library/tutorial/reference/refbib.htm, 31 July 2001. Division of Library Services. 2000, *References, footnotes & compiling a bibliography: A guide to referencing essays, theses & dissertations* (online). 6th edn. Charles Sturt University, Bathurst, NSW.

CHAPTER 10

GRAPHIC COMMUNICATION

COMPETENCIES

This chapter is linked to elements contained in the following competencies which are in the Information Technology Training Package.

- Create User and Technical Documentation ICAITD128A
- Interact with Clients ICAITS009B
- Develop and Present a Feasibility Report ICAITAD043A
- Record Client Support Requirements ICAITS016B
- Assist with Policy Development for Client Support Procedures ICAITS033B
- Apply Skills in Communications BSX154L407
- Guide Application of Communications Management BSX154L507
- Manage Communications BSX154L608
- Apply Occupational Health and Safety Procedures ICAITU00B

The aim of this chapter is to help you develop skills in producing a wide range of graphical material suitable for the documents you may need to develop at work. Information technology enables you to easily incorporate a range of graphical material which you either develop yourself or obtain from a graphic artist. This chapter will help you to be selective about the type of graphics you include to ensure they are appropriate to the purpose of the document.

You will be able to answer questions such as:

- What graphics do I need to include?
- What makes one graphic more effective than another?
- When should I use one kind of graph as opposed to any other sort?
- How do I use computer-generated graphics?
- Should I design the graphics myself?

TOPICS DISCUSSED

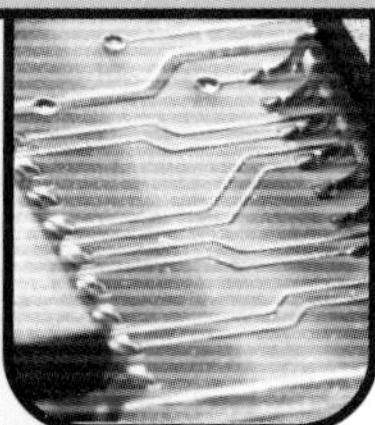

- Producing graphics
- Representing relationships
- Representing quantitative data
- Information through images

INTRODUCTION

Graphics can add to the understanding of complex technical information. The use of technology means that the production of graphics has been made much more accessible. The use of graphics in IT documents adds to their readability.

In many cases, graphics are essential to summarise important information or convey information based on complex written text with high levels of technical jargon. When graphs are used to convey complex technical information it is important that they include reliable data and are clearly constructed so that they can be accurately interpreted. The Moura mine disaster in Figure 10.1 is an example where incorrect graphing techniques, together with poor graphic-interpretation skills, combined to contribute to the death of eleven men.

Figure 10.1

Wrongly drawn graph hid gas build-up in disaster mine

By LEISA SCOTT

A rapid rise in gas levels in the Moura No. 2 mine the day before it exploded was hidden by the incorrect plotting of a graph by a mine fire officer, the inquiry into the cause of the disaster which killed 11 men heard yesterday.

The man responsible for the faulty graph, Mr Alan Morieson, yesterday admitted that if the graph had correctly shown the steep rise in carbon monoxide, he would have been alarmed.

The graph is referred to by mine deputies and under-managers before starting their shifts underground and is meant to alert them to changes in the mine's atmosphere. Mr Morieson has held the position as fire and ventilation officer since July 1990, but told counsel for the Department of Minerals and Energy, Mr Allan MacSporran, that he only learned after the explosion that it 'would have been better' to plot it differently. He had since been taught the correct method of plotting the gas readings by the Australian Coal Industry's Research Laboratory in Ipswich, near Brisbane.

The admission to the inquiry before mining warden Mr Frank Windridge followed heavy questioning from a number of legal counsel about the quality of training given to mine deputies to conduct their duties, which include monitoring gases.

All three mine deputies who have given evidence have told the inquiry they had not been trained to use a gas chromatograph, a specialised instrument used to analyse a number of gases. Two of the deputies have not been able to recall receiving formal training about spontaneous combustion, a feature which a member of the expert panel assisting the mining warden, Mr Peter Neilson, yesterday told the inquiry was 'probably the most hazardous circumstance' that could happen at Moura No. 2 mine.

The inquiry learned yesterday that a section of the mine, known as the 512 panel, had caused concern as far back as June 17. Mr Morieson told the inquiry he had been called in on that day because methane was found to be circulating in the wrong direction. It was the 512 section which had been experiencing a steep rise in carbon monoxide readings the day before the August 7 explosion, a fact hidden by the distorted graph drawn up by Mr Morieson.

The inquiry heard that Mr Morieson did not plot the gas level changes on a daily basis, allowing 'much greater distances' in times between plotting. The inquiry continues today.

Source: © *The Australian*, 21 October 1994.

Well-produced graphics convey information and enhance the appearance of documents, making them more attractive and inviting the reader to engage with the content. Another advantage of good graphics is that visual material such as Microsoft PowerPoint slides, overhead transparencies and handouts look professional and are easier to produce if the source graphic is clear and appropriate. It is also easier for the audience to remember, if all the components of the presentation integrate well.

Good graphics save space because they can substitute for text in a document. The quality of your written documents may be improved because the process of planning and integrating graphics encourages you to look at information from another perspective and perhaps rethink it.

Other advantages of **effective graphics** are that they **help the reader**:

- visualise relationships between things described in the text
- compare data and make judgments based on those comparisons
- save time because they can quickly grasp essential issues through looking at the graphics
- visualise things that written text cannot depict such as trends, complex processes and emotions
- generate a wider range of ideas.

Activity 10.1

Effective graphics

1. Find two articles related to the IT industry in two different magazines or on the internet. Skimread the articles and pay close attention to the use of graphics. What different kinds of graphics did the writers of the articles use? Complete the check list below.

Type of graphic	Article 1	Article 2
Diagrams		
Organisation chart		
Flow chart		
Management chart		
Line graph		
Bar graph		
Pictograph		
Histogram		
Scatter diagrams		
Tables		
Photographs		
Drawings		
Lettering		
Cartoons		
Computer-generated graphics		

2. Describe the audience for each of the articles. Was the article written for IT experts, IT business users or IT home users? What was it about the way the article was written that told you this?
3. What information did the writer communicate in the graphics? (Look at the titles and captions.)
4. Were the graphics essential? Give your reasons. Consider whether the graphics provided information that was not included in the written text. Did they summarise information that appeared in the text? How did they help the reader?

PRODUCING GRAPHICS

Like any form of communication, the effectiveness of graphic communication depends on the quality of planning. It can be harder than writing because, in writing, when you want to ensure that the message is clear you can make the point several times. With graphics you really only get one chance to make your point if it is not reinforced in the text. The steps in Figure 10.2 show a process that will help you produce effective graphics.

Alternatively there are thousands of free pictures and animations available on the internet. It may be faster and easier to use one of these to enhance your argument in written documents or for presentations. If you are going to download graphics from an internet site, be aware of any copyright restrictions that may apply. Just because it is on the internet does not always mean that it is free to use.

Either way, every graphic you use needs to:

- reinforce your argument
- be easily interpreted by the audience
- be relevant.

Planning brief

Developing a good graphic requires planning.

Needless to say, the more time you spend on each step, the more likely it is that the finished plan will be perfect. In practice, most people are constrained by time and money, which means you need to make sure that each stage is only done once, but done well.

The same is true for producing graphics. No matter how much you know about design principles, drafting and reproduction, **without good planning and preparation the graphic will not achieve its potential**.

Important planning steps

1. State your purpose and identify the problem.
2. Describe your audience; focus on their needs and level of written and visual literacy.
3. List the things that might get in the way of the message.
4. Generate a range of options.
5. Decide how you will accomplish your goals.

Factors to take into account

Research

- Is there extra data or information that you need? Where is it available?

Figure 10.2
The process for producing effective graphics

Discrimination issues
- Will people with visual impairment be unnecessarily disadvantaged?
- Will any of the material be incomprehensible to members of the audience from particular cultural backgrounds?
- Will any of the language be hard to comprehend by some of the readers?

Basics of good graphics

Simplicity is the key to an effective graphic. Checklist 10.1 lists the features that should be considered when planning and drafting graphics. Graphics have a wide range of uses such as company identification including letterhead, fax cover sheets, brochures, advertisements and web sites. The checklist can also be applied to graphics used in reports or other documents where the purpose is to convey information.

Checklist 10.1

Graphics

Choose one of the documents from Activity 10.1 and assess its graphics using the following checklist.

	Yes	No
Uncluttered layout	☐	☐
Exciting colour	☐	☐
Readable type	☐	☐
Simple designs	☐	☐
Emphasis used appropriately	☐	☐
Unity of images and placement	☐	☐
Balance between elements in the design	☐	☐
Spacing used effectively	☐	☐
Appropriate scale used:		
• allowing room for titling	☐	☐
• leaving intervals between markers on charts and graphs allowing room for entry of scales	☐	☐
Shade, colour, texture, pattern and line used consciously and sparingly	☐	☐
Accurate and relevant data	☐	☐
Clear and simple labels	☐	☐
Complete legends	☐	☐
Text kept to a minimum depending on the purpose, with detailed explanatory text below the graphic	☐	☐
Lettering:		
• proportional to graphic	☐	☐
• easy to read (font, size)	☐	☐
• uses appropriate case	☐	☐
• legible	☐	☐
Titles:		
• short and descriptive	☐	☐
• subtitle where further description needed	☐	☐
• additional explanatory text follows title	☐	☐
• all text brief	☐	☐

> A clear explanation for symbols　☐ ☐
>
> A clear explanation for abbreviations　☐ ☐
>
> Instructions for artists and editors:
>
> - in circle　☐ ☐
> - different coloured pen　☐ ☐
> - clear and legible　☐ ☐

The following are key questions you should ask about each graphic at the review stage:

1. Is it concise?
2. Is it too complex?
3. Can it be broken up into simpler graphics?
4. Have I obtained another opinion?

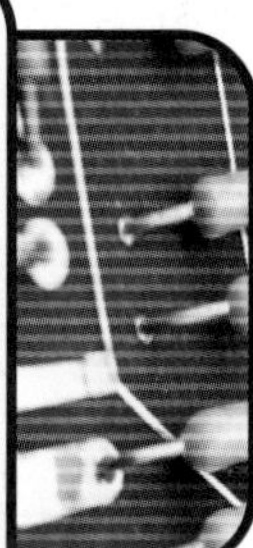

Activity 10.2

Briefing a graphic artist

Your boss has asked you to design a website or a brochure for a series of special deals for home computer users. The sale items include desktop computers, printers, scanners, web cameras and popular computer games.

Prepare the brief for the graphic artist. You will need to consider:

- the purpose of the website/brochure
- information about the audience
- a list of the graphics needed, together with the purpose of each
- a set of sample graphics.

REPRESENTING RELATIONSHIPS

Diagrams

Diagrams usually involve some freehand drawing. Although you may not feel confident to produce a drawing to publication standard, an accurate and clear diagram such as Figure 10.3 can be produced using some simple processes. The use of computer-aided design (CAD) software makes the task of drawing complicated diagrams much easier today.

Organisation charts

Most organisation charts use a pyramid shape such as the one in Figure 10.4. There are a number of techniques for presenting organisation charts that can convey a completely different message. One is to turn the chart on its head so that it looks like an inverted pyramid. Some people add a box indicating customers at the top to give the impression of an organisation driven by the customers. Another technique is to change the height of the pyramid. You can change the way an organisation appears to be structured from hierarchical structure to a flat management structure at the touch of a computer key.

Figure 10.3
Diagram

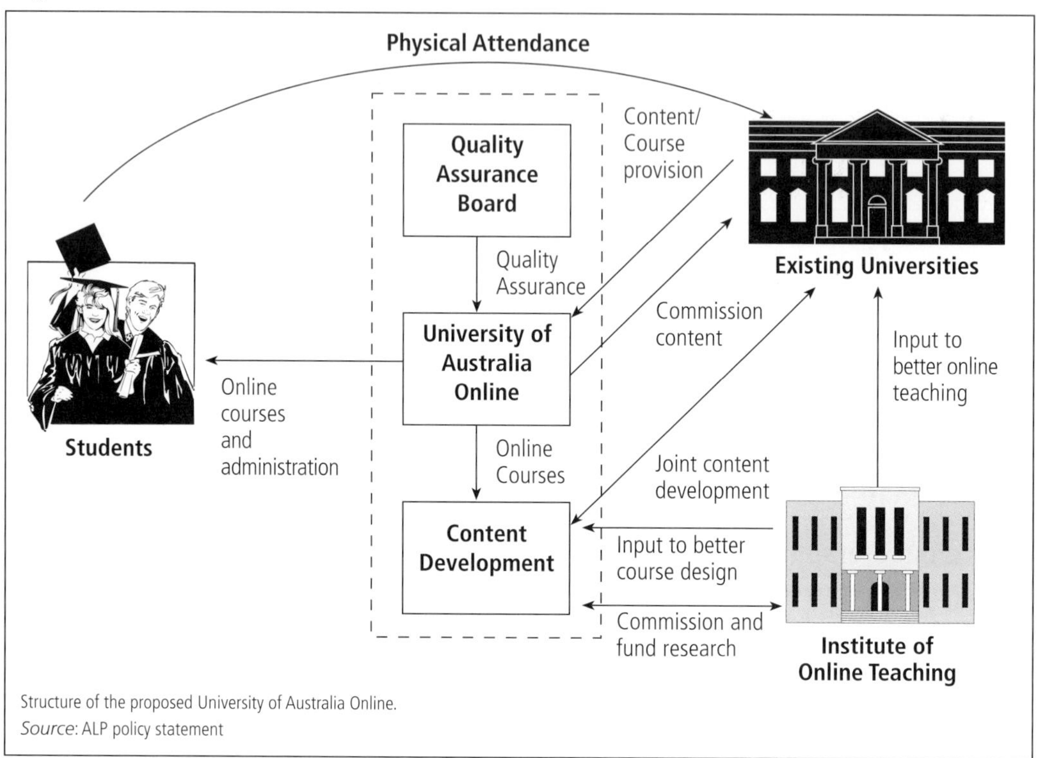

Structure of the proposed University of Australia Online.
Source: ALP policy statement

Figure 10.4
Organisation chart of a company

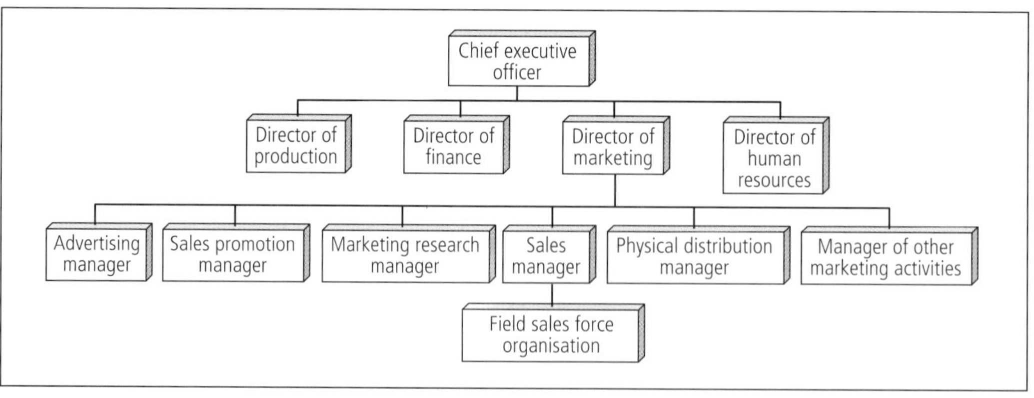

Flow charts

First, sketch the key elements of the flow chart. Second, write next to each element what its role is (options include decision point, action, start of process, end of process, input) and assign a symbol to each type of element. Use the simplest symbols possible. The boundaries of the process should be defined clearly. These days you can produce flow charts using graphics software. Figure 10.5 shows two different flow charts.

Activity 10.3

Designing flow charts

1. Design a flow chart for a simple procedure such as:
   (a) checking for faults in a printer
   (b) designing a macro in Microsoft Word.
2. Draw a flow chart on recycling computer hardware including printer and other peripheral equipment. Show the path of the recyclable components.

Figure 10.5
Flow chart of a production process

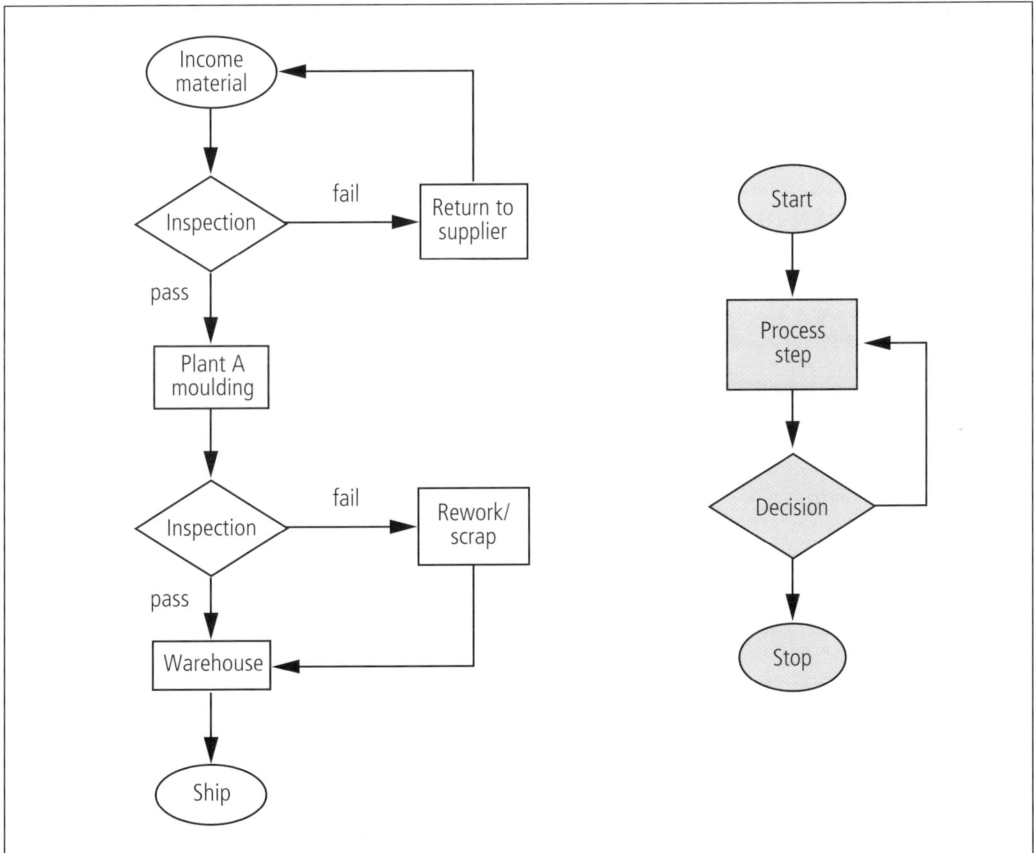

A challenging exercise is to draw a flow chart for setting the recording start and stop times for a video recorder. Very often the material you are working from (the user manual) uses language that is hard to follow, so this exercise can help you develop the skills required to make a graphic image for a complex process. When you have completed the chart, get someone to follow its instructions and give feedback on your work.

The same principles that apply to flow charts apply to Schedule (PERT) charts (see Figure 10.6) and Timeline (Gantt) charts (see Figure 10.7). Their effectiveness depends on your having a clear sense of the process and its boundaries, keeping the chart simple, and testing it on someone who would view it in the same way as your intended audience.

Figure 10.6
PERT chart showing schedule for building a house

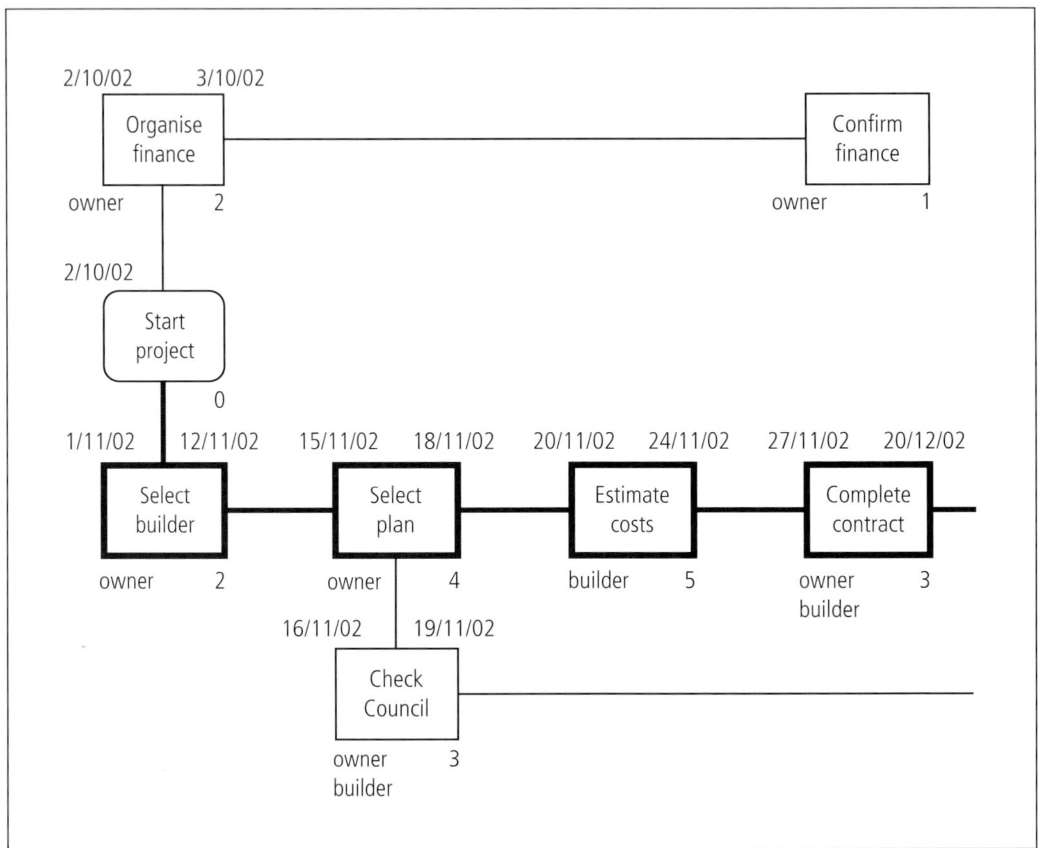

There is an overlap between statistical graphics and other forms of graphic communication. The additional element here is that data has to be represented. This requires a stronger focus on accuracy and clarity.

REPRESENTING QUANTITATIVE DATA

Important points for constructing statistical graphics

- A badly drawn or inaccurate graphic is worse than no graphic.
- Where data is used for comparison, ensure that it is consistent with the data to which it is being compared.

Figure 10.7
Gantt chart for a house-building project

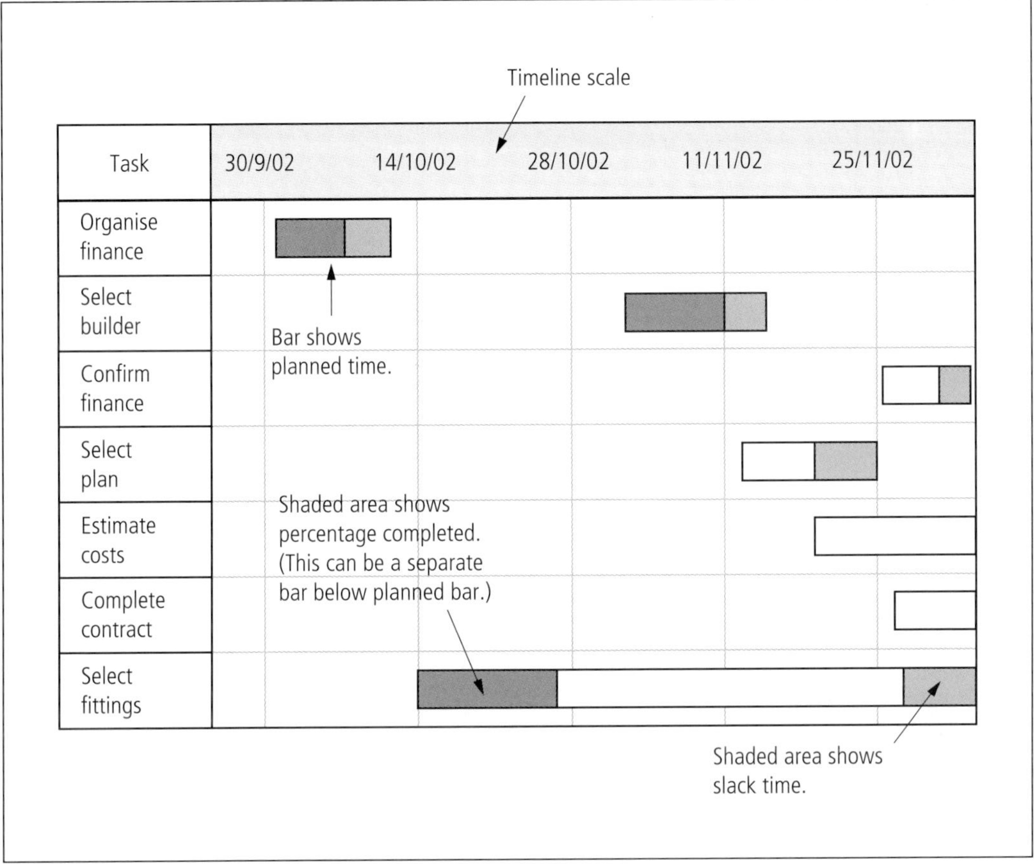

- The graphic or associated text should include:
  —the date that the data was collected
  —the time span covered
  —the location from which the data was collected
  —the instruments used to collect the data.
- Do not make the graphic more complicated than it needs to be.

Graphs

Line graphs

These are used to show trends and provide a basis for inferring what happened between points on the scale. A line graph should not be used to depict discontinuous data where points along the line between the data points do not have any meaning.

A marked point indicates the value of a reading or statistic. It is important that an appropriate scale is used. Line graphs are one of the worst offenders in the game of 'lying with statistics'.

Figure 10.8
Line graph of earnings as a function of sales

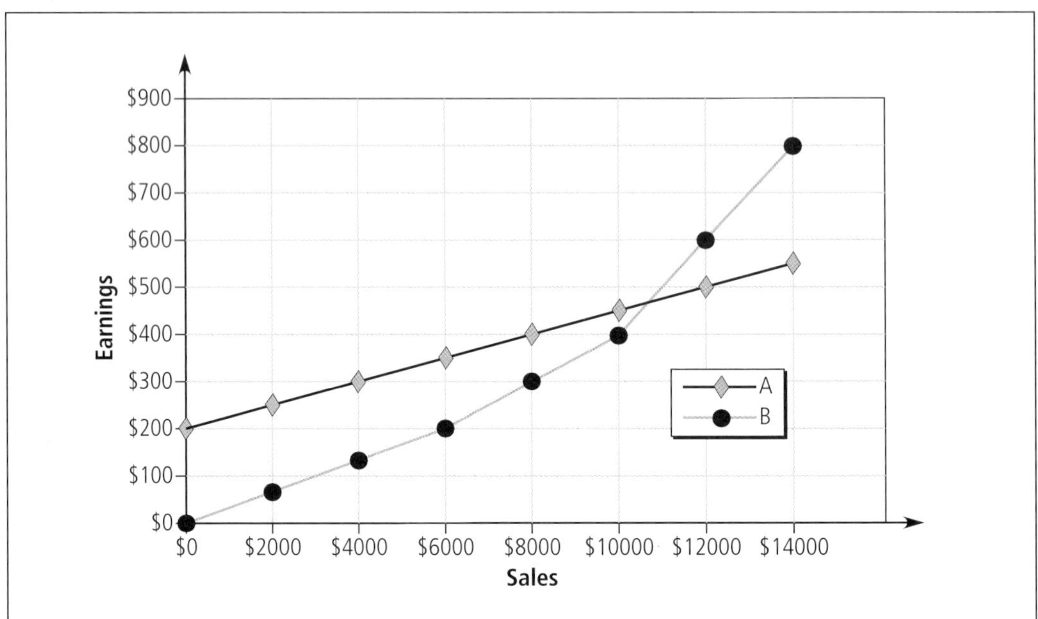

Examples of situations where a line graph is useful include showing relationships between:

- age of user and hours of internet use
- age of purchaser/user of games
- percentage of defects and computer speed.

Other areas where line graphs are useful are in run charts where you measure things like output, down-time and so on over time. Again, the use of an appropriate scale is essential in order to show variation accurately as demonstrated in Figure 10.8

Pie charts

Pie charts show shares of the whole. They should be used to show simple relationships because they become hard to interpret if too complex. If you are trying to convey accurate information, do not use fancy shapes because the proportions are often hard to interpret.

The more elaborate style shown in Figure 10.10 is best suited to embellishing a document rather than providing accurate information. The same is true for most graphics—the moment the picture is distorted, information becomes harder to interpret. Pie charts are best drawn using spreadsheet software such as Microsoft Excel.

Bar graphs

Bar graphs allow you to compare things like expenditure on different categories of items, rainfall, sales figures, population densities, or accident patterns. The main types of bar graph are simple, compound and pictograph. They are sometimes called column graphs.

Figure 10.9
Simple pie chart showing number of ISPs in Australia by State/Territory

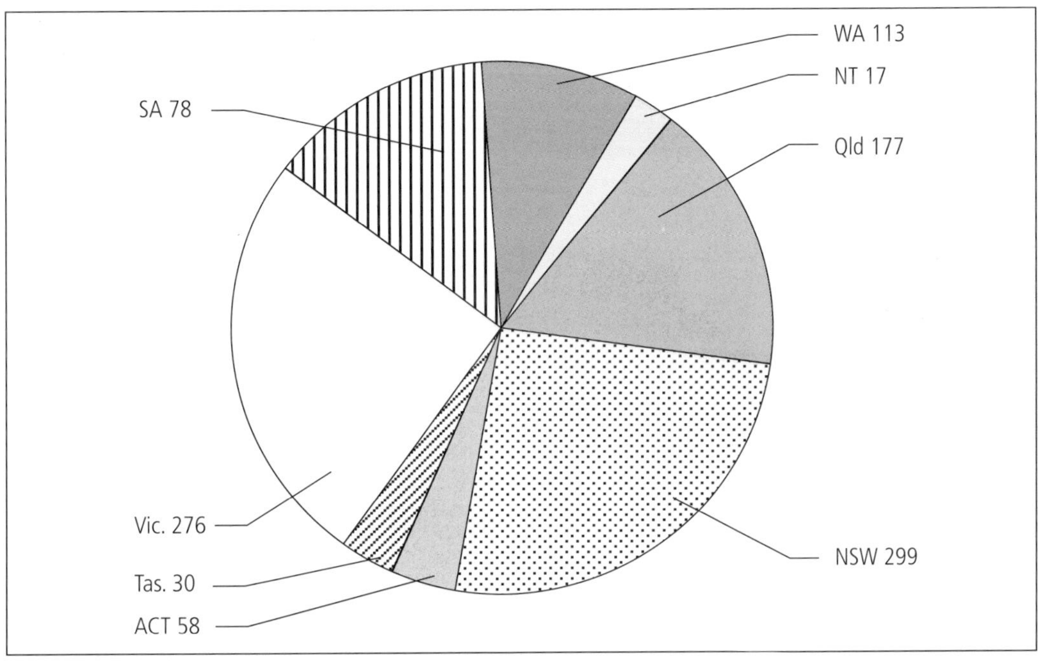

Figure 10.10
Three-dimensional pie chart showing percentage of internet subscribers in Australia by State/Territory

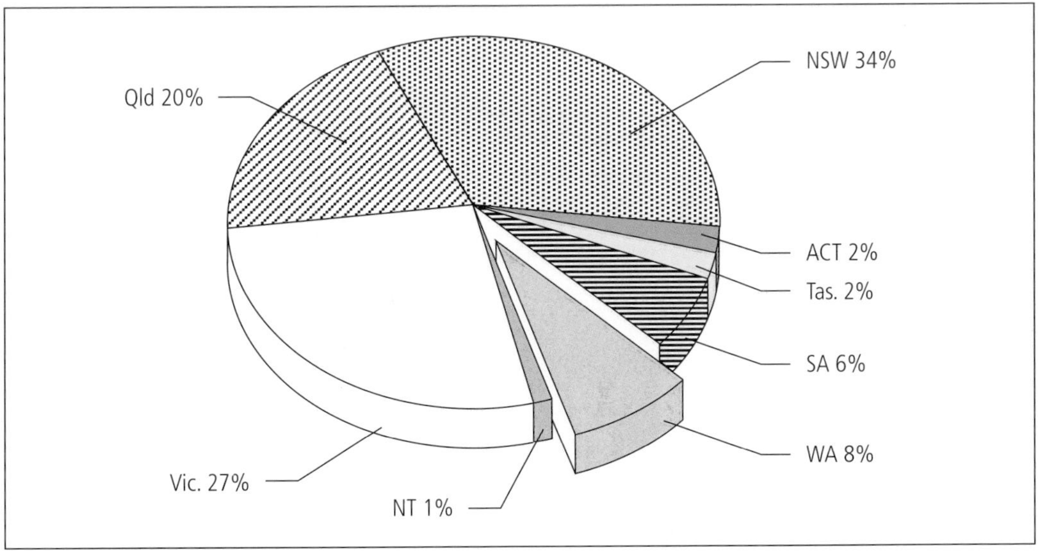

A simple bar graph uses single bars to depict a range of discrete variables. Figure 10.11 shows examples of a range of bar graphs. All of these graphs are easily drawn using a program such as Microsoft Excel.

Figure 10.11
A range of bar graphs

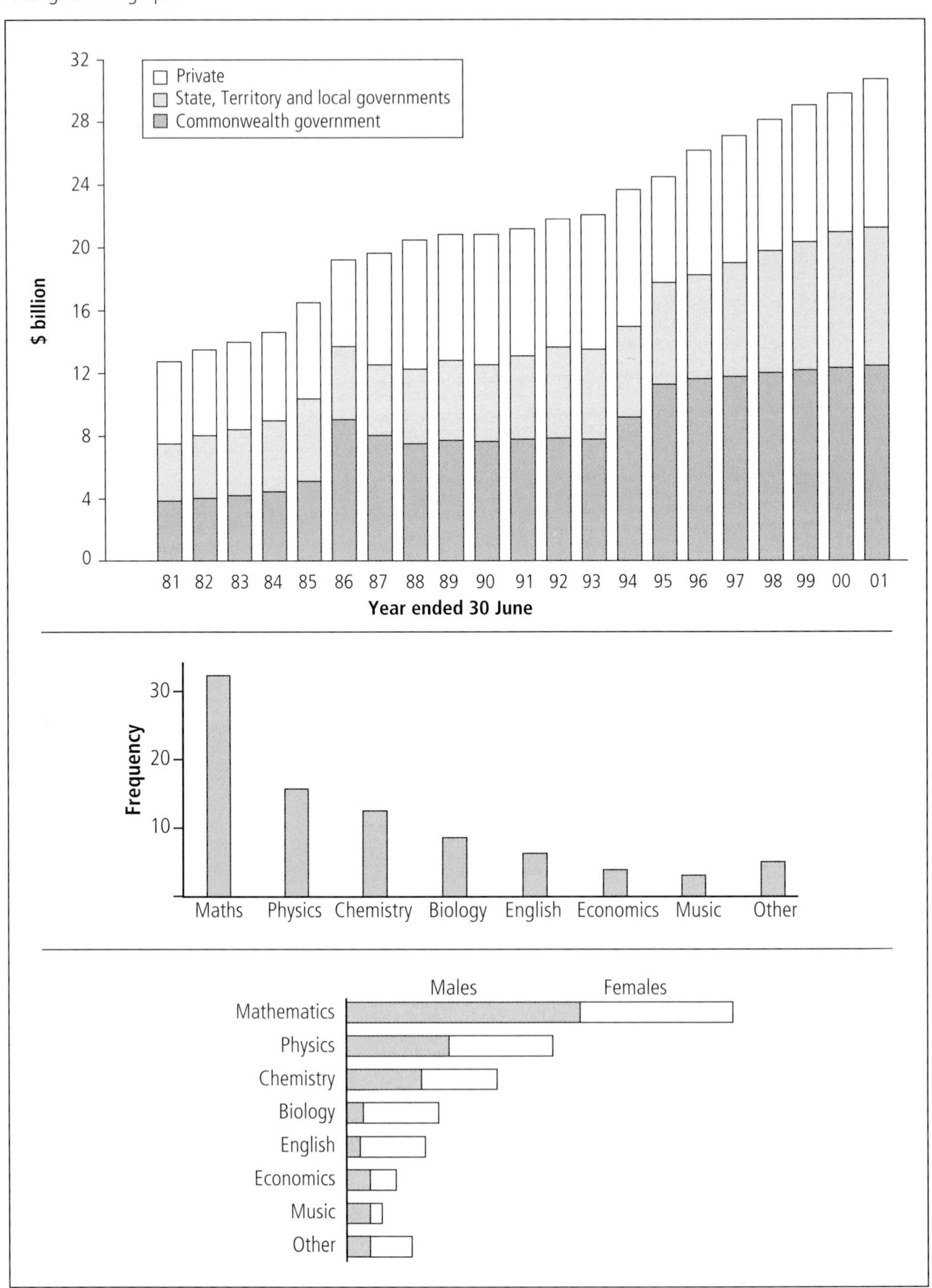

Pictographs

Pictographs use the same principles as bar graphs, but pictures represent the data instead of bars. Care needs to be taken to ensure that proportions are kept consistent, otherwise the different sizes will give a false impression. You can see examples of pictographs in publications by automobile associations when they produce statistics on accidents or vehicle safety tests. Figures 10.12 and 10.13 are examples of pictographs.

Figure 10.12
Pictograph of student study preferences

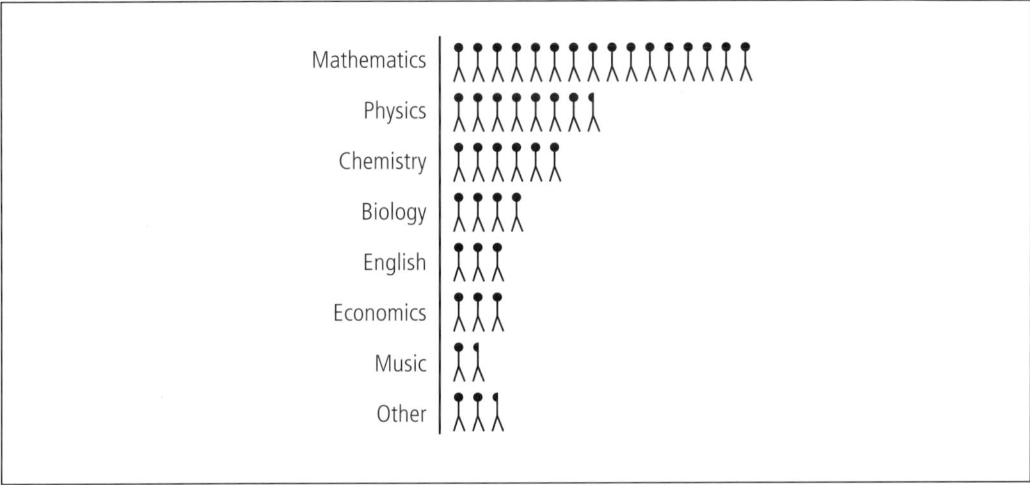

Figure 10.13
A more striking pictograph than that depicted in Figure 10.12

Histograms

A histogram displays the distribution of the data. It reveals the amount of variation in a process, and provides an indication of skewness. Types of data that can be usefully expressed in a histogram include temperature and response times. Types of patterns that emerge from this sort of analysis are depicted in Figure 10.14.

Figure 10.14
Frequency table and histogram of test marks from a group of students

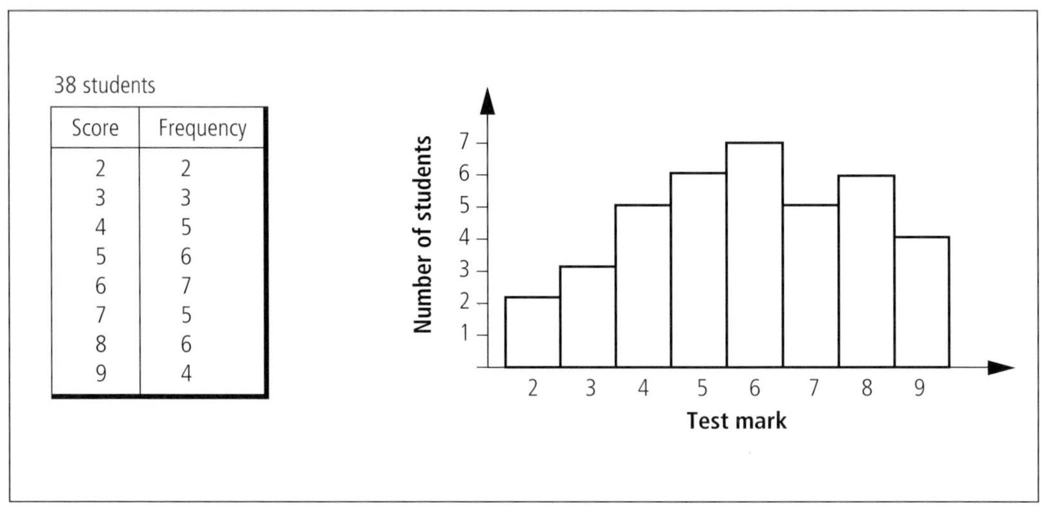

Scatter diagrams and control charts

These are graphics that use the conventions of line graphs to plot sometimes quite sophisticated statistical data. More detailed treatment of how to generate the data for these can be found in texts on quality control and statistics. Their interpretation is quite difficult for a reader with a limited background of the topic discussed.

Tables

Figures in sentences are hard to follow. Figures in columns are easier to comprehend, and therefore more believable. Numeric tables also make comparisons easier, which aids agreement.

Tables are the most common method for displaying large amounts of data in a systematic way. They offer you the flexibility of allowing the data to speak for itself, or to incorporate it into the text. Obviously, complex scientific tables that may confuse the average reader are acceptable for readers of a scientific journal. As a rule, however, simplicity, clear layout and the minimum data necessary to get the message across are recommended.

All word processing programs allow you to format tables in a very simple and efficient way, however, you should always consider the following points.

- **Use clear labels for each unit in the table and include a title** (above the table) or a caption (underneath the table). Choose a title or caption that identifies the content and distinguishes the table from others containing similar data.

- **Use titles to identify content relating to a particular location or period.** For example, 'Sales of New Laptops, Sydney, Jan–June 2001'.
- Do not make a table too cramped or figures too small, even if it means using more space.
- Use headings and subheadings to identify separate units of data.

If you use a computer and spreadsheet or database program to create numeric tables, you can recalculate figures and amend data as new information comes to hand without retyping the whole table. Include all headings and lines as part of the layout on the screen, then print the table as it stands.

Graphics are often reduced in size when printed, particularly in books and journals. This means that if the data is very complex, it will become less intelligible when reduced because it will be harder to read.

Headings should be brief. Detailed explanations should follow the graphic. Only the first letter of each box should be in capitals. Long columns of figures should be doubled-up to improve the appearance of the table.

A table should be accompanied by enough information for the reader to be able to interpret the data and understand the points the author is trying to make.

Table 10.1
Leading causes of drop-out from on line courses on software

Cause of drop-out	1995 (%)	2001(%)
Lack of access to a computer	72	34
Lost interest	13	22
Lack of support	39	42
Course cancelled	6	12

Activity 10.4

Producing graphs and charts

Produce a series of graphs and charts using information from the workplace or home. Sources may include IT publications, websites, product reports, sales figures or human resource data.

Examples of graphical material may include:

- a pie chart showing the types of advertisements on webpages, e.g. books 25 per cent, travel deals 22 per cent, credit cards 8 per cent, computer software 45 per cent
- a bar graph showing energy use for different computer chips
- a graph showing changes in course enrolments in your subject over the past five years (show total, male and female enrolments)
- a table showing pay rates for a range of occupations in the IT industry (include a scale for years of service for each).

INFORMATION THROUGH IMAGES

Key questions you should ask about each graphic at the review stage are:
* Does the graphic simplify the information and make it easier for the reader to understand?
* How useful is the graphic within its context?
* Does it accurately represent information?
* Should it be broken up into simpler graphics?
* What other graphic formats could have been used to present this information?

Photographs

Almost any picture lifts the quality of your page, adds eye appeal and attracts attention, but a striking photograph can focus attention in a way that words and ordinary graphics cannot. People find it hard to disagree with the evidence in front of them. There is no more convincing way to back up an argument. **Photographs make it possible to present a lot of accurate detail in one image**, and they can also incite emotional responses.

Place your photograph as near as possible to the text it refers to, preferably on the same page and following the mention, and beside it put a short, descriptive caption, mentioning also the paragraph to which it relates. In the text, mention the photograph as a cross-reference.

Some of the disadvantages of using photographs are that they are expensive to reproduce and can lose detail in the process. This is especially so when the document is photocopied (although modern photocopiers are reducing this problem). Topical photographs date easily.

Drawings

Drawings can show information simply and clearly, although it can be hard to produce good ones. They can also be uncluttered relative to a photograph. Some of the ideas given earlier in this section will help you develop your drawing skills.

Figure 10.15 shows a simple software-generated drawing that can be easily produced to support text.

Figure 10.15
Simple drawing to support text

Lettering

Lettering plays an important role in graphic communication. It is used in graphics and can convey images or add emphasis in the text.

Roman typefaces with serifs are generally accepted as being the most suitable for continuous reading. Parts of the text can be set in *italics*, **bold**, SMALL CAPITALS or LARGE CAPITALS in order to achieve emphasis. These should be used sparingly or they lose their impact. Bold type can be used for main headings, and italics for subordinate headings, journal titles and quotes.

If the work will be reduced when printed, you should choose an appropriate type size. The normal range of type sizes is 8–12 point. Outside this range the type becomes hard to read or takes up too much room. Obviously, if your audience is likely to have restricted vision, you will modify your type size accordingly.

Layout conventions

People prefer balance in the images they look at. Here are a number of the more generally accepted principles.

- People prefer balance in layout, whether it is symmetrical or asymmetrical.
- **Contrast between visual elements improves recognition**, for example, between:
  —size
  —colour
  —brightness
  —position.
- Simple designs are more easily recalled than complex ones.
- Repeating visual elements verbally improves impact.
- Close things will appear related whereas distant ones will appear unrelated.
- Objects aligned vertically, horizontally or diagonally will appear more related than non-aligned elements.
- Consistent style, shape or size will integrate elements in the image.
- People from Western cultures tend to scan left to right and top to bottom.
- Images that point to each other determine eye flow—this can be achieved by lines, arrows and positioning.

White space is a very important element in many graphics. It separates the graphic from the text and other graphics, inviting the reader to look at it. There is no hard and fast rule, but you should aim to leave at least 2 cm of space around each graphic. The same applies to text, otherwise it appears cramped and uninviting.

Abbreviations and codes

Of course, any abbreviations and codes you use, including most graphic conventions, should be explained at the beginning, in the body, or at the end of the text. Keep abbreviations or codes to a minimum because excessive use fragments the text and, when used in graphics, forces readers to jump from text to glossary and back again.

Computer graphics

The use of graphics software has created new opportunities to present information. Three types of software are desktop publishing, CAD, and painting or drawing software. Images available on the internet can come from any of these types.

CAD and desktop publishing software generally have sophisticated features that are best exploited by people trained to use them. Most word-processing software packages now have an in-built drawing/graphics function together with useful tutorial programs and 'help' facilities that explain many of the features and processes. **Graphics can now be easily imported into your word-processing software and printed out on most printers.**

10.16
Example of computer-generated graphics

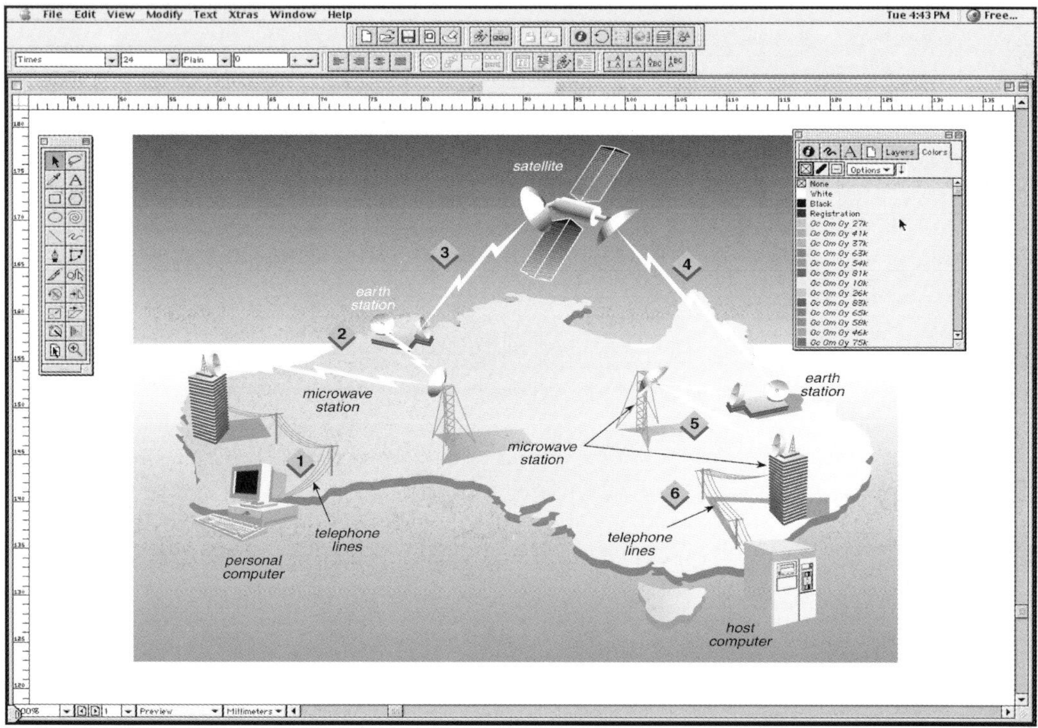

Spreadsheet programs can generate a wide range of graphics from data, including line graphs, pie graphs, bar graphs and scatter plots. In some respects, these are easier to use because many of the features are automated and all you have to do is learn how to enter the data.

Working with artists

In many cases you will produce a graphic for someone else to bring to publication standard. This person is often an artist or graphic designer. The most effective way to ensure that what you produce will make sense to the artist is to ask them what they expect from you. You need to **establish guidelines on things such as**:

- the standard of work you have to produce
- how to differentiate artists' instructions from words that are part of the graphic
- proofreading symbols
- the timetable
- how you will present the graphic (i.e. as part of the text or on a separate sheet).

Activity 10.5

Using graphics

1. What are some of the benefits of using graphics in documents?
2. What are the main planning steps when producing graphics?
3. List the features of well-produced graphics.
4. What layout conventions will improve the effectiveness of graphics?

ACTION POINTS

You will produce effective graphics that enhance the clarity of your message and the visual appeal of your documents if you:

- prepare a plan for complex or very important graphics—your plan should incorporate information about:
  - purpose (ask yourself 'Why is this graphic needed? What am I trying to achieve with it?')
  - the audience (what are their needs and level of written and visual literacy?)
  - anything that might get in the way of the message
  - options for getting the message across
  - resources available to produce the graphic
  - information that has to be gathered
- keep your graphics simple
- use clear headings to identify each graphic
- provide clear, concise explanatory notes wherever necessary—tell the reader what they are looking at
- provide enough information for the reader to be able to interpret the data
- place each graphic as near as possible to the text reference
- use a layout that is balanced and clean to improve visual impact
- provide an adequate amount of white space around graphics and text
- explain all abbreviations and codes
- provide artists with clear guidelines and expectations
- use a checklist for your graphics before sending them for printing
- get a second opinion from someone else before you finish.

SUMMARY

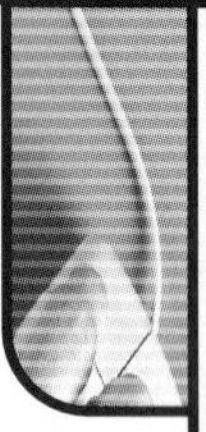

Well-produced graphics convey information and enhance the appearance of documents, making them more attractive and inviting the reader to engage with the content. The quality of your written documents may be improved because the process of planning and integrating graphics encourages you to look at information from another perspective.

The effectiveness of graphic communication depends on the quality of planning. When planning, clearly state your purpose, identify your audience, identify any barriers to communicating your message, produce a range of options, and identify any resources you might need. A badly drawn or inaccurate graphic is worse than no graphic. Where data is used for comparison, ensure that it is consistent with the data to which it is being compared.

Keep graphics simple, using a checklist to make sure all important elements of a good graphic are addressed. It is possible to produce clear diagrams without being an artist if you follow a basic set of guidelines.

The effectiveness of flow charts depends on having a clear sense of the process and its boundaries, keeping the chart simple, and testing it on someone who would view it in the same way as your intended audience.

Avoid overly complicated or fancy shapes in graphs where there is a chance they might mislead the reader. Produce a draft of the graph and ask yourself whether the line accurately reflects the trends. If the reader thinks you are trying to mislead them with graphics, the credibility of the whole document will be compromised.

Tables offer you the flexibility of allowing the data to speak for itself, but depend on clear layout and adequate explanations to be effective.

Computer-generated graphics have the advantage of being easily modified and reproduced. They can, however, take longer to produce if you are not familiar with the software. Most word-processing software packages now have an in-built drawing/graphics function together with useful tutorial programs and 'help' facilities that explain many of the features and processes.

Photographs make it possible to present a lot of accurate detail in one image, and they can also incite emotional responses. Remember that reproduction can be expensive and result in lost quality.

Drawings can show information simply and clearly, and can be uncluttered relative to a photograph. Keep images balanced, simple and close to any text they support. Use adequate white space, and consistent style, shape and size.

The most effective way to ensure that what you produce will make sense to an artist is to ask them what they expect from you. You need to establish guidelines on quality, time lines and cost.

Graphics

Select six different graphics from computer-related websites.
Evaluate each graphic using the checklist below.

TRAINING LOG

	Yes	No
Uncluttered layout	☐	☐
Exciting colour	☐	☐
Readable type	☐	☐
Simple designs	☐	☐
Emphasis used appropriately	☐	☐
Unity of images and placement	☐	☐
Balance between elements in the design	☐	☐
Spacing used effectively	☐	☐
Appropriate scale used:		
• allowing room for titling	☐	☐
• leaving intervals between markers on charts and graphs allowing room for entry of scales	☐	☐
Shade, colour, texture, pattern and line used consciously and sparingly	☐	☐
Accurate and relevant data	☐	☐
Clear and simple labels	☐	☐
Complete legends	☐	☐
Text kept to a minimum depending on the purpose, with detailed explanatory text below the graphic	☐	☐
Lettering:		
• proportional to graphic	☐	☐
• easy to read (font, size)	☐	☐
• uses appropriate case	☐	☐
• legible	☐	☐
Titles:		
• short and descriptive	☐	☐
• subtitle where further description needed	☐	☐
• additional explanatory text follows title	☐	☐
• all text brief	☐	☐
A clear explanation for symbols	☐	☐
A clear explanation for abbreviations	☐	☐
Instructions for artists and editors:		
• in circle	☐	☐
• different coloured pen	☐	☐
• clear and legible	☐	☐

Action plan

1. Design three different graphics to support written information you have prepared for a specific work-related document. Use graphics software and present the graphs within a paper-based, electronic or online document. For example, you may design graphics to support a written report, as in the Action plan for Chapter 9's Training Log.

2. Present your document with and without graphics to a workmate or friend. Ask them to comment on how effective the version with graphics is in communicating the information.

INDEX